The U.S. Constitution

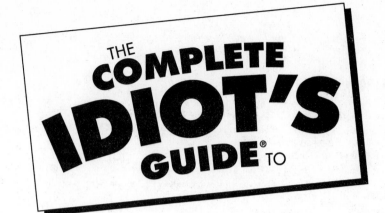

THE COMPLETE IDIOT'S GUIDE® TO

The U.S. Constitution

by Timothy Harper

ALPHA

A member of Penguin Group (USA) Inc.

For my parents, Bud and Eleanor Harper, who taught me the rules and how to challenge them.

ALPHA BOOKS

Published by the Penguin Group

Penguin Group (USA) Inc., 375 Hudson Street, New York, New York 10014, USA

Penguin Group (Canada), 90 Eglinton Avenue East, Suite 700, Toronto, Ontario M4P 2Y3, Canada (a division of Pearson Penguin Canada Inc.)

Penguin Books Ltd., 80 Strand, London WC2R 0RL, England

Penguin Ireland, 25 St. Stephen's Green, Dublin 2, Ireland (a division of Penguin Books Ltd.)

Penguin Group (Australia), 250 Camberwell Road, Camberwell, Victoria 3124, Australia (a division of Pearson Australia Group Pty. Ltd.)

Penguin Books India Pvt. Ltd., 11 Community Centre, Panchsheel Park, New Delhi—110 017, India

Penguin Group (NZ), 67 Apollo Drive, Rosedale, North Shore, Auckland 1311, New Zealand (a division of Pearson New Zealand Ltd.)

Penguin Books (South Africa) (Pty.) Ltd., 24 Sturdee Avenue, Rosebank, Johannesburg 2196, South Africa

Penguin Books Ltd., Registered Offices: 80 Strand, London WC2R 0RL, England

Copyright © 2007 by Timothy Harper

International Standard Book Number: 978-159257-627-2
Library of Congress Catalog Card Number: 2007926850

12   11   10   09   8   7   6   5   4   3

Interpretation of the printing code: The rightmost number of the first series of numbers is the year of the book's printing; the rightmost number of the second series of numbers is the number of the book's printing. For example, a printing code of 07-1 shows that the first printing occurred in 2007.

Printed in the United States of America

Note: This publication contains the opinions and ideas of its author. It is intended to provide helpful and informative material on the subject matter covered. It is sold with the understanding that the author and publisher are not engaged in rendering professional services in the book. If the reader requires personal assistance or advice, a competent professional should be consulted.

The author and publisher specifically disclaim any responsibility for any liability, loss, or risk, personal or otherwise, which is incurred as a consequence, directly or indirectly, of the use and application of any of the contents of this book.

Most Alpha books are available at special quantity discounts for bulk purchases for sales promotions, premiums, fund-raising, or educational use. Special books, or book excerpts, can also be created to fit specific needs.

For details, write: Special Markets, Alpha Books, 375 Hudson Street, New York, NY 10014.

Publisher: *Marie Butler-Knight*
Editorial Director: *Mike Sanders*
Managing Editor: *Billy Fields*
Senior Acquisitions Editor: *Paul Dinas*
Senior Development Editor: *Phil Kitchel*
Production Editor: *Kayla Dugger*

Copy Editor: *Amy Borrelli*
Cover Designer: *Bill Thomas*
Book Designer: *Trina Wurst*
Indexer: *Julie Bess*
Layout: *Ayanna Lacey*
Proofreader: *John Etchison*

Contents at a Glance

Appendixes

Contents

Introduction

The United States Constitution is a sweeping, complex, and daunting subject. How to approach it, how to begin understanding it, has always been a problem, whether for the wizened law professor or the fourth-grader being marched through American history. This book offers a handle on the topic, with options for the reader or student. You can start at the beginning and follow the story of how the Constitution developed. Or if you have a particular interest in some aspect of the Constitution—the Founding Fathers, for example, or the Bill of Rights, or Prohibition—you can dip in and out of the book at those particular chapters and sections.

Given the significance of the Constitution in today's political land-scape, it makes sense that we are in the midst of a national discussion about the rule of law as it relates to the future of America's national culture and character. The goal of this book is to present history and today's perspective in an even-handed, fact-based manner that both informs you and helps you do your own analysis of the day's headlines. Rather than the classic case-and-argument style of law books, this guide is written in a conversational style aimed at being accessible for a broad range of readers. The emphasis is on telling stories—the stories of what happened, and of the people who were involved. Let's look at what's in the book, and how it is organized.

We begin with a breezy history lesson that looks at both the development of our American legal principles, mostly from English common law, and the development of our American society, beginning in the colonies. The opening chapter of the book takes us through the American Revolution—the colonists regarded themselves as freedom fighters and patriots, while the British rulers regarded them as rebels—and the Declaration of Independence into the first tentative steps of a new nation. We look at the foundations of the Constitution—the people give the government rights, not the other way around—and the historic convention that produced this remarkable set of ideas in Philadelphia during the sultry summer of 1789.

Next we look at Articles I, II, and III of the Constitution, which laid out the framework for history's boldest experiment in democracy. We look at the reasons behind the separation of powers between three equal branches of government—executive, legislative, judicial—and the elaborate system of checks and balances that the framers of the Constitution designed to keep any one branch of government from assuming too much power.

The remaining parts of the original Constitution, Articles IV, V, VI, and VII, look at the blueprint for how the new federal system is supposed to work, including the relationship between the individual states and the national government. This section also looks at the wisdom of the framers of the Constitution who, in recognizing that a society must move forward and change and adapt to succeed, prescribed a way to amend the Constitution.

Much of the book, naturally, is devoted to the Bill of Rights—the first 10 amendments to the Constitution, the amendments that define so many of the individual rights that have become so important to Americans and are synonymous with the American ideal. We examine all 10 amendments in the Bill of Rights, but focus primarily on the most significant, including: the First Amendment, the so-called "great" amendment, guaranteeing freedom of speech, religion, and the press; the Second Amendment and its controversial "right to bear arms" wording; the Fourth Amendment, which protects us against unlawful searches and seizures by authorities; the Fifth Amendment, which gave us the right against self-incrimination and Miranda warnings; the Sixth, Seventh, and Eighth amendments, which guarantee fair trials and punishment; and the Ninth Amendment's personal privacy protections.

Moving on, the book discusses each of the subsequent amendments individually, but concentrates more on those that had a major impact on society or that continue to have implications for today, including the amendments that ended slavery and granted civil rights, at least in theory, to African Americans. We'll examine the far-reaching U.S. Supreme Court interpretations and applications of the Fourteenth Amendment and its Equal Protection Clause. There are some good stories—and some grumbling that continues today—behind the Sixteenth Amendment, which led to the national income tax, and the Seventeenth Amendment, which let Americans vote directly for their senators for the first time.

The early twentieth century was a time of striking change in America as we became the world's dominant nation, but it is unlikely that the framers of the Constitution ever saw their amendment process being used to outlaw alcohol or give women the vote—the results of the Eighteenth and Nineteenth amendments. We'll look at how Prohibition backfired and led to repeal in the Twenty-First Amendment, and at the women's suffrage movement.

Besides the other amendments passed in the last century—including one to limit presidents to two terms and another that gave the vote to 18-year-olds—we'll recap some of the amendments that came close to ratification but failed, notably the Equal Rights Amendment. The text will close with some thoughts on the future of the Constitution, including shifts in the balance of power among the three branches of government, and some speculation about future proposed amendments. Finally, there will be a glossary that defines many of the terms commonly used in discussions of constitutional law and a list of references for further reading.

As you go through the book you'll notice a number of sidebars, little nuggets of information, asides that are aimed at adding to your knowledge and illustrating the main points. There are four types of sidebars:

Cases
Summaries of landmark cases that have changed the course of American history.

def•i•ni•tion
Common legal terms and concepts.

People
Brief profiles of those who played pivotal roles in constitutional cases, along with pithy quotes from many of those people.

What It Means to You
Pointed commentary that explains the main points of constitutional law in simple terms.

This book is intended to be informative, thoughtful, and thought-provoking. It does not pretend to be comprehensive, and it is by no means the last word in understanding or appreciating the Constitution.

Rather, it is more of an overview and an introduction, providing the basics of what you need to know to be an informed citizen who understands the principles that underpin our legal system and our society. There is much more to be learned and considered about each and every aspect of the Constitution put forth here. If this is your first step in learning about the Constitution, we hope it's the start of a long and rich journey.

Acknowledgments

My professors at the University of Wisconsin Law School, especially noted Supreme Court and constitutional scholar Mark Tushnet, deserve appreciation for putting up with a journalist who came back to school not to be a lawyer but to be a better journalist. Law school would not have been as profitable, nor nearly as enjoyable, without the support and friendship of too many classmates to mention here, but especially Jeff Mohr, Ed Manydeeds, Al Olson, and Jim Grau. They are good lawyers and good guys. In addition, my North Jersey neighbor and fellow author Jim Tosone, an amateur constitutional scholar, was generous with his knowledge and insights on a number of key points.

Thanks to my American Society of Journalists and Authors colleague George Sheldon for connecting me with his agent, Robert Diforio, and to Bob for bringing me to the editors at Penguin who oversee the series. Thanks to Paul Dinas, the senior editor who recruited me and provided considerable encouragement and advice and showed remarkable patience as he shepherded the book through the process. Thanks also to development editor Phil Kitchel and copy editor Amy Borrelli, whose catches and comments and questions were most welcome and most valuable. Thanks to production editor Kayla Dugger, and to Trina Wurst for the book design and Bill Thomas for the cover design.

Finally, thanks to my family for their forbearance for several months as I worked on tight deadlines on this and other assignments: my wife, Nancy Bobrowitz, and our kids, Lizzie and Jon. Together, we've learned a lot over the years about the value of rights, responsibility, rules, and especially flexibility—whether in a national constitution or in a family.

Birth of the Constitution

In This Chapter

- ◆ The rule of law in history
- ◆ The American Revolution
- ◆ The 1787 Constitutional Convention
- ◆ The Preamble

The United States Constitution is a master document, the paramount or overriding set of laws laying out the foundation of American democracy and the rule of law. The Constitution does not grant us rights, but rather gives our government the power to protect those rights.

The Constitution establishes the three branches of the national government and the system of checks and balances that keeps any one branch from dominating. The Constitution also creates the framework for electing federal officials, and limits their power. Finally, the Constitution lists individual rights that are the heart of democracy.

Theory and History

American democracy is a grand experiment based on a relatively new and radical idea: a government by and for all citizens. Various forms of participatory and representative government have been tried throughout history; however, until the United States was formed, democracy was a failed theory. We have made it work, more or less, largely through our Constitution, the document upon which we base our rule of law. It's important for us to remember, though, that the words of the Constitution—what it says—are not as significant as the fact that we have agreed as a society to live by the spirit of the rules laid down in the Constitution.

Theory: Society's Agreement to Live by Rules

Ever since our ancestors began to gather in tribes and villages, we have been looking for the best way to live together—how to create civilization. Chieftains and kings handed down laws and enforced them, often according to their own whims. But even when the leader was kind and just, people wanted to know the rules. And they wanted assurances that the rules would be applied fairly and equally for everyone. In other words, they wanted the rule of law—a government of laws rather than men.

A constitution, whether for a powerful nation or for a local garden club, is a set of charter rules, a supreme or paramount law that outlines how the organization will operate. In terms of a nation, the constitution sets forth political principles, establishes power and authority, and defines rights and responsibilities. The constitution proscribes the general principles for what a government can and cannot do. Specific laws enacted by the government, also called statutory law, spell out the details. For example, the U.S. Constitution gives the government the authority to collect taxes, but leaves it to the government to decide who and what will be taxed and how much.

Our Constitution establishes a federal system of state governments that operate with a certain amount of self-rule under a single national government. There is a constant balancing of interests to preserve the rule of law and prohibit any person or group of people from dominating the government. There are balances among the three branches of government, between the states and the federal government, and among individual states.

Not all constitutions are codified, or written. Israel, New Zealand, and the United Kingdom have constitutional governments, but instead of a single written document, their constitutional laws derive from a number of different documents and unwritten principles that are sometimes called *common law*.

def•i•ni•tion

Common law is the body of law, largely unwritten, that evolved in England through prevailing customs, widely accepted principles, and decisions by courts rather than through administrative rule or legislative action.

Written or not, it's important to remember that a constitution is so much more than its actual words. The former Soviet Union had a beautifully written constitution, full of the same sort of high-minded language that the U.S. Constitution uses to guarantee liberty. But the Soviet constitution was little more than lip service; instead of the rule of law, the Soviet Union was ruled by a single political party that imposed what many Soviet citizens thought was a particularly harsh brand of communism.

The U.S. Constitution is based on what can be described as a free-market premise: society should be a marketplace of ideas, and people should be able to use their knowledge and their energy to make better lives for themselves. The rationale is that no government can know what's best for all its citizens; instead, people know what's best for themselves. At the same time, it's important to recognize that democracy does not necessarily mean individual liberty. Democracy can mean tyranny by the majority if individual rights are not protected. Instead, our form of democracy, as outlined in the Constitution, strives to preserve and protect individual rights: I have the right to do whatever I want as long as it's not prohibited by law and it doesn't violate anyone else's individual rights.

People

"The rule of law is a solution to a problem, and as the classical liberal tradition has always recognized, the problem is tyranny." —*Political scientist Noel B. Reynolds*

History: Back to the Magna Carta

The earliest written laws we know about date back to ancient Babylon (now Iraq) and King Hammurabi, who had his Hammurabi Code carved into stone and put on public display in the eighteenth century B.C.E. In the seventh century B.C.E., Draco became the first law scribe in ancient Greece, though the laws he codified were extraordinarily harsh by today's standards and often carried the death penalty for even minor crimes (hence the modern word "draconian"). Another Greek lawgiver, Solon, put forth the idea that laws should be equal for rich and poor. Whether or not people lived in a democracy, he believed they should be able to rely on the rules being applied fairly and equally to everyone. Aristotle advanced the notion of a constitutional form of government based on a set of master laws. In Rome, Cicero promoted the idea that rather than taking away individual freedom, laws promote freedom when everyone agrees to live by the rules.

The Germanic tribes that dominated Europe in the Dark and Middle ages had various sets of laws, sometimes written and sometimes not, but the precedents for our Constitution were not confined to Europe. Japan had an early constitution based on Buddhist lessons on morality, Mohammed drafted the Constitution of Medina, and the Iroquois nation had a constitution that was said to inspire the early American settlers.

For the American colonists, however, perhaps the most important legal document in history was the Magna Carta, signed reluctantly by King John in 1215. The king was waging foreign wars against Muslims, and members of the nobility were upset at the cost in taxes and men. England's barons objected to the way the king used his authority, and threatened him with rebellion unless he signed.

It's worth remembering that the Magna Carta actually did little or nothing for common citizens; it was strictly for the benefit of the feudal lords who supported the king. But for the first time the king was subject to law, instead of making the law, and the Magna Carta became the foundation for our rule of law. The Magna Carta put some limits on the king's ability to levy taxes, but its most important provision was the right of habeas corpus, which said that the king could not imprison or execute anyone without *due process*. Article 39 of the Magna Carta said, "No free man shall be arrested, or imprisoned, or deprived of his property, or outlawed, or exiled, or in any way destroyed, nor shall we go against him or send against him, unless by legal judgment of his peers, or by the law of the land."

def•i•ni•tion

Due process is the catchall term for procedures that guarantee that all a person's legal rights are recognized and considered properly and fairly under the law.

The Magna Carta was short-lived (so was King John), but the principles became a cornerstone over the following centuries into the so-called Age of Enlightenment. English common law increasingly recognized the rights of individuals, particularly when kings abused their power by granting economic favors—such as monopolies over certain aspects of trade and industry—to their friends. Public dissatisfaction with both crown and cronies, particularly in the way the courts came to be controlled by politicians, helped inspire the English Civil War—also called the Glorious Revolution—in 1688.

While the American colonists were carving out their own brand of rugged individualism on the other side of the Atlantic, thinkers such as John Locke helped England embrace the idea of more individual rights and less government authoritarianism. Locke stressed that a government's role was to protect the property of its citizens. Locke and others also stressed that certain rights are natural to humankind and cannot be given or taken away by kings or governments. Those ideas were embraced on our side of the Atlantic.

People

"The end of the law is, not to abolish or restrain, but to preserve and enlarge freedom. For in all the states of created beings capable of laws, where there is no law there is no freedom." —*John Locke*

The American Revolution

Like many colonies throughout history, the Americans of the first half of the 1700s had a love-hate relationship with their mother country. They were proud to be British, but they resented the way their distant rulers seemed to take advantage of them. The British, meanwhile, were at the height of their imperial haughtiness. Great Britain prized its American possessions for their vast natural resources and for the way the developing American middle class of shopkeepers and farmers was becoming an important market for trade. But to the British, Americans weren't even second-class citizens because they weren't citizens. Besides, India was the real jewel in the crown of the empire.

Taxation Without Representation

The British had handed a number of laws across the Atlantic that weren't well received in America, largely because they were seen as being economically unfair. For example, the British put strict limits on the colonial iron industry, in order to protect sales of British iron products in America. If Americans were allowed to operate their own forges and produce their own iron tools, they wouldn't buy them from Britain—and pay import taxes for them on top. Similar laws restricted American production, forced Americans to buy only from Britain, or imposed high taxes on everyday items such as newspapers, playing cards, textiles, wine, beer, coffee, and tea.

Resentment toward British rule began to peak after 1760 when King George III assumed the throne. Parliament began taxing the colonies directly to help pay for "Mad" King George's wars against France and Spain and for the British troops sent to America to keep order against an increasingly rebellious colonial population. New "quartering" laws required colonists to open their homes and kitchens to shelter and feed British troops. The Americans organized boycotts, became enthusiastic smugglers, gave rousing speeches, and printed treasonous pamphlets. Some of them organized themselves into the Sons of Liberty and made violent attacks on the crown's property and agents. In today's language, we would call them freedom fighters; the British would call them terrorists.

People

Wealthy Boston merchant and patriot John Hancock, best known today for that big signature on the Declaration of Independence, was a committed smuggler who defied British tax laws. When he finally got caught, his sloop *Liberty* and all its cargo were seized, and a judge—the British wouldn't allow a jury to hear the case—fined him 9,000 pounds, three times the value of the cargo.

As the British imposed more taxes, the colonists protested more, the British sent more troops to America to maintain order, and then they imposed more taxes to pay for the additional troops. New taxes on paper, glass, paint, and tea fueled the protests, and American juries began finding accused smugglers innocent even when they were caught red-handed. The British then stopped allowing jury trials. In 1773, a group of patriots clownishly dressed like Mohawk Indians boarded three ships in Boston Harbor and threw the cargo overboard rather than submit to new rules that said only agents of the crown could sell tea.

As Parliament moved to take away the colonies' limited self-rule authority, the first Continental Congress convened in Philadelphia. The representatives of 12 colonies (Georgia did not attend) declared their opposition to rule by Parliament and vowed to go home and promote the forming of local militia. In 1775, the first shots were fired at Lexington and Concord, Massachusetts, and the colonial minutemen—they could grab their rifles and be out the door in a minute—sent the redcoats fleeing back to Boston.

George Washington, who had been one of the leaders of the British-Colonial military forces that defeated the French in the French-Indian War a few years earlier, assumed command of the Continental Army as full-fledged war broke out.

People

"In America the law is king. For as in absolute governments the king is law, so in free countries, the law ought to be king ...."
— *Thomas Paine, in* Common Sense

The Declaration of Independence

In June 1776, the Continental Congress appointed a Committee of Five to draft a statement that would explain to the British (and the rest of the world) why the Americans wanted and deserved independence. The other four members of the committee asked Thomas Jefferson to take it on and get back to them. In a mere 17 days, Jefferson worked up a draft. He showed it to two other members of the committee, Benjamin Franklin and John Adams. They made a few suggestions, the full Committee of Five made a few more, and the document went before the Continental Congress on July 2. The Congress tinkered and debated that day, all the next, and into the late morning of the following day. When the people of Philadelphia heard all the city's church bells pealing at once, they were exhilarated and terrified. Independence had been declared.

> **People**
>
> "Men do not make laws. They do but discover them. Laws must be justified by something more than the will of the majority. They must rest on the eternal foundation of righteousness. That state is most fortunate in its form of government which has the aptest instruments for the discovery of law."
> —Calvin Coolidge, 1914

The Declaration of Independence, for all practical purposes little changed from Jefferson's original draft, opened: "When in the Course of human events, it becomes necessary for one people to dissolve the political bands which have connected them with another, and to assume among the powers of the earth, the separate and equal station to which the Laws of Nature and of Nature's God entitle them, a decent respect to the opinions of mankind requires that they should declare the causes which impel them to the separation."

And then came the second paragraph, the words we all remember for their simple power: "We hold these truths to be self-evident, that all men are created equal, that they are endowed by their Creator with certain unalienable Rights, that among these are Life, Liberty and the pursuit of Happiness." Simply and directly, the declaration set out the rights claimed by the colonists—rights that anybody who read them would agree were natural rights that should be afforded all people.

The foundation of the Declaration of Independence, and subsequently the Constitution, was straightforward and powerful: individual rights are inalienable, natural, and cannot be granted or taken away by governments.

The declaration went on to cite a list of wrongs by the British crown, violations of those rights. As soon as the 56 signatures on the declaration were dry—maybe before they were dry—runners carried the document to printers for copies to be made and sent to the other colonies and to the commanders of the Continental Army. Within five days, all 13 colonies had approved the Declaration of Independence.

It was a long and difficult war, marked by numerous defeats and retreats for the Continental Army. There were mass desertions and a handful of mutinies. The odds were against the Americans, but shrewd generalship by Washington, the fact that the British were fighting far from home and the Americans were literally defending their homes, and some sheer luck led to Lord Cornwallis' ignominious surrender at Yorktown, Virginia, in 1781. The following year, the British Parliament voted to cease hostilities with America and urged King George to negotiate for peace. The British troops began returning from the former colonies. The Treaty of Paris, in which Britain recognized the United States of America, was signed in 1783, the same year that the Continental Army disbanded and Washington, to the surprise of many who wanted him to become king of America, returned to private life. He had been one of the richest men in the colonies, but he had neglected his farm and business back home in Mount Vernon during the war years, and he was eager to restore his fortune and live the life of a country gentleman.

The Articles of Confederation

While the war was still raging, the Congress of the new nation decided its formal name should be the United States of America and began work on a framework for how the states would get along. The members of Congress hesitated to call their new master document a constitution, largely because of widespread misgivings about identifying the states as part of a single nation. "Independence" being the watchword, the new states preferred to think of themselves as separate republics in an alliance of convenience. The Articles of Confederation, the charter document produced by Congress in 1781, instead described "a firm league of friendship."

Article II made it clear that the individual states were not subject to the United States: "Each state retains its sovereignty, freedom, and independence, and every power, jurisdiction, and right, which is not by this Confederation expressly delegated to the United States, in Congress assembled." In the Articles of Confederation, the states agreed to defend each other against outside attacks "on account of religion, sovereignty, trade, or any other pretense whatever."

> **People**
>
> "The great aim of the struggle for liberty has been equality before the law." —*Constitutional scholar F. A. Hayek*

The Articles of Confederation was at best an emergency constitution, better suited to war than peacetime. But the articles afforded a transition, letting the 13 states dip their toes into new nationhood with little more than vague promises to help each other if needed. There was no executive branch to enforce laws, nor any taxing authority. Instead, the Congress financed its fledgling central government by asking the states for contributions. Sometimes the states contributed, and sometimes they didn't.

Most of the new country's problems arose not because of conflicts between the states and outsiders, but because of conflicts among the states themselves. Without any overriding rules on how they would co-exist, various states insisted on imposing their rules and laws on the other states. One of the big problems with the Articles of Confederation was the requirement that all 13 states had to approve any major laws. It seemed that at least one state was always willing to cast a veto.

Most of the conflicts were over trade and commerce. For example, treaty talks over rights to use the Mississippi River faltered because of squabbling among Northern and Southern states. And there were many other disputes. Who could buy and sell what goods and commodities across which borders? Could states regulate prices for products and commodities bought and sold in other states? Could states tax each other?

It became clear that the states needed to do business with each other to prosper, but their conflicting rules got in the way. So in true American fashion, they agreed to change the rules. A conference was called at

Annapolis, Maryland, in 1786, and the states agreed to a proposal by Alexander Hamilton for a convention in Philadelphia the following year to revise the Articles of Confederation.

The 1787 Constitutional Convention

Not everyone was in favor of amending the Articles of Confederation. Patrick "Give me liberty or give me death!" Henry was one of a number of prominent Revolutionary leaders who refused to attend the Constitutional Convention because he was uneasy about any sort of national government that might take power away from the states.

Twelve of the 13 states sent at least two delegates to Philadelphia in May; Rhode Island did not participate. The 55 delegates, all men, ages 26 to 81 (the oldest being Benjamin Franklin), met throughout the long hot summer. Most of them participated regularly, and some rarely missed the sessions that ran from 10 in the morning until 3 in the afternoon, 6 days a week. A number appeared sporadically, and a handful showed up rarely.

The delegates elected George Washington to serve as president of the Constitutional Convention. Washington reluctantly returned to public life because he was convinced the country needed a stronger central government both to make things run smoothly among the 13 states and to oversee expansion to the west and the creation of new states. Washington, who called the Articles of Confederation "little more than the shadow without the substance," quickly assumed control of the convention, and his dignity and gravitas no doubt had a lot to do with keeping the proceedings civil and productive.

Washington presided over the Constitutional Convention in Independence Hall—where the Declaration of Independence had been signed—from a chair that had a sun carved into the backrest. Delegates wondered whether the sun was rising or setting on their new nation. James Madison stepped up as the unofficial architect of the Constitution, with Gouverneur Morris as the chief draftsman. The actual sessions were held in secret, so we don't know as much as we might like about the back-and-forth discussion. But we know that there were many debates on many aspects of the Constitution, and they were often spirited.

The Compromise Constitution

The delegates were originally supposed to merely amend the Articles of Confederation, primarily to grease the wheels of interstate commerce. But the representatives quickly agreed to scrap the Articles of Confederation and start over with a constitution that would set the course for the new nation.

There were several areas of serious contention—so many, in fact, that the delegates agreed that a constitution might never be approved if they held out for unanimous ratification. So they agreed that only 9 of the 13 states would have to approve the constitution for it to go into effect. The delegates also agreed in principle that they should more clearly establish some sort of federal government, but in a form that would keep power from being concentrated in a single branch—particularly the kind of power that a king might have. They agreed to establish separate branches of government with a system of checks and balances not only among the three branches of government, but also between the federal government and the individual states.

> **People**
>
> Gouverneur Morris was a true member of the small American aristocracy, but unlike many of the patrician class he was also committed to independence and liberty. Serving as the primary writer of the Constitution was the highlight of his political career, which suffered on a number of occasions because of his penchant for sarcasm. For example, when discussing the role of the presidency at the convention, Morris announced that he "had no doubt that our Executive like most others would have too much patriotism to shrink from the burden of his office, and too much modesty not to be willing to decline the promotion."

Yet another issue, an echo of the misgivings that kept Patrick Henry back home in Virginia, was how power would be apportioned among the states. In the Continental Congress, each state had one vote, regardless of its size. Yet Congress asked the states to contribute taxes based on their population. At the Constitutional Convention, the small states wanted to stick with one state, one vote, while the large states wanted voting to be proportional. In the end, of course, the compromise was for a divided Congress, with two senators from each state and a House of Representatives elected proportionally by population.

The question of an army was also hotly contested. Would there be a European-style standing army? Or should the national government rely on state militia, as it had during the Revolution? Another compromise, vague in its terms, was reached: the states could maintain their own militia, but there also would be a national military force. The national force, however, would be under the ultimate control of the civilian government.

One issue that the delegates could not reach a compromise on was slavery. Some delegates, mostly from Northern states, wanted to abolish slavery. Most delegates from Southern states with slavery wanted to leave it up to each state. The convention agreed that the importing of slaves could not be banned until 1808 at the earliest; no limitations were agreed on owning slaves. It would take a bloody civil war decades later to make it illegal for one human being to claim ownership over another.

> **People**
>
> "It is much to be wished that slavery may be abolished. The honour of the States, as well as justice and humanity, in my opinion, loudly call upon them to emancipate these unhappy people. To contend for our own liberty, and to deny that blessing to others, involves an inconsistency not to be excused." —John Jay, *statesman, diplomat, politician, and the first Chief Justice of the Supreme Court*

The Agreement to Add a Bill of Rights

Besides the authority of the states within the federal system, there was also great concern among the anti-federalists over whether a central government would limit the rights of individuals. A final draft of the proposed Constitution was not presented until the delegates had agreed upon a compromise that called for adding a Bill of Rights in the form of a series of amendments protecting individual liberties. The fact that amendments were to be added almost immediately is no doubt one of the reasons that the Constitution was viewed from the beginning as a flexible document designed to be changed according to changes in society.

> **People** _____
> Benjamin Franklin was an octogenarian, frail in body but not
> mind, in 1787. Too weak to join the verbal jousting, he was some-
> times carried to Independence Hall on a sedan chair. But his written
> notes and comments were influential. He swayed other delegates before
> the final vote by saying the Constitution wasn't perfect, but it was good
> enough. And he concluded that the sun carved into Washington's chair
> was rising, not setting.

The convention approved the proposed new Constitution of the United
States of America on September 17, 1787, 11 years after the bells of
Philadelphia had rung out to mark the signing of the Declaration of
Independence. Thirty-nine of the 55 delegates—some call them the
Founding Fathers, but in legal circles we have come to think of them as
the "framers" of the Constitution—signed the document and submitted
it to Congress, which then offered it to the state legislatures for ratifi-
cation.

There were bitter fights over the Constitution in a number of states,
but supporters undertook an aggressive public relations program,
giving speeches and distributing pamphlets to educate the public.
Supporters of the new Constitution seized on three themes that struck
a chord with the public: national security, the economy, and pride in
being American. Delaware was the first state to vote for ratification,
in December 1787, on a unanimous vote. New Jersey and Georgia followed soon after. Massachusetts narrowly approved, 187 to 168. New
Hampshire, by 57 to 47, became the ninth state to approve, thereby
officially ratifying the Constitution in June 1788.

Alexander Hamilton and John Jay, writing under the pen name
"Publius," promoted the Constitution in New York by publishing a
series of 85 essays that came to be known as The Federalist Papers.
Despite the opposition of the popular governor, George Clinton, New
York ultimately endorsed the Constitution 30 to 27. The Constitution
went into effect in 1789, and George Washington took office as the
first president under the new form of government. The thirteenth and
final state approval did not come until 1790 when Rhode Island, the
only state not to send delegates to the convention, finally gave grudging
approval by a vote of 34 to 32.

The Preamble

"We the People of the United States, in Order to form a more perfect Union, establish Justice, insure domestic Tranquility, provide for the common defence, promote the general Welfare, and secure the Blessings of Liberty to ourselves and our Posterity, do ordain and establish this Constitution for the United States of America."

When you think about it, those early American colonists participated in two revolutions—one military and one ideological. In many ways, the military war against England was easier. We're still fighting our other revolution, the one that for the first time established a government by and for the people, based on "popular sovereignty" rather than on the sovereignty of a king or any other form of government. By our standards today, however, the framers of the Constitution were not especially enlightened. They were white guys, most of them old and rich, and their Constitution was written for themselves and the other old, rich, white guys who ran the states and the country. They did not envision women voting. Some of them may have envisioned black men being free someday, but many of them were themselves slave owners.

> **People**
>
> "'We the People.' When the Founding Fathers used this phrase in 1787, they did not have in mind the majority of America's citizens ...."
> —*Thurgood Marshall, the first African American justice on the U.S. Supreme Court*

not true

The Preamble sets a tone and lays out the goals of the Constitution, but it is worth noting that the Preamble itself, unlike the rest of the Constitution, is not regarded as part of the supreme law of land. It is merely an introduction. You cannot sue based on the Preamble in the same way that you can sue, for example, on the First Amendment if your rights to free speech are violated or on the Fourth Amendment if the police search your house illegally.

Nonetheless, the Preamble to the Constitution, with Gouverneur Morris's elegant "We the People" phrasing, is an important prelude for the way it emphasizes the democratic nature of the new nation. The Preamble speaks of justice and liberty, and offers lofty aspirations of peace and prosperity. It sets the tone for a Constitution that was written to offer hope, in 1787 and today.

The Least You Need to Know

◆ The United States is an ongoing experiment in democracy, and the Constitution is the blueprint for that experiment.

◆ The power of the U.S. Constitution comes not from the document itself, but rather from our society's agreement to live under the rule of law.

◆ The Constitution does not grant rights to the people; rather, it identifies the powers that the people grant to the government.

◆ The government's role under the Constitution is to protect both the United States as a nation and individual rights.

◆ The Constitution is the supreme law of the land, dealing less in specifics than in the spirit of the law.

Articles I–III: Separation of Powers

In This Chapter

- Article I: The Legislative Branch
- Article II: The Executive Branch
- Article III: The Judicial Branch

The first three original Articles of the Constitution, also called the "Powers" section of the Constitution, set out the three branches of government: legislative, executive, and judicial. This part of the Constitution also sets up the separation of powers, a sort of rock-paper-scissors arrangement aimed at keeping any one branch of government from amassing too much power.

The legislative branch can pass legislation for the president to sign into law, but the legislature has the authority to override a presidential veto. The president has broad powers to appoint government administrators and regulators, but many of the top appointees are subject to approval by the legislative branch. The president makes appointees to sit on the federal courts, also subject to legislative approval. And federal judges and Supreme

Court justices can overturn laws approved by the legislative branch and regulations enforced by the executive branch if they are ruled unconstitutional.

Article I: The Legislative Branch

This article establishes the branch of government that includes the elected representatives of the people, where laws are proposed, debated, and voted up or down.

The framers of the Constitution had choices for how to set up the new nation's Congress. At first they considered a unicameral system—a single legislative body, like the old Continental Congress. But how to pick the representatives? Should each state have the same number of representatives? Or should representation be based on population?

Balancing and compromising, as they so often did, the framers ended up with a bicameral legislature with two houses: the House of Representatives, with members chosen according to population, and the Senate, which allowed two members for each state no matter what their population.

In quoting from the text of the Constitution, here and elsewhere, we've preserved the quaint original punctuation, grammar, and spelling, such as "chuse" for "choose." In addition, the phrases in italics represent language that was not in the original articles, but was later added by amendments.

Section 1: Congress

"All legislative Powers herein granted shall be vested in a Congress of the United States, which shall consist of a Senate and House of Representatives."

The "vesting" language in effect prohibits direct voting by citizens and prohibits the other branches of government, the executive and the judicial, from enacting laws. Most states have a mechanism for referendum voting, allowing citizens to vote directly on proposed state legislation, but this clause prohibits national referendum voting.

Section 2: The House of Representatives

"The House of Representatives shall be composed of Members chosen every second Year by the People of the several States, and the Electors in each State shall have the Qualifications requisite for Electors of the most numerous Branch of the State Legislature.

"No Person shall be a Representative who shall not have attained to the age of twenty five Years, and been seven Years a Citizen of the United States, and who shall not, when elected, be an Inhabitant of that State in which he shall be chosen.

"*Representatives and direct Taxes shall be apportioned among the several States which may be included within this Union, according to their respective Numbers, which shall be determined by adding to the whole Number of free Persons, including those bound to Service for a Term of Years, and excluding Indians not taxed, three fifths of all other Persons.* The actual Enumeration shall be made within three Years after the first Meeting of the Congress of the United States, and within every subsequent Term of ten Years, in such Manner as they shall by Law direct. The Number of Representatives shall not exceed one for every thirty Thousand, but each State shall have at Least one Representative; and until such enumeration shall be made, the State of New Hampshire shall be entitled to chuse three, Massachusetts eight, Rhode-Island and Providence Plantations one, Connecticut five, New-York six, New Jersey four, Pennsylvania eight, Delaware one, Maryland six, Virginia ten, North Carolina five, South Carolina five, and Georgia three.

"When vacancies happen in the Representation from any State, the Executive Authority thereof shall issue Writs of Election to fill such Vacancies.

"The House of Representatives shall chuse their Speaker and other Officers; and shall have the sole Power of Impeachment."

Section 2 establishes the House of Representatives, the "people's house," and specifies that elections will be held every two years for all members of the House. When a vacancy occurs between regular elections, the governor of that state can call a special election. This section allowed the states to set the requirements for citizens to be eligible to vote for House candidates, but later amendments said states could not

A **poll tax** is a fee that a voter must pay before being allowed to vote. Historically, poll taxes have been used to keep poor people from voting.

keep people from voting because of their race or their sex, if they are at least 18 years old, or if they did not pay a *poll tax*.

Interestingly, there is no requirement that members of the House of Representatives actually live in the district they represent, though they are supposed to be at least 25 years old and have been a citizen of the United States for at least 7 years.

Each state must have at least one representative, but otherwise House districts (there have been 435 since 1911) are spread proportionately across the nation by population. A sparsely populated state such as Wyoming will have only one representative, while a densely populated city such as Chicago will have five members of the House, plus several others from the outlying suburbs. The Constitution called for a census every 10 years to reconfigure congressional districts in response to population shifts.

Note the language in the third paragraph of Section 2 that mentioned "three fifths of all other persons," in determining population for the purposes of deciding how many representatives each state would send to Congress. In effect, the framers of the Constitution were counting a slave as "three fifths" of a person as a compromise designed to limit the power of slave-holding states in Congress. The Fourteenth Amendment, after slavery was abolished, removed the three-fifths clause, and today all inhabitants of a state are counted, whether they are citizens or not.

When a House seat becomes vacant, a new election is held. When a Senate seat becomes vacant, the governor of the state can appoint a replacement.

That same clause, beginning "Representatives and direct taxes shall be apportioned ...," was aimed at making sure each state's share of any taxes collected by the federal government would be proportionate to the state's population. The Sixteenth Amendment changed this so that individual income taxes could be collected.

The Constitution borrows the British Parliament's procedure for impeaching a president; only the House can vote to impeach, and it is up to the Senate (Section 3) to put an impeached president on trial. Finally, this section allows the House to choose its own Speaker. Nothing says the Speaker actually has to be a member of the House, but so far every one in American history has been.

Section 3: The Senate

"The Senate of the United States shall be composed of two Senators from each State, chosen by the Legislature thereof, for six Years; and each Senator shall have one Vote.

"Immediately after they shall be assembled in Consequence of the first Election, they shall be divided as equally as may be into three Classes. The Seats of the Senators of the first Class shall be vacated at the Expiration of the second Year, of the second Class at the Expiration of the fourth Year, and of the third Class at the Expiration of the sixth Year, so that one third may be chosen every second Year; *and if Vacancies happen by Resignation, or otherwise, during the Recess of the Legislature of any State, the Executive thereof may make temporary Appointments until the next Meeting of the Legislature, which shall then fill such Vacancies.*

"No Person shall be a Senator who shall not have attained to the Age of thirty Years, and been nine Years a Citizen of the United States, and who shall not, when elected, be an Inhabitant of that State for which he shall be chosen.

"The Vice president of the United States shall be president of the Senate but shall have no Vote, unless they be equally divided.

"The Senate shall chuse their other Officers, and also a president pro tempore, in the Absence of the Vice president, or when he shall exercise the Office of president of the United States.

"The Senate shall have the sole Power to try all Impeachments. When sitting for that Purpose, they shall be on Oath or Affirmation. When the president of the United States is tried the Chief Justice shall preside: And no Person shall be convicted without the Concurrence of two thirds of the Members present.

"Judgment in Cases of Impeachment shall not extend further than to removal from Office, and disqualification to hold and enjoy any Office of honor, Trust or Profit under the United States: but the Party convicted shall nevertheless be liable and subject to Indictment, Trial, Judgment and Punishment, according to Law."

Senators were originally chosen by state legislatures, but that was later changed so that voters chose them directly for six-year terms. Unlike House seats that came up for re-election every two years, roughly one third of the Senate seats come open every two years. Senators need to be older than representatives—30 years old, and a citizen for 9 years. In addition, senators, unlike members of the House, must be residents of the states from which they are elected. The vice president was named president of the Senate, but can vote only to break ties.

> **People**
>
> The most recent president to be impeached was Bill Clinton, for perjury and obstruction of justice in connection with the dalliance he eventually admitted having with a White House intern. Only 45 senators voted to convict, far short of the 67 votes needed to remove him from office.

When the House votes to impeach a president, or any other federal official or judge, the Senate in effect acts as a jury; a two-thirds majority is needed to convict. If a president has been impeached, the chief justice presides over the trial in the Senate. Someone who is convicted is tossed out of office, can be barred from holding any other office, and may still face criminal charges.

Section 4: Elections and Sessions

"The Times, Places and Manner of holding Elections for Senators and Representatives, shall be prescribed in each State by the Legislature thereof; but the Congress may at any time by Law make or alter such Regulations, except as to the Places of chusing Senators.

"The Congress shall assemble at least once in every Year, and such Meeting shall be *on the first Monday in December*, unless they shall by Law appoint a different Day."

The states oversee federal elections, but this section allowed Congress to set a standard date for congressional elections. That turned out to be the Tuesday following the first Monday in November of even-numbered years. Congress could simply have specified the first Tuesday in November, but didn't want to conflict with November 1, the religious holiday All Saints' Day, when it falls on a Tuesday.

In the second paragraph, the requirement to meet on the first Monday meant that since the new Congress originally was not sworn in until the following March, the gathering in December was a *lame duck* Congress. The Twentieth Amendment changed the rules so that newly elected or re-elected members of the House and Senate took office in early January.

> **def•i•ni•tion**
>
> A **lame duck** is an elected official or body of officials whose terms in office are expiring.

Section 5: Housekeeping

"Each House shall be the Judge of the Elections, Returns and Qualifications of its own Members, and a Majority of each shall constitute a Quorum to do Business; but a smaller Number may adjourn from day to day, and may be authorized to compel the Attendance of absent Members, in such Manner, and under such Penalties as each House may provide.

"Each House may determine the Rules of its Proceedings, punish its Members for disorderly Behaviour, and, with the Concurrence of two thirds, expel a Member.

"Each House shall keep a Journal of its Proceedings, and from time to time publish the same, excepting such Parts as may in their Judgment require Secrecy; and the Yeas and Nays of the Members of either House on any question shall, at the Desire of one fifth of those Present, be entered on the Journal.

"Neither House, during the Session of Congress, shall, without the Consent of the other, adjourn for more than three days, nor to any other Place than that in which the two Houses shall be sitting."

This is a housekeeping section for Congress, allowing the Senate and House to make their own rules. For example, when a 29-year-old won election to the Senate, the Senate bent its rules to let the young senator-elect wait a few months until his thirtieth birthday to assume his seat.

The quorum clause requires each chamber to have a majority present to do business, but in fact this rule is widely ignored.

Each house can censure one of its own members by a simple majority vote, but it takes a two-thirds majority to expel a member.

Each chamber must keep a journal of what happens on the floor, but it can keep anything out of the journal, or put things into the journal that didn't actually happen. For example, members of Congress sometimes have speeches entered in the *Congressional Record* without ever actually giving the speech. Neither house can adjourn without the consent of the other for more than three days, but this simply means that the House and the Senate frequently meet the constitutional requirement simply by calling themselves to order every three days—often for less than a minute—without actually doing any business.

Section 6: Pay and Privileges

"The Senators and Representatives shall receive a Compensation for their Services, to be ascertained by Law, and paid out of the Treasury of the United States. They shall in all Cases, except Treason, Felony and Breach of the Peace, be privileged from Arrest during their Attendance at the Session of their respective Houses, and in going to and returning from the same; and for any Speech or Debate in either House, they shall not be questioned in any other Place.

"No Senator or Representative shall, during the Time for which he was elected, be appointed to any civil Office under the Authority of the United States, which shall have been created, or the Emoluments whereof shall have been encreased during such time; and no Person holding any Office under the United States, shall be a Member of either House during his Continuance in Office."

Members of Congress are allowed to set their own pay under this section of the Constitution, but it prevents them from starting to collect the raise until after the next election. To prevent harassment from the executive branch, special privileges granted to members of Congress include immunity from arrest for minor crimes—in effect, this barred "civil" arrests, which are rare these days—while they are in session or on their way to or from Congress. Members of Congress, however, can be arrested on criminal charges, either misdemeanors or felonies. They can't, however, be sued for slander for remarks on the floor.

In another move toward financial propriety, and to shore up the separation of powers, members of Congress must wait until their terms expire to take higher-paying jobs in government; they can't resign one day and start collecting the higher pay the next day.

Section 7: Legislation

"All Bills for raising Revenue shall originate in the House of Representatives; but the Senate may propose or concur with amendments as on other Bills.

"Every Bill which shall have passed the House of Representatives and the Senate, shall, before it become a law, be presented to the president of the United States: If he approves he shall sign it, but if not he shall return it, with his Objections to that House in which it shall have originated, who shall enter the Objections at large on their Journal, and proceed to reconsider it. If after such Reconsideration two thirds of that House shall agree to pass the Bill, it shall be sent, together with the Objections, to the other House, by which it shall likewise be reconsidered, and if approved by two thirds of that House, it shall become a Law. But in all such Cases the Votes of both Houses shall be determined by Yeas and Nays, and the Names of the Persons voting for and against the Bill shall be entered on the Journal of each House respectively. If any Bill shall not be returned by the president within ten Days (Sundays excepted) after it shall have been presented to him, the Same shall be a Law, in like Manner as if he had signed it, unless the Congress by their Adjournment prevent its Return, in which Case it shall not be a Law.

"Every Order, Resolution, or Vote to which the Concurrence of the Senate and House of Representatives may be necessary (except on a question of Adjournment) shall be presented to the president of the United States; and before the Same shall take Effect, shall be approved by him, or being disapproved by him, shall be repassed by two thirds of the Senate and House of Representatives, according to the Rules and Limitations prescribed in the Case of a Bill."

Senators or representatives can introduce bills, but all legislation raising revenue—tax bills, in other words—must originate in the House. The House also claims that it must initiate appropriations bills—spending bills, in other words. The Senate historically has disagreed, but in practice all appropriations bills do originate in the House: if the Senate initiates a spending bill and sends it to the House, the House simply returns it without any action.

The Presentment Clause sets forth the way a bill becomes law: when both chambers have approved a bill in exactly identical forms, it is sent to the president, who has 10 days (not counting Sundays) to sign it so that it becomes law or veto it—send it back to the originating chamber with an explanation of his objections. The bill can still become law if both chambers, by two-thirds majorities instead of the usual simple majorities, override the veto. If a president does not return a Congress-approved bill within 10 days, it becomes law—unless Congress has adjourned in the meantime. If Congress has adjourned, this is called a pocket veto, and the bill dies because the president could not return it to the House or Senate.

This section of the Constitution also includes one of its most important provisions—the procedure for changing the Constitution itself. Two thirds of both houses of Congress can approve a proposed amendment and send it to the states for ratification. The president doesn't get a crack at a veto—a clear example of the framers' intentions to limit the power of the executive branch. The states then vote on ratification. This is usually done by each state's legislature, but an amendment can instead call for each state to hold a ratification convention. Either way, a simple majority is needed for ratification. When three fourths of the states have ratified an amendment, it becomes part of the Constitution.

Cases

Clinton v. City of New York (1998): In 1996, Congress approved the Line Item Veto Act, which allowed the president, instead of vetoing or signing a bill, to veto certain spending provisions. President Clinton used the line-item veto to trim spending for health programs in New York City, the city sued, and the Supreme Court declared the act unconstitutional.

Section 8: Enumerated Powers

"The Congress shall have Power To lay and collect Taxes, Duties, Imposts and Excises, to pay the Debts and provide for the common Defence and general Welfare of the United States; but all Duties, Imposts and Excises shall be uniform throughout the United States;

"To borrow Money on the credit of the United States;

"To regulate Commerce with foreign Nations, and among the several States, and with the Indian Tribes;

"To establish an uniform Rule of Naturalization, and uniform Laws on the subject of Bankruptcies throughout the United States;

"To coin Money, regulate the Value thereof, and of foreign Coin, and fix the Standard of Weights and Measures;

"To provide for the Punishment of counterfeiting the Securities and current Coin of the United States;

"To establish Post Offices and post Roads;

"To promote the Progress of Science and useful Arts, by securing for limited Times to Authors and Inventors the exclusive Right to their respective Writings and Discoveries;

"To constitute Tribunals inferior to the supreme Court;

"To define and punish Piracies and Felonies committed on the high Seas, and Offences against the Law of Nations;

"To declare War, grant Letters of Marque and Reprisal, and make Rules concerning Captures on Land and Water;

"To raise and support Armies, but no Appropriation of Money to that Use shall be for a longer Term than two Years;

"To provide and maintain a Navy;

"To make Rules for the Government and Regulation of the land and naval Forces;

"To provide for calling forth the Militia to execute the Laws of the Union, suppress Insurrections and repel Invasions;

"To provide for organizing, arming, and disciplining, the Militia, and for governing such Part of them as may be employed in the Service of the United States, reserving to the States respectively, the Appointment of the Officers, and the Authority of training the Militia according to the discipline prescribed by Congress;

"To exercise exclusive Legislation in all Cases whatsoever, over such District (not exceeding ten Miles square) as may, by Cession of Particular States, and the Acceptance of Congress, become the Seat of the Government of the United States, and to exercise like Authority over all Places purchased by the Consent of the Legislature of the State in which the Same shall be, for the Erection of Forts, Magazines, Arsenals, dock-Yards and other needful Buildings;—And

"To make all Laws which shall be necessary and proper for carrying into Execution the foregoing Powers and all other Powers vested by this Constitution in the Government of the United States, or in any Department or Officer thereof."

The sweeping provisions of this part of the Constitution, known as the "enumerated powers," give Congress a laundry list of its authority. For example, 1 of the 17 powers specifically listed allows Congress to establish a national post office. But Congress, obviously, has also established a Social Security system, a Department of Education, and many other government agencies and functions that are not enumerated. How?

The opening clause of Section 8 is known as the General Welfare Clause, allowing Congress to provide for the common defense and general welfare, without defining either. Under a broad interpretation of this clause, Congress has been able to decide what's good for the country and then pass laws and spend money to make it happen. A narrow interpretation of the Constitution, particularly among those who are critical of the welfare state, maintains that a broad interpretation would in effect give Congress unlimited power—something that the framers did not contemplate.

The third clause is the wide-ranging Commerce Clause, allowing Congress to regulate trade with foreign nations and among the states. It originally was intended to keep the 13 states from erecting trade barriers or tariffs that would prevent the free flow of goods and services within the new nation. It also gave federal laws and regulations precedence over conflicting states' rules.

In the twentieth century, as the government began regulating more aspects of everyday life and work, the clause provided Congress much of its authority to impose rules on companies that do business across state borders. Libertarians protest that Congress has assumed more regulatory power than the Constitution intended, including to some noncommercial activities conducted entirely within states. In several cases the Supreme Court has ruled that Congress has gone too far, particularly in limiting New Deal programs in the 1930s, but in a more recent case the Supreme Court ruled that the Commerce Clause applied to a person growing marijuana for personal medical use, even though no profits or interstate commerce was involved.

Cases
NLRB v. Jones & Laughlin Steel Co. (1937): This case expanded Congress's authority under the Commerce Clause by approving the authority of the National Labor Relations Board to punish employers for "unfair labor practices," including firing workers for trying to unionize.

Other clauses in Article I, Section 8, of the Constitution give Congress the power to pass laws relating to a broad range of areas: bankruptcy, coining money, counterfeiting, the value of U.S. dollars on the foreign currency exchanges, the post office, standards for weights and measures, copyrights, and patents. It is up to the federal government, not the states, to determine who is and who is not a citizen.

The War Powers Clause says only Congress can declare war, though the specifics of how and when this can happen are left unsaid. Congress has declared war only five times in U.S. history, always at the request of the president, most recently for World War II in 1941.

After presidents waged undeclared wars in Korea in the 1950s and Vietnam in the 1960s and '70s, Congress passed the War Powers Resolution of 1973. In theory, this act was designed to have Congress and the president share the power to declare war, but in practice it has given the president more authority—perhaps more than the Constitution intended, according to some critics—to wage war with or without the approval of Congress. The president has engaged in military conflicts several times since then with Congress's approval but without a formal declaration of war, including in Iraq in 1991, Afghanistan in 2001, and Iraq again in 2003.

Congress has the authority to establish and finance an army, but the framers' misgivings about standing armies led them to require that military funding not be for more than two years at a time—which is irrelevant today, since military budgets are routinely approved each year. Congress still has the superior authority over the executive branch in terms of rules and regulations for the land and naval military forces, though in practice the executive branch, through the Pentagon, has much more to do with overseeing the military. The president has the authority to call out a state's militia, as when National Guard troops were used to enforce desegregation in the 1950s and to quell urban unrest in the 1960s.

This section also gives Congress authority to oversee the District of Columbia's locally elected government, though many residents of the nation's capital believe they would be better off if their city had more autonomy.

The last clause of Section 8 is the Necessary-and-Proper Clause, which affords Congress broad authority to do whatever it needs to do to carry about the section's enumerated powers—including reorganizing the executive or judicial branches. A landmark case was *McCulloch v. Maryland* in 1819, when the Supreme Court endorsed the concept of a national bank despite strong opposition from those who feared that a federal banking system would weaken the states. Justice John Marshall said all the powers in the clause need not be enumerated, and that the General Welfare and the Commerce clauses gave Congress authority to decide a national bank was necessary and proper.

People

Late in their lives, 40 years after the Constitutional Convention, two of the most venerated Founding Fathers took opposite sides of the public debate over the national bank issue ultimately decided in *McCulloch v. Maryland*. Thomas Jefferson said a bank was not necessary, so therefore unauthorized. Alexander Hamilton said a bank was necessary to collect taxes, borrow money, and regulate trade. The Supreme Court agreed with Hamilton's position.

Section 9: Restrictions on Congress

"The Migration or Importation of such Persons as any of the States now existing shall think proper to admit, shall not be prohibited by the Congress prior to the Year one thousand eight hundred and eight, but a Tax or duty may be imposed on such Importation, not exceeding ten dollars for each Person.

"The Privilege of the Writ of Habeas Corpus shall not be suspended, unless when in Cases of Rebellion or Invasion the public Safety may require it.

"No Bill of Attainder or ex post facto Law shall be passed.

"No Capitation, or other direct, Tax shall be laid, *unless in Proportion to the Census of Enumeration herein before directed to be taken.*

"No Tax or Duty shall be laid on Articles exported from any State.

"No Preference shall be given by any Regulation of Commerce or Revenue to the Ports of one State over those of another: nor shall Vessels bound to, or from, one State, be obliged to enter, clear or pay Duties in another.

"No Money shall be drawn from the Treasury, but in Consequence of Appropriations made by Law; and a regular Statement and Account of the Receipts and Expenditures of all public Money shall be published from time to time.

"No Title of Nobility shall be granted by the United States: And no Person holding any Office of Profit or Trust under them, shall, without the Consent of the Congress, accept of any present, Emolument, Office, or Title, of any kind whatever, from any King, Prince or foreign State."

This section is noted, or notorious, for the compromise that allowed the importing of slaves to continue until 1808. Most of the members of the Constitutional Convention in 1787 abhorred slavery—even the slave owners such as Ben Franklin said it was immoral—but they needed to keep the slave-owning states on board. They also allowed a tax of up to $10 per year per slave. On January 1, 1808, the first day it was possible to outlaw bringing new slaves into the country, Congress did so.

There's a bit of irony, perhaps, in one brief phrase in this section. The colonists cherished the right of habeas corpus under British rule, and in fact it was one of the reasons for the Revolution. This part of the Constitution prohibits suspending the *writ of habeas corpus* except in cases of rebellion or invasion. The Supreme Court later shored up this provision by holding that habeas corpus could not be suspended as long as the civil courts were operating. This section also bans *bills of attainder* and *ex post facto laws*.

The provision against "direct" taxes led the Supreme Court to declare income taxes unconstitutional until they were expressly legalized by the Sixteenth Amendment.

This section also prohibits Congress from taxing exports from any state, prohibits Congress from granting any titles of nobility, and prevents any American government official from accepting any office or title—or any meaningful gift—from a foreign country. That's why a president can't keep all the loot collected on those grand foreign tours; it all belongs to the people of the United States, and is turned over to the government.

def•i•ni•tion

A **writ of habeas corpus,** from the Latin "you have the body," is a legal order, known as "the Great Writ," from a judge that orders a prisoner to be brought in front of the court to determine whether the prisoner is being held legally.

Bills of attainder are laws passed by a legislative body to single out one person or group of people for punishment without the usual protections of due process in the judicial system.

Ex post facto laws are passed "after the fact," and punish people—or increase previous punishments—for actions taken before the laws were passed.

Section 10: Restrictions on the States

"No State shall enter into any Treaty, Alliance, or Confederation; grant Letters of Marque and Reprisal; coin Money; emit Bills of Credit; make any Thing but gold and silver Coin a Tender in Payment of Debts;

pass any Bill of Attainder, ex post facto Law, or Law impairing the Obligation of Contracts, or grant any Title of Nobility.

"No State shall, without the Consent of the Congress, lay any Imposts or Duties on Imports or Exports, except what may be absolutely necessary for executing its inspection Laws: and the net Produce of all Duties and Imposts, laid by any State on Imports or Exports, shall be for the Use of the Treasury of the United States; and all such Laws shall be subject to the Revision and Controul of the Congress.

"No State shall, without the Consent of Congress, lay any Duty of Tonnage, keep Troops, or Ships of War in time of Peace, enter into any Agreement or Compact with another State, or with a foreign Power, or engage in War, unless actually invaded, or in such imminent Danger as will not admit of delay."

This section aims to make it clear to states that some powers are solely the providence of Congress and the federal government. States are not allowed to enter into treaties or alliances, coin money, tax imports or exports, or have their own warships or standing armies. States were, however, allowed to have local militia—today's National Guard—with federal oversight. States also may not declare war or grant titles of nobility. (Presumably a Kentucky colonel is not noble enough to violate the Constitution.)

The first paragraph contains the sometimes controversial Contracts Clause, which bars states from interfering with contract law. In an infamous 1810 case, the Supreme Court ruled that the state of Georgia could not annul contracts made by corrupt members of the state legislature to sell off state lands—even though the deals were blatant with bribery.

Article II: The Executive Branch

Article II sets out the executive branch of government, including the president and vice president, and defines their authority.

Section 1: President and Vice President

"The executive Power shall be vested in a president of the United States of America. He shall hold his Office during the Term of four Years, and, together with the Vice president, chosen for the same Term, be elected, as follows:

"Each State shall appoint, in such Manner as the Legislature thereof may direct, a Number of Electors, equal to the whole Number of Senators and Representatives to which the State may be entitled in the Congress: but no Senator or Representative, or Person holding an Office of Trust or Profit under the United States, shall be appointed an Elector.

"The Electors shall meet in their respective States, and vote by Ballot for two Persons, of whom one at least shall not be an Inhabitant of the same State with themselves. And they shall make a List of all the Persons voted for, and of the Number of Votes for each; which List they shall sign and certify, and transmit sealed to the Seat of the Government of the United States, directed to the president of the Senate. The president of the Senate shall, in the Presence of the Senate and House of Representatives, open all the Certificates, and the Votes shall then be counted. The Person having the greatest Number of Votes shall be the president, if such Number be a Majority of the whole Number of Electors appointed; and if there be more than one who have such Majority, and have an equal Number of Votes, then the House of Representatives shall immediately chuse by Ballot one of them for president; and if no Person have a Majority, then from the five highest on the List the said House shall in like Manner chuse the president. But in chusing the president, the Votes shall be taken by States, the Representatives from each State having one Vote; a quorum for this Purpose shall consist of a Member or Members from two thirds of the States, and a Majority of all the States shall be necessary to a Choice. In every Case, after the Choice of the president, the Person having the greatest Number of Votes of the Electors shall be the Vice president. But if there should remain two or more who have equal Votes, the Senate shall chuse from them by Ballot the Vice president.

"The Congress may determine the Time of chusing the Electors, and the Day on which they shall give their Votes; which Day shall be the same throughout the United States.

"No Person except a natural born Citizen, or a Citizen of the United States, at the time of the Adoption of this Constitution, shall be eligible to the Office of president; neither shall any person be eligible to that Office who shall not have attained to the Age of thirty five Years, and been fourteen Years a Resident within the United States.

"In Case of the Removal of the president from Office, or of his Death, Resignation, or Inability to discharge the Powers and Duties of the said Office, the Same shall devolve on the Vice president, and the Congress may by Law provide for the Case of Removal, Death, Resignation or Inability, both of the president and Vice president, declaring what Officer shall then act as president, and such Officer shall act accordingly, until the Disability be removed, or a president shall be elected.

"The president shall, at stated Times, receive for his Services, a Compensation, which shall neither be encreased nor diminished during the Period for which he shall have been elected, and he shall not receive within that Period any other Emolument from the United States, or any of them.

"Before he enter on the Execution of his Office, he shall take the following Oath or Affirmation:—'I do solemnly swear (or affirm) that I will faithfully execute the Office of president of the United States, and will to the best of my Ability, preserve, protect and defend the Constitution of the United States.'"

The chief executive is called president. Both president and vice president are elected to four-year terms. The Constitution originally set no limit on the number of terms a president could serve, and George Washington may well have been able to serve as many four-year terms as he wanted. Washington thought no more than two terms were proper, and every president followed that tradition until Franklin Delano Roosevelt, who was elected four times. After his death, the Twenty-second Amendment officially limited the president to two terms.

The president and vice president are not elected directly by the people but instead by electors chosen by the state legislatures. Each state has the same number of electors as it has members in Congress—representatives and senators combined. However, no representatives or senators can serve as electors.

Today there are 538 electors in what came to be known as the Electoral College, representing 100 senators, 435 representatives, and 3 representatives from the District of Columbia. A presidential ticket—president and vice president—that wins a state is presumed to win all the electoral votes from that state. On election night, returns are counted unofficially, state by state, and a presidential candidate is declared the winner by amassing 270 or more electoral votes, a majority.

The original language, calling for each elector to vote for two candidates, one of them from a different state, proved cumbersome as the House struggled before declaring Thomas Jefferson the new president after a tie vote with Aaron Burr in 1800. Under changes implemented by the Twelfth Amendment, after a national election in November, electors officially cast their ballots in December for both president and vice president, and Congress formally counts those votes in January. If no candidate has a majority of the electoral votes, the House of Representatives chooses the next president and vice president.

In practice, the actual popular vote does not count, and there have been instances of a presidential candidate getting the most votes nationally, but losing the election. That's what happened in 2000, when George W. Bush won more electoral votes even though more people voted for Al Gore across the nation.

Section 1 of Article II also requires that both the president and the vice president be "natural born" citizens who are at least 35 years and who have lived in the United States for at least 14 years. However, no courts have ruled on what "natural born" means, and whether it applies to citizens born in overseas territories or to parents who are citizens living in other countries. The eligibility requirements have ruled out presidential bids for a number of popular figures over the years; for example, it would take a Constitutional amendment to allow Austrian-born Arnold Schwarzenegger to become president. Two other prominent popular public figures who were considered presidential timber at least in some circles but were ineligible for being born abroad included statesman and lawyer Frederick Lehman in the nineteenth century and comedian Bob Hope in the twentieth century.

> **People**
>
> When George Washington took the oath of office, he ad-libbed, "So help me God," at the end, and every president since then has added it, too.

The Twenty-fifth Amendment superseded the section on succession, providing for the vice president to assume the presidency if the president is disabled or leaves office. This section also prohibits Congress from changing a president's salary ($400,000 a year as of the four-year term expiring in 2008) during that term, and prohibits the president from accepting any other pay while in office.

The familiar oath of office administered by the chief justice at the inauguration, beginning, "I do solemnly swear that I will faithfully executive the office of the president ...," is also spelled out in this section.

Section 2: Presidential Powers

"The president shall be Commander in Chief of the Army and Navy of the United States, and of the Militia of the several States, when called into the actual Service of the United States; he may require the Opinion, in writing, of the principal Officer in each of the executive Departments, upon any Subject relating to the Duties of their respective Offices, and he shall have Power to Grant Reprieves and Pardons for Offences against the United States, except in Cases of Impeachment.

"He shall have Power, by and with the Advice and Consent of the Senate, to make Treaties, provided two thirds of the Senators present concur; and he shall nominate, and by and with the Advice and Consent of the Senate, shall appoint Ambassadors, other public Ministers and Consuls, Judges of the supreme Court, and all other Officers of the United States, whose Appointments are not herein otherwise provided for, and which shall be established by Law: but the Congress may by Law vest the Appointment of such inferior Officers, as they think proper, in the president alone, in the Courts of Law, or in the Heads of Departments.

"The president shall have Power to fill up all Vacancies that may happen during the Recess of the Senate, by granting Commissions which shall expire at the End of their next Session."

The president is commander in chief of the military, has the authority to grant pardons or reprieves, and may require "the principal officer" of executive departments—Cabinet officers, in other words—to offer written advice. The president can make treaties with the approval of the Senate, and can appoint judges and ambassadors, also with the approval of the Senate.

This section specifically authorizes the "recess" appointments that have become controversial under recent presidents; rather than risking a tough confirmation battle and possible rejection, presidents can appoint judges and other officials while the Senate is in recess and cannot confirm the nominations. The political thinking holds that it is more difficult for the Senate to reject a nominee who is already serving.

The president—this article specifies "he" but presumably applies if and when a woman is elected president—can fire many appointed officials but not federal judges, who are appointed for life in order to insulate them from political pressures.

Section 3: Executive Responsibility

"He shall from time to time give to the Congress Information on the State of the Union, and recommend to their Consideration such Measures as he shall judge necessary and expedient; he may, on extraordinary Occasions, convene both Houses, or either of them, and in Case of Disagreement between them, with Respect to the Time of Adjournment, he may adjourn them to such Time as he shall think proper; he shall receive Ambassadors and other public Ministers; he shall take Care that the Laws be faithfully executed, and shall Commission all the Officers of the United States."

> **People**
>
> Thomas Jefferson thought delivering a State of the Union speech personally was too much like a king making an address. Instead, he sent a written summary to Congress that was read by a clerk. Every subsequent president did the same until Woodrow Wilson returned to Congress and made the speech himself, and that's what every president since then has done.

This section lists a number of presidential responsibilities, including making an annual State of the Union speech to Congress, calling the House or Senate or both into special session, commissioning military and Foreign Service officers, receiving foreign ambassadors, and generally executing or enforcing the laws of the United States.

The "missing clause" from this section covers executive privilege—a president's authority to withhold information from the courts, Congress, and the public. The

Supreme Court has agreed that the president does have limited executive privilege, but cannot withhold information simply by claiming that releasing it would harm the presidency or threaten national security. Richard Nixon, for example, tried to withhold the secret tapes from his office on the grounds of executive privilege, but the Supreme Court rejected his claim and ordered the tapes released, which led to Nixon's resignation in the face of possible impeachment.

Section 4: Impeachment

"The president, Vice president and all Civil Officers of the United States, shall be removed from Office on Impeachment for and Conviction of, Treason, Bribery, or other high Crimes and Misdemeanors."

This section allows Congress to remove the president, vice president, and other members of the executive branch, as well as federal judges. The House votes for impeachment, and the Senate then sits as the jury at a trial. If convicted, the official is removed from office and may be barred from holding any other federal government post. The contentious part of this section is what constitutes "high crimes and misdemeanors," but in practical matters the House decides what are or aren't high crimes and misdemeanors.

Article III: The Judicial Branch

This article sets forth the federal court system, including the Supreme Court. It outlines the rules for appointing judges and establishes the authority of the courts.

Section 1: Federal Courts

"The judicial Power of the United States, shall be vested in one supreme Court, and in such inferior Courts as the Congress may from time to time ordain and establish. The Judges, both of the supreme and inferior Courts, shall hold their Offices during good Behaviour, and shall, at stated Times, receive for their Services, a Compensation, which shall not be diminished during their Continuance in Office."

This section makes it clear that there will be one, and only one, Supreme Court, and leaves it to Congress to create the lesser federal courts. The main courts today are the District Courts, but there are also regional Circuit Courts of Appeal, an intermediate level where losers in the District Courts can appeal. The Supreme Court generally hears only cases that have been appealed from the Circuit Courts.

Federal judges are appointed by the president with the approval of the Senate and can be removed only through impeachment, which is so rare that it has happened only a handful of times in American history.

Section 2: Jurisdiction and Judicial Review

"The judicial Power shall extend to all Cases, in Law and Equity, arising under this Constitution, the Laws of the United States, and Treaties made, or which shall be made, under their Authority;—to all Cases affecting Ambassadors, other public ministers and Consuls;—to all Cases of admiralty and maritime Jurisdiction;—to Controversies to which the United States shall be a Party;—to Controversies between two or more States;—between a State and Citizens of another State;— between Citizens of different States;—between Citizens of the same State claiming Lands under Grants of different States, and between a State, or the Citizens thereof, and foreign States, Citizens or Subjects.

"In all Cases affecting Ambassadors, other public Ministers and Consuls, and those in which a State shall be Party, the supreme Court shall have original Jurisdiction. In all the other Cases before mentioned, the supreme Court shall have appellate Jurisdiction, both as to Law and Fact, with such Exceptions, and under such Regulations as the Congress shall make.

"The Trial of all Crimes, except in Cases of Impeachment, shall be by Jury; and such Trial shall be held in the State where the said Crimes shall have been committed; but when not committed within any State, the Trial shall be at such Place or Places as the Congress may by Law have directed."

This section makes it clear that the federal courts have jurisdiction for all cases arising from the Constitution or from federal law, and for all conflicts that cross state lines, such as disputes between different states or lawsuits between citizens of different states. However, the Eleventh Amendment prevents a state from being sued in federal court. Federal courts also have jurisdiction over all cases involving foreign governments and admiralty and maritime cases. This section also guarantees the right to trial by jury in criminal cases and lists certain cases that can be taken up directly by the Supreme Court without appeal from lower courts.

One of the biggest issues surrounding the federal judiciary, from the earliest days of the United States through today, is the authority of the courts to review—and overturn—laws and regulations enacted by other branches of the government. On one hand, the Constitution never specifically mentions judicial review; on the other hand, the system of checks and balances would not work nearly as effectively if it was up to Congress and the president to decide whether their actions were constitutional or not.

Cases

Marbury v. Madison (1803): Without the principle set forth in this landmark case, the system of checks and balances might not work as well, or at all. The decision by Chief Justice John Marshall established the concept of judicial review by declaring an act of Congress unconstitutional for the first time. Since then, the Supreme Court has reinforced its authority to overrule laws and regulations approved by the other branches of government in more than 120 other cases.

A court can overturn existing law—literally throw it out, and wipe it off the books—by finding that the law is itself illegal. This is what happens, for example, when a law is declared unconstitutional. Besides nullifying legislation, a court can also declare administrative regulations and procedures illegal. Sometimes the courts offer suggestions or guidelines about how to correct the procedures. This is what has happened in a series of court rulings that shaped the way the death penalty is administered by states. A new set of rules or guidelines set forth by a court stand as the law unless and until superseded by legislative action or a higher-court ruling.

A court can overturn existing laws, regulations, and procedures by finding that they violate existing law, including the Constitution. Our judicial system follows precedent, which means that courts also can overturn all or part of existing laws because of conflicts with previous court rulings. Courts are typically reluctant to overturn their own precedents, and the Supreme Court has been known to go through gymnastics of creative reasoning to reach a desired result without flatly overruling an earlier court decision.

In truth, however, courts can find many reasons for overturning existing law, including "public policy." Whatever the reason, critics often complain about judicial activism and criticize "activist judges" for overturning legislation approved by the public's elected representatives. The debate continues today, from law schools to blogs to courtrooms to the chambers of the Supreme Court itself: when and how the courts can and should exert the authority to review legislation.

People

A Yale University study into judicial activism looked at the 64 U.S. Supreme Court decisions overturning congressional legislation between 1994 and 2005. These are the percentages for the justices on the court at that time (before justices Roberts and Alito replaced justices Rehnquist and O'Connor) in voting to overturn Congress:

Thomas: 66 percent
Kennedy: 64 percent
Scalia: 56 percent
Rehnquist: 47 percent
O'Connor: 47 percent
Souter: 42 percent
Stevens: 39 percent
Ginsburg: 39 percent
Breyer: 28 percent

Section 3: Treason

"Treason against the United States, shall consist only in levying War against them, or in adhering to their Enemies, giving them Aid and Comfort. No Person shall be convicted of Treason unless on the Testimony of two Witnesses to the same overt Act, or on Confession in open Court.

"The Congress shall have Power to declare the Punishment of Treason, but no Attainder of Treason shall work Corruption of Blood, or Forfeiture except during the Life of the Person attainted."

Treason, the only federal crime specified in the Constitution, is defined as an act of war against the United States, or lending "aid and comfort" to its enemies. Cases of treason have been rare in American history, though there are some notable instances. Former vice president Aaron Burr, fleeing murder charges after killing Alexander Hamilton in a duel in 1804, was tried and acquitted of treason in 1807 after being accused of trying to muster an army to establish a rival nation, perhaps in Mexico, with himself as president.

Many wanted the so-called American Taliban, John Walker Lindh, to be charged with treason after being captured fighting American troops in Afghanistan in 2001, but Walker ended up accepting a 20-year sentence and agreeing to plead guilty to lesser charges.

The Least You Need to Know

- The three branches of government—executive, legislative, and judicial—operate in a system of checks and balances designed to keep any one branch from exerting too much power.

- The legislative branch is the bicameral Congress, made up of the House of Representatives, with 435 districts set by population, and the Senate, that includes two members from each state; it is empowered to approve federal laws.

- The president is the chief executive, whose power comes from the constitutional obligation to administer the government, and to execute and enforce its laws.

- The judiciary's ultimate power in the system of checks and balances comes from the principle of judicial review, which allows the federal courts to throw out laws and regulations for violating the Constitution.

3

Articles IV–VII: Making the Federal System Work

In This Chapter

- ◆ Article IV: Full Faith and Credit
- ◆ Article V: Amending the Constitution
- ◆ Article VI: The Supreme Law of the Land
- ◆ Article VII: Ratification

Articles IV, V, VI, and VII together erect a framework for relationships among the states and their relationships with the federal government, including provisions for admitting new states and amending the Constitution.

Article IV: Full Faith and Credit

The original 13 colonies in many ways viewed themselves, and each other, as more like independent mini-nations than as part of a single entity. One colony did not necessarily have to respect the laws of another colony. The Articles of Confederation allowed the fledgling states to maintain much of that independence from each other. Article IV of the Constitution, however, redefined the relationships among the states, requiring them to recognize and honor each other's laws.

Section 1: Full Faith and Credit

"Full faith and credit shall be given in each state to the public acts, records, and judicial proceedings of every other state. And the Congress may by general laws prescribe the manner in which such acts, records, and proceedings shall be proved, and the effect thereof."

The Full Faith and Credit Clause is one of the most important in the Constitution. The clause requires the states to honor each other's laws, records—including licenses—and court decisions. If you win a legal case in one state, that same case cannot be reopened in another state. One of the key factors back when the Constitution was being debated was that this provision would allow a plantation owner from a slave-holding state to travel with his slave to a nonslave state, and the slave would not become free merely by setting foot in a free state. Without this provision today, your driver's license might not be recognized by the next state.

The Full Faith and Credit Clause has had a major significance on domestic law, including marriage and child custody issues. For example, it presents a major obstacle to a divorced parent who is unhappy with a court's child-custody orders and takes the kid to another state seeking a new custody order.

And without this section of the Constitution, your spur-of-the-moment marriage in Las Vegas might not be recognized back home. Hawaii sent ripples across the mainland's legal landscape in 1993 when the state courts recognized gay marriage. Three years later, Congress enacted the Defense of Marriage Act, which defined marriage as between a man and a woman. The act also said that despite the Full Faith and Credit

Clause, states could refuse to recognize same-sex marriages recognized as legal in other states.

The arguments continue, however, over whether the Constitution allows states to deny recognition to same-sex marriages that are legal in other states. Opponents of gay marriage want a federal marriage amendment to the Constitution to make it clear that marriage can be between a man and a woman only.

Cases

"The primary purpose of this clause," the Supreme Court said of the Full Faith and Credit Clause in a 1948 case, "was to help fuse into one Nation a collection of independent sovereign States."

Section 2: Privileges and Immunities

"The citizens of each state shall be entitled to all privileges and immunities of citizens in the several states.

"A person charged in any state with treason, felony, or other crime, who shall flee from justice, and be found in another state, shall on demand of the executive authority of the state from which he fled, be delivered up, to be removed to the state having jurisdiction of the crime.

"No person held to service or labor in one state, under the laws thereof, escaping into another, shall, in consequence of any law or regulation there, be discharged from such service or labor, but shall be delivered up on claim of the party to whom such service or labor may be due."

The Privileges and Immunities Clause was a key part of the framers' desire to create a seamless nationwide economic union, where residents of one state could work and travel and do business in other states, too. It ensures that when you visit another state, you have the same rights and privileges as the residents of that state. States you are visiting cannot discriminate against you just because you are a nonresident. For example, a state cannot say you have to be a resident of that state to get a job there. However, the courts have outlined some exceptions. For example, you cannot vote in another state without meeting that state's requirements, including residency.

What It Means to You

Despite the Privileges and Immunities Clause, the courts have ruled that states can charge nonresidents higher fees for services or privileges that residents support with their taxes. For example, nonresidents can be required to pay more for their fishing licenses and out-of-state tuition can be higher at state-funded colleges and universities.

The second part of this section provides for extradition—the return of an accused criminal to the state where the alleged crime occurred. If you commit a crime in one state and run away to another state, the police in that state can arrest you and hold you. The state where the offense allegedly occurred can then request extradition. You can fight it in court, but accused prisoners are usually extradited routinely.

Cases

Mahon v. Justice (1888): When an armed posse from Kentucky captured a suspected criminal in West Virginia and took him back to Kentucky for trial, the accused man appealed. The Supreme Court nonetheless ruled that he could be tried and convicted in Kentucky.

The final part of this section, the Fugitive Slave Clause, allowed slave owners to pursue runaways into nonslave states and bring them back. It was overturned by the Thirteenth Amendment.

Section 3: The Equal Footing Clause

"New states may be admitted by the Congress into this union; but no new states shall be formed or erected within the jurisdiction of any other state; nor any state be formed by the junction of two or more states, or parts of states, without the consent of the legislatures of the states concerned as well as of the Congress.

"The Congress shall have power to dispose of and make all needful rules and regulations respecting the territory or other property belonging to the United States; and nothing in this Constitution shall be so construed as to prejudice any claims of the United States, or of any particular state."

The framers envisioned the United States growing. More states could be created as the Western frontier—areas such as what is now Tennessee and Ohio—was settled. And perhaps the new nation would acquire more of the foreign-held land west of the Mississippi River. This section of the Constitution allows for Congress to admit new states to the Union. But Congress has to give permission. The District of Columbia, for example, tried to become the fifty-first state but was turned down by Congress in 1993.

This section says no new state could include land that had been within another state, unless that state approved. In addition, a new state could not be formed by a merger of two states unless they both approved. No hostile takeovers, in other words. Five states were created out of the original 13 colonies: Vermont was originally part of New York, Kentucky was part of Virginia, Tennessee was part of North Carolina, Maine was part of Massachusetts, and West Virginia was part of Virginia.

In the latter case, Virginia didn't actually approve of creating West Virginia. But when West Virginia declared independence and asked Congress for approval to become a state soon after the Civil War ended, the Reconstruction Congress said Virginia had forfeited its right to keep West Virginia by fighting on the Confederate side in the war.

This section doesn't specifically address the issue, but subsequent court cases have held that new states would have equal status to the other states. "Equality of constitutional right and power is the condition of all the States of the Union, old and new," the Supreme Court ruled in an 1883 case. Similarly, new states cannot have more powers than the other states. Texas was an independent nation before it joined the Union and, like most independent nations, claimed authority over waters up to three miles from its shore. When Texas became a state, however, it ceded that authority to the federal government, just like the other states. The federal government also has control of all public lands within the states, and authority over American-owned territories, including American Samoa, Guam, Puerto Rico, and the Virgin Islands.

There are no provisions in the Constitution for a state to withdraw or secede. So just as Northern California cannot secede from the rest of

California and declare itself a state, it cannot secede and declare itself an independent nation. The courts have held that the Constitution stands for the "perpetuity and indissolubility if the Union"—and, of course, the federal government launched the bloodiest war in American history when the Confederate states, using the same reasoning and even some of the same language as the Declaration of Independence, tried to declare themselves a new and separate nation.

Section 4: The Guarantee Clause

"The United States shall guarantee to every state in this union a republican form of government, and shall protect each of them against invasion; and on application of the legislature, or of the executive (when the legislature cannot be convened) against domestic violence."

> **Cases**
>
> **Luther v. Borden (1849):** In this case from Rhode Island, the Supreme Court said it is up to Congress, not the courts—not even the Supreme Court—to decide whether a state has a "republican" form of government. In effect, if Congress admits a state's representatives and senators, then it has a republican form of government.

The Guarantee Clause says that the federal government will make sure each and every state has a "republican" form of government, but doesn't define republican. One theory is that it simply means that there can never be a king of Nebraska, but a more practical view is that every state must have a government of representatives elected by the people.

Section 4 of Article IV also provides for the federal government to protect the states against invasion and domestic violence. The president's authority to call in troops even without a state's request was established in 1894. Pullman railroad workers went on strike in Chicago and severely disrupted the nation's commercial transportation system. President Grover Cleveland sent in 2,000 Army troops to end the strike on the grounds that the strike was interfering with the delivery of the U.S. mail.

A president also has the authority to call on a state militia—the National Guard—but this power took an odd turn in 1957 in Arkansas. A federal court had ordered the public schools in Little Rock to desegregate, but Gov. Orval Faubus vowed to block any attempt to allow black children to integrate white-only schools. President Dwight Eisenhower nationalized the Arkansas National Guard not to enforce the integration, but to temporarily remove the Guard from Faubus's control. Eisenhower then sent in regular Army troops to make sure the schools were integrated. Ironically, this provision of the Constitution was originally approved back in 1787 because of Southern states' fears of slave uprisings.

Article V: Amending the Constitution

"The Congress, whenever two thirds of both Houses shall deem it necessary, shall propose Amendments to this Constitution, or, on the Application of the Legislatures of two thirds of the several States, shall call a Convention for proposing Amendments, which, in either Case, shall be valid to all Intents and Purposes, as Part of this Constitution, when ratified by the Legislatures of three fourths of the several States, or by Conventions in three fourths thereof, as the one or the other Mode of Ratification may be proposed by the Congress; Provided that no Amendment which may be made prior to the Year One thousand eight hundred and eight shall in any Manner affect the first and fourth Clauses in the Ninth Section of the first Article; and that no State, without its Consent, shall be deprived of its equal Suffrage in the Senate."

The framers of the Constitution wanted to make it difficult to change the Supreme Law of the Land. They established two methods of amending the Constitution. One has never been used: a new Constitutional Convention. Two thirds of the states (34 of 50) can petition Congress for a new convention, but there have always been misgivings that a convention might have the authority to go beyond the amendment on the table. The Constitution has always held such a sacrosanct place in American democracy that few people would want to open it up to a wholesale retinkering. If and when a full-blown Constitutional Convention would take place, three quarters of the states (38 of 50) would have to ratify an amendment for it to go into effect.

The more common and accepted manner of amending the Constitution calls for both houses of Congress to approve the proposed amendment by two-thirds majorities. The proposed amendment is then sent to the states for ratification. A proposed amendment is usually considered by the state legislature, and again, three quarters of the states must approve for ratification.

The Constitution sets no time limit on the ratification process, except to say it must be "reasonable." In practical terms, this means it is up to Congress. Ordinarily in recent times Congress has said that a proposed amendment must be ratified within seven years to take effect, or else it expires. However, the Twenty-seventh Amendment, limiting congressional pay raises, was originally proposed in 1789 but not approved until 1992, more than 200 years later.

Article VI: The Supreme Law of the Land

"All Debts contracted and Engagements entered into, before the Adoption of this Constitution, shall be as valid against the United States under this Constitution, as under the Confederation.

"This Constitution, and the Laws of the United States which shall be made in Pursuance thereof; and all Treaties made, or which shall be made, under the Authority of the United States, shall be the supreme Law of the Land; and the Judges in every State shall be bound thereby, any Thing in the Constitution or Laws of any state to the Contrary notwithstanding.

"The Senators and Representatives before mentioned, and the Members of the several State Legislatures, and all executive and judicial Officers, both of the United States and of the several States, shall be bound by Oath or Affirmation, to support this Constitution; but no religious Test shall ever be required as a Qualification to any Office or public Trust under the United States."

Article VI is an incongruous mix of a centuries-old bookkeeping footnote and a sweeping historical precedent that is called the "linchpin of the Constitution." The first part of the Article is straightforward bean counting: the new United States government will assume the debts of the old government that operated under the Articles of Confederation.

The second part, however, is the Supremacy Clause, the glue that holds together the whole crazy idea of a democracy wrapped in a republic wrapped in a federal system wrapped in a system of checks and balances. In effect, the clause holds that the Constitution and federal laws and treaties take precedence over state laws, and all judges must follow that rule. In other words, any law in conflict with the Constitution is invalid. Without the Supremacy Clause, states could be mini-nations unto themselves, passing any laws of their own, refusing to acknowledge the laws of other states, and ignoring the federal laws of the United States.

The final section of Article VI buttresses the Supreme Clause by requiring all government officials, both state and federal, to give precedence to the U.S. Constitution over any state constitution or other laws. The "religious test" phrasing prohibits any sort of religious requirement or restriction on holding any federal office. This requirement was extended to state officeholders under the Equal Protection Clause of the Fourteenth Amendment.

Article VII: Ratification

"The Ratification of the Conventions of nine States, shall be sufficient for the Establishment of this Constitution between the States so ratifying the same."

The article that specifies how the proposed new Constitution will be ratified offers another of those delicious little ironies and contradictions from 1787. The Constitutional Convention was held under the Articles of Confederation, right? And the Articles of Confederation required the approval of all 13 states for any major changes, right? So why did the framers at the Constitutional Convention decide that only 9 of 13 states needed to approve the new Constitution? And what gave them the authority to change the rules in midstream?

The answers are pretty simple. The men who gathered in Philadelphia that hot summer were not confident that all the states would vote for ratification. They didn't even want to take a chance by requiring 10 states—enough for the three-quarters majority they specified for approving any future amendments—to vote to ratify. They thought nine had a decent chance, so they said nine. And their only authority to change the rule was that they went ahead and changed the rule. And, like the Constitution itself, everybody agreed to go along.

The Least You Need to Know

◆ The Constitution prohibits any state you visit, whether for work or leisure, to discriminate against you simply because you are not a resident.

◆ States can charge more for some services, such as out-of-state tuition at state universities, that are supported by residents' tax dollars.

◆ If Congress approves a constitutional amendment, then three quarters of the states (38 of 50) must ratify before it changes the Constitution.

◆ The Constitution and federal laws take precedence over state laws.

4

The First Amendment: Freedom of Expression

In This Chapter

◆ Freedom of religion

◆ Freedom of speech

◆ Freedom of the press

◆ Freedom of assembly

◆ Freedom to petition

"Congress shall make no law respecting an establishment of religion, or prohibiting the free exercise thereof; or abridging the freedom of speech, or of the press; or the right of the people peaceably to assemble, and to petition the Government for a redress of grievances."

At the 1787 convention, the framers argued vehemently over whether their new Constitution needed provisions that specifically protected individual rights. On one hand, the anti-federalists wanted a list of individual liberties—a Bill of Rights—to restrain the authority of the new national government. On the other hand, the Federalists argued that a national government could enhance rather than inhibit individual liberty. The Federalists believed the premise of the Constitution—that people grant rights to the government rather than the other way around—provided adequate protection for "natural" rights. The Federalists were also afraid that if the framers tried to list individual liberties in the Constitution, anything that wasn't listed would not be protected: that listing individual rights might actually lead to more limitations on personal freedom.

As a result of the anti-federalist sentiment, and in response to calls from the states for specific protections for individual liberties, the Bill of Rights was proposed in the form of the first 10 amendments to the Constitution. Ratified in 1791 (though Georgia, Massachusetts, and Connecticut did not formally ratify the amendments until 1939), the Bill of Rights strives to establish a delicate balance within a democracy. Yes, the will of the majority should rule. But no, the majority should not be able to limit personal freedom as long as it doesn't intrude upon other individuals or society. Individual rights should not be subject to the domination of the majority and should not be limited by a popular vote.

The First Amendment, also called the Great Amendment, is in many ways the cornerstone of America's free, open, and tolerant society. It is the basis of a democracy that prizes individual liberty. The amendment protects the freedom of religion, press, speech, assembly, and petition. It guarantees that Americans can share the information they need for a robust public debate on the issues, and to act on the issues.

> **People**
>
> In a 1943 Supreme Court case, Justice Robert Jackson noted that "if there is any fixed star in our constitutional constellation, it is that no official, high or petty, can prescribe what shall be orthodox in politics, nationalism, religion, or force citizens to confess by word or act their faith therein."

The five freedoms specifically protected in the First Amendment are not mutually exclusive, of course, so there has been considerable overlap in real-life cases. Freedom of religion is sometimes also freedom of speech, for example, and freedom of speech is sometimes also freedom of the press or freedom to petition. Taken together, the rights protected in the First Amendment are categorized as freedom of expression.

Beginning with "Congress shall make no law …," the First Amendment originally applied only to federal limitations on individual rights. However, the Fourteenth Amendment, ratified in 1868, granted equal protection under the laws to all citizens. Under the Fourteenth Amendment's Incorporation Doctrine, the Supreme Court eventually extended the protections of the First Amendment, along with virtually all the rest of the Bill of Rights, to apply to state actions, too.

Perhaps no other part of the Constitution reflects the changes we have seen in American government, society, and culture. As times have changed, our standards have changed for the way we look at many aspects of society, including what is obscene, what is offensive, what is dangerous, and what is a threat to national security. Largely because of its tension between individual rights and the protection of society, the First Amendment remains controversial and is often the battle-ground for arguments over what is right and wrong, and good and bad, in our culture. That is why First Amendment cases are so often where legal scholars lock horns over the two widely different views of the Constitution in modern society: if you disagree with a ruling, you are more likely to say that the "activist" court went too far in making a new law that was not intended by the Constitution; if you agree with a ruling, you are more likely to say the court did a proper job of merely interpreting the Constitution.

It has frequently been left to the Supreme Court, the court of last resort, to decide exactly what is or is not legal or illegal under the First Amendment. It is remarkable to think that so many of those decisions are made, and will be made, by nine middle-aged to elderly lawyers, and sometimes the most momentous cases are determined by 5–4 decisions. If one justice would change his or her vote, the result would be the opposite. Indeed, it is not hard to find similar court cases, with comparable sets of facts and decided by the same nine justices, where one case has been decided 5–4 on one side of an issue, and the other case has been decided 5–4 on the other side of the issue after a single justice changed votes.

Freedom of Religion

Many early colonists came to the New World to escape religious perse-cution, but once they got here they did not necessarily practice religious freedom or tolerance. Many early American communities ostracized and sometimes punished people for not following their religion or even their sect of a shared religion. They came to America to practice *their* religion, not to let you practice yours. From Massachusetts to Virginia, the colonial Baptists seemed particularly prone to persecution; they were thrown in jail for offenses as varied as failing to follow the official Church of England teachings, to refusing to pay taxes to support other churches preferred by colonial officials.

> **People**
>
> "No man shall be compelled to frequent or support any religious worship, place, or ministry whatsoever." — *Thomas Jefferson*

In 1663, the Charter of Rhode Island guaranteed religion freedom; in 1708, Connecticut guaranteed "full liberty of worship"; and by the time the framers were considering a new constitution, they were in general agreement that there would not be a national religion. Jefferson, Madison, and other framers talked up separation of church and state, using those words.

The First Amendment guarantees that the government will not prefer one religion over another. It also guarantees that the government will not prefer religion in general over nonreligion or the lack of religion, and that it will not prefer nonreligion over religion. One example is a 1994 case in which the Supreme Court struck down a New York state law that outlined a school district conforming to the borders of Kiryas Joel, a settlement of Hasidic Jewish families, to create its own school district. The court said that amounted to special treatment to a religious group, and was therefore unconstitutional.

The protections for religion in the First Amendment are two-pronged. The Establishment Clause says, "Congress shall make no law respecting an establishment of religion," while the Exercise Clause says, "or prohibiting the free exercise thereof." The Establishment Clause is considered to be absolute; the government cannot prohibit you or anyone else from establishing or following your own religion. There are many limitations, however, in the interpretations of the Exercise Clause: you can believe in your religion, but that does not give you the right to practice it any way you want, and there may be restrictions on what you can do in the name of your religion.

Religious Practices

In one of the first religion cases to come before the Supreme Court, a Utah man asked the justices to overturn a federal law prohibiting polygamy; he said having more than one wife was part of his Mormon religion. The court upheld the polygamy law, reasoning that religion was not a license for extreme behavior. After all, some ancient religions allowed human sacrifice.

The Supreme Court considered a spate of First Amendment religion cases in the mid-twentieth century, many of them involving Jehovah's Witnesses appealing against local laws aimed at keeping them from practicing the "witness" part of their faith by going door to door and handing out leaflets. One law that was overturned required them to have permits, and another let authorities charge them with littering for leaving their leaflets around town.

What It Means to You

The freedom of religion, like the rest of the First Amendment, is designed primarily to protect beliefs, not actions. The government cannot punish you for what you think, but it can punish you for committing illegal acts because of what you think or believe.

In general, the courts must find a "compelling interest" for the government to overcome a religious practice, as in a 1972 case, *Wisconsin v. Yoder,* where the Supreme Court said that Amish children cannot be required to stay in school beyond the eighth grade if it violates their religion. On the other hand, in a 1990 case the court denied the appeal of two workers who were fired for using peyote on the job; they said it was part of their religion, but the court said that does not give them immunity from "an otherwise valid law prohibiting conduct the State is free to regulate." A later court case struck down a Hialeah, Florida, ordinance banning ritual animal slaughter by Santeria followers while at the same time allowing kosher butcher shops to operate.

Evolution

It never got to the Supreme Court, but a famous 1925 trial in Dayton, Tennessee, drew the lines in the ongoing debate in American society over teaching evolution and creationism—science versus religion—in public schools. In the so-called Scopes Monkey Trial, famed orator and four-time presidential candidate William Jennings Bryan led the prosecution of schoolteacher John Thomas Scopes for violating a state law against teaching evolution. Clarence Darrow, one of the most highly regarded defense attorneys in U.S. legal annals, represented Scopes in a trial that riveted the nation's attention. In the end, Scopes was convicted.

In 1968, the Supreme Court overturned an Arkansas law prohibiting the teaching of evolution. The court ruled that the law, which made it illegal "to teach the theory or doctrine that mankind ascended or descended from a lower order of animals," was a violation of the Establishment Clause. In a 1987 case, *Edwards v. Aguillard*, the Supreme Court struck down a Louisiana law that said if teachers talk about evolution, they must also talk about creationism. In 2005, in *Kitzmiller v. Dover Area School District*, the Supreme Court held that it was an unconstitutional establishment of religion for schools to require the teaching of intelligent design.

What It Means to You

The First Amendment does not prohibit prayer, Bible readings, or other expressions of religion in private schools—only in public schools that receive government funding from tax revenues.

No *Dist Court.*

Parochial Schools

Financial aid to private schools with religious affiliations has been and continues to be an issue. In a 1970 case, the court said religious organizations could be exempt from income and property taxes, and the following year it held that government financial aid to religious schools is permissible under the First Amendment as long as the aid has a secular purpose, neither advances nor inhibits religion, and does not "excessively tangle" government and religion. However, local governments cannot pay part of the salaries of parochial school teachers and cannot "purchase" services from parochial schools as a way of providing financial support.

In one of the church-and-state questions that has not been fully decided, the Supreme Court has ruled that it may sometimes be permissible for state and local government authorities to provide financial aid to parents who send their children to parochial schools, provided the aid goes to the parents rather than to religious schools. In a pair of 1973 cases, the Supreme Court held that public funding could not be allocated to help low-income families pay their children's tuition at parochial schools. But that ruling was modified in a 1983 Minnesota case, *Mueller v. Allen*, that granted tax breaks to parents for sending their kids to private schools.

In a number of cases, the courts have said the First Amendment does not prevent government financial assistance to colleges and universities with religious affiliations. In more recent cases, the high court has approved state use of federal money for a program providing educational materials and equipment to both public and private schools, and a Cleveland school vouchers program. In the Cleveland case, opponents said it was unconstitutional government support for religious education, but the Supreme Court said that vouchers, like tax breaks, were legal as long as they went to parents rather than to churches or church schools.

School Prayer

In 1962, the Supreme Court ruled that the New York Board of Regents violated the First Amendment by requiring a prayer, written to be non-denominational, to be recited in public schools. The following year, the court ruled that public schools cannot require daily Bible readings or recitations, including the Lord's Prayer. Justice Tom Clark wrote, "They are religious exercises, required by the States in violation of the command of the First Amendment that the Government maintain strict neutrality, neither aiding nor opposing religion."

A 1985 Supreme Court case overturned an Alabama law allowing schools to have a one-minute period of silence at the start of the school day; it might have been permissible if the minute of silence was for nonreligious purposes—secular meditation, for example—but the court found that it was for prayer. Subsequent cases have held that invocations at public-school graduation ceremonies are unconstitutional, even if attendance is voluntary and the students vote to have an opening prayer, and so are student-initiated prayers before public-school football games.

In 2000, a California father challenged a school district's practice of having students recite the Pledge of Allegiance. He said the phrase "under God" was akin to forcing his daughter to pray in school. A federal appeals court agreed with him in 2002, but the Supreme Court reversed that decision not on First Amendment grounds but on a technicality—that the father did not have custody of his daughter and therefore did not have legal standing to sue over her education.

Religious Displays

A religion-oriented display, such as a crèche or manger scene at Christmas, is not necessarily a violation of church and state. On a number of occasions the Supreme Court has held that it is, depending on whether it seems to be presented to benefit or promote a particular view of religion, or whether it is part of a more secular display to celebrate the season. A manger scene in a county courthouse has been held unconstitutional, for example, while a Christmas tree and a menorah have been allowed.

Similarly, displays of religious symbols such as the Ten Commandments may or may not violate the First Amendment. The court pointed out the distinction, by a pair of 5–4 rulings, in two cases in 2005. The cases were distinguished by a single swing vote—Justice David Souter. Souter said a Ten Commandments monument in a Texas park at the state capitol in Austin was all right because there were other nonreligious symbols of law and justice in the park. On the other hand, he said Ten Commandments plaques placed in Kentucky courthouses appeared to be religious symbols because they stood alone, rather than as part of a larger secular display.

One of the most highly publicized cases involving religious symbols began in 2001, when Alabama Chief Justice Roy Moore installed a large Ten Commandments monument in the state judicial building. The ACLU and others filed suit, claiming the monument violated the separation of church and state, and the federal courts ordered the monument removed. Moore refused, and was removed from office—along with the monument. He appealed to the U.S. Supreme Court, which refused to take the case and let the lower court orders stand.

Cases

Glassroth v. Moore (2002): Former Alabama Supreme Court Justice Roy Moore merely wanted to demonstrate his faith in God; he argued that the Ten Commandments were the moral foundation for the American legal system. The courts said the First Amendment would allow him to express his faith in many ways, but installing a 5,280-pound monument in the lobby of a public building was not one of them.

Freedom of Speech

We have a participatory democracy. Every citizen has a right, and maybe even a responsibility, to participate in civic affairs. That means we've got to share our thoughts and opinions and ideas. We've got to communicate. We've got to talk. And that's why the First Amendment guarantees free speech. Without freedom of speech, life would not only be boring, but we'd not be exposed to the theories and ideas—along with the criticisms and complaints—that make us think about how our government is doing and how our elected officials are representing us. Could they be doing a better job? Let's talk about it with other people and see what they think. That is freedom of speech.

Political Speech

Historically, governments put limits on free speech in order to maintain control of society and stay in power. If a king or dictator didn't like what people were saying, those people were tossed behind bars—or worse. That's what the English governors in the colonies did in the name of the king. The First Amendment was supposed to keep that from happening, but it only took seven years, until 1798, for Congress to pass the Alien and Sedition Act at the behest of President John Adams, who wanted a way to go after the people who were criticizing his government.

It was an ironic piece of legislation, considering that the country had been created not long before by a handful of radicals—including *Adams* himself—who criticized the government to the point of advocating and then leading a violent overthrow. The act made it illegal to say or write anything "false, scandalous, or malicious" about the government; in other words, anything the government didn't like. The act expired three years later, and when Thomas Jefferson became president he pardoned the 10 people who had been convicted of sedition.

Freedom of speech is not absolute; you cannot say anything you want, anytime, anywhere. And the definition of free speech, always evolving, is often defined more by what you are told you cannot say than by what you can say. Free speech, like other civil liberties, can be affected by the times, such as war or some other national crisis. From 1836 until 1844, for example, the House of Representatives had a gag rule preventing debate on abolition of slavery.

In 1917, Congress passed the Espionage Act, aimed at peace activists who tried to talk potential World War I recruits out of enlisting in the military. The following year another Sedition Act was enacted, making it a crime to speak or write anything negative about the government, the Constitution, or the American flag. The Supreme Court upheld a series of convictions growing out of opposition to U.S. participation in the Great War, as it was called at the time. Not everybody, however, thought it was a good idea to send people to prison for being peace activists during World War I. In a dissent in a Supreme Court case that upheld a portion of the Espionage Act against criticizing the government, Justice Oliver Wendell Holmes wrote that "the ultimate good desired is better reached by free trade in ideas—that the best test of truth is the power of the thought to get itself accepted in the competition of the market."

> **People**
>
> One of Oliver Wendell Holmes's frequent allies on the court, Justice Louis Brandeis, expanded on his colleague's "marketplace of ideas" principle in another opinion a few years later, suggesting that the answer to falsehoods and fallacies should be "more speech, not enforced silence."

In another case, *Schenk v. United States* in 1919, which upheld the conviction of an activist passing out leaflets urging potential recruits not to join the military, Holmes enunciated a famous First Amendment doctrine: speech could be limited if it created a "clear and present danger" of criminal acts. In that case, Holmes also wrote one of the best-known misquotes in history. The commonly cited phrase is that free speech does not extend to "shouting fire in a crowded theater." Actually, Holmes wrote that the First Amendment does not protect "a man falsely shouting fire in a theater and causing a panic." He included "falsely," but not "crowded."

In response to the crackdown on free speech, the American Civil Liberties Union was formed in 1920, and could claim an early victory the following year when the Sedition Act was repealed. Just as Thomas Jefferson pardoned those convicted under the first Sedition Act more than a century earlier, Franklin Delano Roosevelt later issued presidential pardons to those convicted under the World War I Espionage and Sedition acts.

The end of the war, however, did not end the tension between free speech and government interests, particularly in silencing critics such as anarchists and communists who advocated the overthrow of the government. In the 1925 case *Gitlow v. New York*, the Supreme Court ruled that the free speech guarantees of the First Amendment apply to state law via the Fourteenth Amendment, but nonetheless upheld a pamphleteer's conviction under New York's anti-anarchy law.

Cases

Stromberg v. California (1931): In this case, the Supreme Court reversed the conviction of a young woman who had displayed a red flag to show her support for the Young Communist League. It was the first time that the court regarded nonverbal, symbolic expression as free speech. But not the last.

At one point the Supreme Court ruled that "fighting words," the kind of statement that might make anybody punch the speaker in the nose, were not free speech. The court later backed away, though, from the idea that it's sometimes okay to resort to violence in response to someone else's statement. Instead, the court acknowledged that outrageous or inflammatory speech may be protected if it makes you think. In a 1949 case, Justice William O. Douglas wrote, "It may indeed best serve its high purpose when it induces a condition of unrest, creates dissatisfaction with conditions as they are, or even stirs people to anger."

In 1940, as World War II was heating up in Europe, the Supreme Court upheld a Pennsylvania law requiring children to salute the flag and recite the Pledge of Allegiance. "National unity is the basis of national security," Justice Felix Frankfurter wrote. But that decision was overturned three years later in another Jehovah's Witness case: kids were no longer required to pledge or salute at school. It is worth noting that around the same time, the salute that schoolchildren used for the Pledge of Allegiance was changed to the hand over the heart. It had been a straight-arm, "Heil Hitler" salute, except with the palm up instead of down.

With another war came another set of laws aimed at limiting free speech. In 1940, the United States enacted the Smith Act, formally the Alien and Registration Act, which again made it a crime to advocate the violent overthrow of the government. After World War II, the Smith Act became a Cold War tool for the government. It was used at the urging of J. Edgar Hoover, the FBI director, to prosecute suspected Communist activists. In 1951, the Supreme Court upheld a series of convictions under the Smith Act, ruling that it did not violate the First Amendment. The Smith Act technically remains on the books today.

The Vietnam War era sparked a flurry of First Amendment confrontations over free speech. In 1968, the Supreme Court upheld the conviction of a protestor who argued that burning his draft card was free speech, but the following year the court overturned the convictions of a group of Des Moines students who went to high school wearing black armbands to protest the war. In 1971, the court overturned the conviction of a protestor who wore a jacket bearing the words "F--- the Draft" into a courthouse. The backlash against flag burning that began during the Vietnam protests has simmered since then. In 1989, Congress passed the Flag Protection Act, and the Supreme Court soon after made two rulings, one voiding the new federal law and another striking down a comparable state law in Texas, that said burning or otherwise abusing Old Glory is a legitimate expression of free speech.

Unpopular views, including those that are racist, may be protected by the umbrella of free speech, but there are limits. In a 1969 case, *Brandenburg v. Ohio*, the Supreme Court upheld the conviction of a Ku Klux Klan member, saying that that speech is not protected if it is "likely to incite or produce" violence. The court opinion noted that "the constitutional guarantees of free speech and free press do not permit a State to forbid or proscribe advocacy for the use of force or of

law violation except where such advocacy is directed to inciting or pro-
ducing imminent lawless action and is likely to incite or produce such
action." In 2003, the high court ruled that a KKK cross-burning prohibition can be legal because it is so intimidating to black people that it
effectively amounts to violence against them.

Cases

Red Lion Broadcasting v. FCC (1969): The Supreme Court in this case
endorsed the Federal Communications Commission's "fairness doctrine,"
saying that Congress and FCC are authorized to require broadcasters
to provide opportunities for opposing views to be aired in response to
personal attacks and political editorializing. Later, however, the FCC and
the courts abandoned the fairness doctrine. The "equal time" doctrine
for political opponents remains in effect, though the Supreme Court has
ruled that a TV station does not have to invite every candidate running in
an election to participate in a televised debate.

In 1982, in *Board of Education v. Pico,* the Supreme Court held that officials cannot pull books off the shelves of school libraries merely because
they disagree with the ideas in those books. The decision said that
"the right to receive ideas is a necessary predicate to the recipient's
meaningful exercise of his own rights of speech, press, and political
freedom." However, just as the federal government can withhold grants
from artists, the Supreme Court ruled in 1991 that the government can
withhold funding from health centers that discuss abortion as a method
of birth control. The discussion is free speech, but that doesn't mean
the government has to support it with federal funding.

The early 1990s spawned a wave of so-called political correctness—
the very phrase would seem to be a violation of at least the spirit and
perhaps the letter of the First Amendment—that resulted in attempts
around the country to ban "hate speech." Those efforts were largely
snuffed out after a 1992 Supreme Court ruling overturned a local hate-
speech ordinance.

More recently, Congress and the courts have grappled with campaign
finance issues, and in *Buckley v. Valeo* the Supreme Court upheld the
part of the Federal Election Campaign Act that limited campaign contributions but struck down the part of the law that limited how much

candidates can spend on their campaigns. Restricting campaign expenditures, the court held, was a restraint on freedom of expression.

In a May 2006 California case, *Garcetti v. Ceballos*, the Supreme Court rejected the First Amendment claim of an assistant district attorney who said he was passed over for a promotion because he criticized his boss in public. He said he was a whistle-blower, but the court said the Constitution does not protect "every statement a public employee makes in the course of doing his or her job."

Obscenity

Obscenity is not protected by the First Amendment's guarantees of free speech. A series of federal and state laws approved in the latter part of the 1800s were the first widespread effort to control obscenity in American culture. Known as Comstock laws, after anti-obscenity campaigner Anthony Comstock, the laws made it criminal to sell or distribute "obscene, lewd or lascivious" materials, including "any article or thing" providing information on contraception or abortion. The federal law and many of the state Comstock laws remain on the books and are still used to prosecute those who sell obscene material, but the age-old question remains: what is obscene? After all, one man's pornography may be another man's artistic erotica.

> **People**
>
> In 1964, Supreme Court Justice Potter Stewart spoke for most of us when he acknowledged that it was difficult to define pornography, but added, "I know it when I see it."

The courts have made a number of attempts to define obscenity and balance it against the guarantees of free speech. In the nineteenth century, the Supreme Court defined obscenity as material that would "deprave or corrupt those whose minds are open to such immoral influences." In other words, if material offended the most sensitive people in society—if it offended pretty much anyone—it was obscene.

The standards have loosened over the decades, but it has been a continual struggle to define when, where, how, and why words may be of "prurient interest," which means "too dirty" to those of us who do not sit on the U.S. Supreme Court. But again, what is too dirty? Justice William Brennan offered the "utterly without redeeming social value" standard: something could be obscene, but if it had artistic or cultural value, it might be protected by the First Amendment.

What It Means to You _____

The Supreme Court ruled in 1969 that "private possession of obscene material" is legal. Authorities cannot burst into your house and arrest you merely for possessing pornography. Justice Thurgood Marshall wrote, "If the First Amendment means anything, it means that a State has no business telling a man sitting in his own house what books he may read or what films he may watch." *except.*

A 1973 Supreme Court case, *Miller v. California*, offered a three-part test for whether speech is obscene:

◆ If the "average person applying contemporary community standards" would find that the material, taken as a whole, appeals to prurient interests.

◆ If the depiction or description is patently offensive sexual conduct that is defined and prohibited by state law.

◆ If, taken as a whole, the material lacks serious literary, artistic, political, or scientific value.

The current standards for obscenity do not include a national standard, except for child pornography. The courts have agreed that child pornography is never acceptable. In other types of obscenity, however, the courts are supposed to consider local or community standards. The 1973 Miller provision for considering the literary, artistic, political, or scientific value allows for a nude stripper or live-sex performer in a bar to be regarded differently under the First Amendment than a nude actor appearing in *Hair*, a life study in an art gallery, or anatomical depictions in a medical journal. Another factor is the audience; material that can be viewed by children is treated differently than material restricted to adult eyes only, but even adult-only material can be obscene. The wider the audience, the more oversight: the FCC is allowed to regulate indecent speech because broadcasting's "uniquely pervasive presence" means that children might see or hear it. It is also legal for local governments to impose zoning restrictions that control where adult businesses may operate. A 1998 court case upheld federal requirements for the National Endowment for the Arts to consider decency standards when awarding grants to artists; merely denying government funding does not infringe upon an artist's freedom of expression.

As a society, we're still trying to figure out how to handle child pornography and the Internet. The Supreme Court found the Child Pornography Prevention Act of 1996 unconstitutional in 1997; the court said it was overbroad, with the potential authority for law enforcement officials to punish legal speech in the name of protecting children. A subsequent law, the Child Online Protection Act, also ran into a series of First Amendment setbacks in federal courts. The Supreme Court said there may be "a number of plausible, less restrictive alternatives," and said the government needed to justify COPA. Campaigners for Internet safety for kids could claim a victory, however, when the Supreme Court upheld the 1998 Children's Internet Protection Act, which withholds federal money from schools and libraries that do not have antipornography filtering software on their computers with Internet access.

Freedom of the Press

Freedom of the press is closely linked to freedom of speech. If it is okay to say it, it's probably okay to publish it, too. Our form of democracy relies on the press to perform the necessary but unofficial function of spreading around all that free speech so that we have an informed citizenry capable of participating in the debates and electing the leaders we want to address the issues we care about. That's why the press is called the Fourth Estate, informally supplementing the three official branches of government.

Censorship

The First Amendment's guarantee of a free press, it should be noted, says nothing about press responsibility. The primary goal is to protect the press from government censorship, whether direct or indirect. But there are limits on what the press can do, and penalties for violating the public trust conferred by the First Amendment. A good example is libel law, which allows individuals who are harmed by the press to sue for damages.

The 1735 trial of New York printer John Peter Zenger marked the beginning of the American free press. Zenger was jailed for publishing criticism of the royal governor, but a jury of colonists, responding to stirring arguments by defense attorney Alexander Hamilton, ignored the instructions of the governor's court and acquitted Zenger. It was an important milestone in showing the colonists the power of the press— and the law—in fighting imperial rule from London. In practical terms, the case also laid down early precedents for American law: a jury can decide what is libel and what isn't, and truth is a defense to libel. Later, in the Federalist Papers, Alexander Hamilton wrote, "The liberty of the press shall be inviolably preserved."

As with free speech, times of national crisis often provide stern tests for freedom of the press. During the Civil War, President Lincoln ordered temporary suspension of the *Chicago Tribune* and later two New York newspapers for printing stories he viewed as disloyal to the Union effort in the Civil War. The Supreme Court's first free-press case was decided in 1907, when the justices upheld the contempt conviction of a Denver publisher who had run criticisms of the Colorado Supreme Court.

In a 1931 case, *Near v. Minnesota,* the Supreme Court overturned a state court's *prior restraint* order on the grounds that the First Amendment was designed primarily to prohibit government censorship. That case also extended the protections of the First Amendment to the states through the Equal Protection Clause of the Fourteenth Amendment. A 1936 high-court decision outlawed a state tax on advertising in newspapers with circulation of more than 20,000 a week. The court said such a tax

def•i•ni•tion

Prior restraint is the term for preventing publication or broadcast. A plaintiff will ask a court to block the publication because of the potential harm it might cause, whether to national security or to a private individual or corporation.

could restrict the flow of "information to which the public is entitled in virtue of the constitutional guarantees." It could be a form of censorship, in other words.

Censorship has been permitted, however, in instances such as wartime—in 1941 Franklin Delano Roosevelt opened, with Congress's approval, an Office of Censorship—and there have been numerous examples of courts issuing gag orders to prevent pretrial publicity. A major precedent for controlling pretrial publicity was the 1966 case *Sheppard v. Maxwell*, when the Supreme Court overturned the conviction of Dr. Sam Sheppard—the real-life inspiration for *The Fugitive* TV series and movie—on the grounds that newspaper publicity had kept him from getting a fair trial. Another example of censorship, sometimes in response to legal requirements but often voluntary self-censorship, is when the news media withholds the names of certain people involved in crimes, such as minors or rape victims.

Cases
New York Times Co. v. U.S. (1971): The Nixon administration tried to stop the *Times* and the *Washington Post* from publishing the so-called "Pentagon Papers," 7,000 pages of leaked documents recounting U.S. involvement in Vietnam. The Supreme Court decided by a 6–3 vote, with 9 separate opinions, that the injunctions sought by the government amounted to prior restraint violating the First Amendment.

Libel

The case that shaped our modern law of libel—when someone sues for defamation, or damage to his or her reputation—was *New York Times v. Sullivan* in 1964. Previously, the main defense to libel allegations was truth: if you said your reputation had been damaged by something I wrote about you, I had to prove it was true. The Sullivan case, however, set new standards for people who are public officials. Instead of proving that the allegation was true, a defendant merely had to show that the allegation was not made with "actual malice."

Actual malice is defined as knowledge that the allegation was false or reckless disregard for whether it was false or not. The court's reasoning was that society needs to be able to comment on and talk about public officials, and that officials open themselves up to criticism and commentary when they enter the public arena. If the press makes a mistake, the public official who has been wronged can collect money damages only by proving that the press either knew or should have known that the allegation was false. The Supreme Court recognized that mistakes can be made in the press, particularly under deadline pressure, but reasoned that keeping accuracy standards too high could be a form of censorship and therefore a violation of the First Amendment. The "public official" standard for libel was subsequently expanded to include public figures, too, including celebrities.

Sometimes the best way to avoid libel damages, especially if you know what you're saying is false, is to be as outrageous as possible. In a 1988 case, evangelist Jerry Falwell sued *Hustler* magazine for running a fake liquor ad showing Falwell in a lewd pose. The Supreme Court rejected the libel suit on the grounds that it was legitimate political satire, which has played "a prominent role in public and political debate" in American history. In other cases, however, the court has made it clear that not only facts, but opinions, too, can be the basis for a successful libel suit.

Cases

Miami Herald Publishing v. Tornillo (1974): Print publications are not subject to the same "equal time" provisions required of broadcasters. In this case, the Supreme Court struck down a Florida law requiring newspapers to give free rebuttal space to political candidates they criticize. The ruling said an equal-time provision would inhibit editorial decision making—whether to print something or not.

One of the continuing issues in the American press is where the role of reporter ends and the role of citizen begins. In a 1972 case, *Branzburg v. Hayes*, the Supreme Court said that reporters are not exempt from the normal responsibilities of citizenship just because they are reporters, including testifying before a grand jury. We've also seen, in recent cases such as the investigation into the leaking of a CIA spy's identity and the use of steroids in baseball, how reporters can be sent to jail—in theory indefinitely, since contempt of court need not carry a set term of imprisonment or even a maximum sentence—for refusing to provide law enforcement authorities and courts with information about confidential sources. Reporters argue that freedom of the press allows them to protect their sources and that giving up their sources would discourage other whistle-blowers and leakers, but the courts have said that civic responsibility and the integrity of the legal system may be more important.

School-funded student newspapers have presented a number of First Amendment dilemmas. The courts generally have ruled that while student editors and reporters have First Amendment rights, school officials can impose editorial controls as long as the decisions are justified for legitimate teaching and educational purposes.

Looking ahead, the rapid changes in communications technology in recent years are presenting new challenges to the First Amendment and the concepts of freedom of the press. Instead of being in an office that can be searched or seized or shut down, new technology allows almost anyone to "publish" from almost anywhere. And the new world of self-publishing is forcing us to rethink and redefine just who is a journalist and who is deserving of First Amendment free-press protection. Is a blogger a journalist? The rest of the world is watching China's attempts to control the new media, including creating its own vast national intranet, limiting access to the World Wide Web, and jailing surfers who visit sites that are deemed pornographic or politically subversive.

Freedom of Assembly

The freedom to assemble—to talk, march, plot against the government, or cheer for your team—is closely linked to free speech. Also sometimes called the right of association, it means we can hang out with whomever we want—mostly. We can form political parties, special interest groups, clubs, and unions, but the First Amendment won't necessarily protect us if those organizations, or some of the members we associate with, undertake illegal activities. Terrorist groups, for example, can be banned. As with other aspects of the First Amendment, the tension is between freedom of expression and the need to protect society. It may be your right to organize a protest march, but the government may have the right to require you to get a parade permit and follow a certain route at a certain time in order to keep from snarling traffic and causing safety problems.

Throughout history, totalitarian governments have banned the right to assemble just as they have banned free speech and the free press. And we're not talking about ancient history. In Iran in 1978, amid fears about the exiled Ayatollah Khomeini returning to lead a revolt, the late Shah's government banned any public gathering of more than two people. In 2001, amid fears of a Montagnard uprising, Vietnam banned gatherings of more than four people in its Central Highlands. In September 2006, Thailand banned gatherings of more than five people.

If people cannot get together, repressive leaders reckon, they cannot plan a revolution. On a smaller scale, American officials have sometimes limited the right of assembly—such as through parade permits—solely to discourage causes they do not agree with. The Supreme Court has overturned state laws against being a member of the Communist party, ruling that "peaceable assembly for lawful discussion cannot be made a crime. The holding of meetings for peaceable political action cannot be proscribed." In 1958, the court ruled that the NAACP did not have to turn over its membership roster to authorities, and later that Communist party members could be state employees in Arizona and public school teachers in New York.

Cases
Boy Scouts of America v. Dale (2000): Sometimes the right of association can protect you from associating with people you don't want to be around. The Supreme Court, emphasizing that it did not agree or disagree with the Boy Scouts' position on gays, agreed in a 5–4 decision that the Scouts do not have to accept gay scoutmasters.

The suburbanization of America in the second half of the twentieth century led to a First Amendment debate over whether groups must be allowed to assemble—and speak—on private property such as malls and shopping centers. The reasoning is that malls have become the new town squares and village greens, where people historically would gather to talk about the issues of the day. The federal courts generally have said the right of association does not extend to private property and have sided with mall managers who want to keep out people chanting or handing out leaflets. In contrast, state courts have been more likely to recognize the "new town square" argument and give groups the right to assemble in malls as long as they behave themselves.

The tension between law enforcement and the right to assemble was in the headlines in the spring of 2003 when women's groups converged on Georgia to protest the no-females membership policy of the Augusta National Golf Club, the home of the Masters tournament. Local authorities quickly made new rules requiring 20 days' notice for a permit to stage a public protest, leaving it up to the local sheriff to approve or deny permits and to tell protesters when and where they could protest. The sheriff refused to let the women protest at the entrance to the club, and instead moved them a half mile away.

Freedom to Petition

This is the freedom to protest against the government, to ask for changes, and to ask that wrongs done in the name of the government be corrected. Sounds sort of like the Declaration of Independence, doesn't it? It gives everyday citizens the right to protest and to sue in a court of law to correct wrongs.

The right to petition often overlaps with free speech and free assembly, and the courts sometimes prefer to focus on those or other constitutional rights when lawsuits are brought over the right to sue. For example, the Supreme Court in 1963 overturned a Virginia rule prohibiting people from soliciting lawyers; the court ruled that it was permissible for the NAACP to seek attorneys to handle civil rights lawsuits. The right to petition was an issue, but the court decided the case on free-speech and free-association grounds.

> **People**
>
> "We have recognized this right to petition as one of the most precious of the liberties safeguarded by the Bill of Rights," Justice Sandra Day O'Connor wrote in a 2002 case, "and have explained that the right is implied by the very idea of a government, republican in form."

In a 1971 Connecticut case, the Supreme Court said an indigent couple seeking a divorce should not have to pay the usual court fees. The couple had filed their appeal on the grounds of the right to petition, but the court instead said that denying them a divorce for financial reasons was a violation of their right to due process—the right to have their case heard fully and fairly. The due process rationale, rather than the right to petition, is also why prisoners are allowed access to law libraries when working on their own appeals.

In 1980, the Supreme Court ruled in *Missouri v. NOW* that the state of Missouri could not claim damages from the National Organization for Women because of economic damage resulting from a NOW boycott to protest opposition to the proposed Equal Rights Amendment. The court said that the boycott was a form of petition and was therefore protected by the First Amendment. In a 1981 case, the court made it clear that the right to petition, at least in terms of the right to sue, does not extend to frivolous claims; the justices found in favor of a property developer who complained that his plans to build a shopping center were being blocked by lawsuit after lawsuit filed by other property owners and existing shopping centers.

The Least You Need to Know

- The First Amendment protects freedom of expression, including freedom of religion, speech, and the press.

- Freedom of religion is the basis for the separation of church and state.

- The First Amendment protects your right to believe whatever you want, but your beliefs do not allow you to break laws or violate the rights of others.

- The First Amendment prohibits you from imposing your beliefs on others.

- The Constitution protects freedom of the press as a foundation of democracy.

Chapter 5

Second and Third Amendments: Arms and Armies

In This Chapter

◆ The Second Amendment: the right to bear arms

◆ The Militia Clause

◆ The Right to Arms Clause

◆ The gun control debate today

◆ The Third Amendment: quartering troops

The Second Amendment, often cited for "the right to bear arms," is at the heart of the national debate over gun control and is one of the most controversial portions of the Bill of Rights. The Third Amendment, which guarantees that citizens do not have to feed and shelter soldiers, is one of the least controversial parts of the Bill of Rights.

Second Amendment: The Right to Bear Arms

"A well regulated militia, being necessary to the security of a free state, the right of the people to keep and bear arms, shall not be infringed."

The Second Amendment occupies an odd little corner of constitutional law—a corner that not many legal scholars or Supreme Court justices have cared to visit since 1787. Discussions about the Second Amendment do not take up many pages of law books, and there are only a handful of court decisions on the Second Amendment in the federal courts. The controversy—the right of every American to own a gun versus society's need to get guns off the streets to prevent violent crime—seems like too much of a hot potato even for the biggest legal brains.

The amendment is divided into two clauses: the Militia Clause and the Right to Arms Clause. Various experts, depending on whether they are for or against more gun control, argue back and forth over which clause is more important. Does the amendment guarantee an absolute right for individuals to own guns? Or does it mean only that the states can form militias that may allow citizens to have firearms? If the Militia Clause is more important, then perhaps the Right to Arms Clause has a limited meaning: that citizens have the right to bear arms only if they are part of the National Guard or some equivalent. If the Right to Arms Clause is superior, then perhaps the government has much less authority to make laws regulating the sale, possession, and use of guns.

We don't know, because the courts have never decided just exactly what the Second Amendment means. Meanwhile, we have plenty of legal authorities, real and imagined, who tell us what the framers of the Constitution were thinking about guns and gun control back in 1787— and how, even if the framers really did mean for every citizen to have guns in the closet and over the mantle, the changing times have made their intentions obsolete.

To be prepared - need arms

> **People**
>
> "The right of self defense is the first law of nature: in most govern-
> ments it has been the study of rulers to confine this right within the
> narrowest limits possible. Wherever standing armies are kept up, and
> the right of the people to keep and bear arms, is under any colour
> or pretext whatsoever, prohibited, liberty, if not already annihilated,
> is on the brink of destruction." —Henry St. George Tucker, American
> Revolutionary gunrunner and legal scholar

The Militia Clause

The Articles of Confederation said that the states should have militias, but made no mention of individual gun ownership. At the
Constitutional Convention in 1787, there were obvious reasons for
including something about guns. Hunting was an important source of
food for many people. Personal security was a factor in an era when
society felt the need to protect itself not only from ordinary crime, such
as armed robbery, but also in certain areas of the country from Indian
attacks and slave uprisings.

But there were also political motivations for ensuring gun rights.
Americans mistrusted standing armies. Europe had powerful standing
armies whose main role, to Americans, seemed to be to keep monarchs
in power. When they looked across the Atlantic, the Americans saw
that virtually every monarchy in Europe had strict gun control laws,
and the Americans believed it was to head off armed insurrections.
After all, fresh in everyone's mind was the Revolutionary War, when
the nation's independence had been earned through bloody victories
fought largely by citizen-soldiers using the muskets they grabbed off
the mantelpiece or from the closet. To early Americans, guns were
more than a symbol of freedom. They *were* freedom. A well-armed citizenry within a state was a reminder and a warning not only to foreign
countries but also to other states and the new federal government: don't
tread on our inalienable rights!

The history of militias in America goes back to the seventeenth century, and eventually every colony had its own militia that required
every able-bodied white male to be a member. But being a member
didn't necessarily mean marching and carrying a rifle; there were other

duties, such as fund-raising and record keeping, that a militiaman could do instead of actually picking up a gun—especially if he was rich or had political connections.

Massachusetts' militia, known as the minutemen for the way they could leave their shops and farms and be ready to fight in a minute, became the model for the other colonies. They were an inspiration for the growth of the militia across the colonies after firing "the shots heard 'round the world" to announce the war of independence against the redcoats at Lexington and Concord in 1775.

The importance of militias ebbed and flowed in the 1800s, depending on whether we were at war or not, but during the Civil War states in both North and South sent their militias into battle as units under their state flags. Indeed, rebel soldiers typically thought of themselves as fighting not for the Confederate States of America, but for old Virginia or old South Carolina. Every state's militia has evolved into its version of the modern National Guard, which began in the early 1900s in the populous Northeastern states and gradually spread across the country to become today's professional, highly trained military force under shared state and federal control.

> **People**
>
> When gun control advocate Al Gore was running for president in 2000, actor Charlton Heston, president of the National Rifle Association, held a Revolutionary War–era rifle over his head and told 20,000 cheering delegates at the NRA convention that Gore would have to pry his gun "from my cold, dead hands." The phrase became a popular NRA bumper sticker.

Today, of course, with our professional full-time Army, Navy, Air Force, and Marines, society's attitude toward a standing army and state militias is much different than it was in 1787. Most of us cannot imagine ever needing to grab a rifle off the mantle to defend ourselves against foreign invaders or occupying forces, but guns remain a part of American culture and heritage.

The Right to Arms Clause

Unlike some other provisions of the Bill of Rights, such as the right to free speech and the right to due process, the Second Amendment does not apply to the states under the Fourteenth Amendment's equal protection provisions. That means that private organizations, such as housing associations, can ban guns. It also means that states can be as restrictive or permissive as they want with their gun control laws. An estimated 20,000 local, state, and federal laws are already on the books controlling gun sales, possession, and use.

Groups that oppose any sort of gun control, most notably the National Rifle Association, would argue that all or most of those existing laws are unconstitutional under the Second Amendment. The courts have never agreed, however. The most important U.S. Supreme Court ruling on the Second Amendment so far was *United States v. Miller*, a 1939 case viewed by gun control advocates as the foundation for all existing federal gun control laws. That case represented a challenge to a federal law that taxed sawed-off shotguns—in effect making them illegal. The high court ruled that the law did not violate the Second Amendment since the sawed-off shotgun was not used by state militia nor in preserving the peace—it was more commonly used by gangsters and armed robbers because it had a lot of firepower but could be hidden in clothes or small packages.

But neither the Miller case nor any other case decided by the Supreme Court has directly addressed the question of whether the Second Amendment guarantees citizens the right to own guns, or how far the federal government can go in terms of legislation to control guns. That leaves our legal system walking a tightrope: it seems that we want to allow gun ownership, but we want to restrict and regulate the use of some guns by some people.

> **Cases**
>
> **Lewis v. U.S. (1980):** This was the only other significant Second Amendment case before the Supreme Court in recent years, and the court ruled that it was permissible under the Constitution for states to prohibit convicted felons from possessing firearms.

The Gun Control Debate Today

Gun control became a hot-button issue in America only in the second half of the twentieth century, amid growing concern over the increase in crime and the more frequent use of guns by criminals. Since both sides cite public policy in their legal arguments, we can't really look at the legal issues surround the Second Amendment without looking at the real-world arguments:

On one hand, polls sponsored by pro-gun organizations indicate that people want to be able to own guns. On the other hand, polls sponsored by anti-gun groups indicate that people like the idea of reasonable restrictions on gun ownership.

On one hand, if you have a gun in your house, it is more likely to be used to kill a friend or family member than an intruder. On the other hand, studies show that cities with higher-than-average gun ownership have less armed robbery. And a Justice Department study in the 1990s said that children who get guns from their parents are less likely to commit crimes or use drugs than children who don't have access to guns, or obtain them illegally.

Let's take a brief look at the legal positions of the two sides. The anti-gun control position first, as put forth by the National Rifle Association:

- The framers of the Constitution were clear, both in their intent and their language. They intended for the Second Amendment to guarantee that citizens have the right to have guns for self-defense, and the government cannot take away that right.

- The Second Amendment also guarantees the right of citizens to own guns in order to participate in militia to defend their states or the national government.

- The framers of the Constitution distrusted government, especially any government that would not trust its own citizens with firearms.

- The Bill of Rights spells out individual rights that the government cannot take away, and the right to bear arms is just as specific and clear as free speech and other rights.

> **People** _____
>
> "The biggest hypocrites on gun control are those who live in upscale developments with armed security guards—and who want to keep other people from having guns to defend themselves. But what about lower-income people living in high-crime, inner-city neighborhoods? Should such people be kept unarmed and helpless so that limousine liberals can 'make a statement' by adding to the thousands of gun laws already on the books?" —*Thomas Sowell, legal scholar and commentator*

On the other side of the argument is the Brady Center to Prevent Gun Violence, created by James Brady, the former press secretary to President Reagan who suffered brain damage when he was shot along with Reagan during a 1981 assassination attempt. The Brady Center puts forth the following argument:

◆ The Second Amendment was enacted to make sure states could have militias, but those militias are no longer needed because of the standing U.S. military forces and the National Guard.

◆ Nothing in the Constitution or the historical record of 1787 shows that the framers intended for the Second Amendment to allow firearms for self-defense or any purpose other than to raise a militia.

◆ The Second Amendment pertains to federal laws only, and does not prohibit local and state governments from imposing their own controls—including outright bans—on guns.

◆ Federal gun laws that don't interfere with the National Guard are not a violation of the Second Amendment.

> **People** _____
>
> "We're not talking about banning or confiscating guns that people buy and own for hunting, collecting, or personal protection. The issue isn't whether someone is 'pro-gun' or 'anti-gun' but why there is a reluctance from some of our elected officials to take moderate steps that would make our homes and neighborhoods safer." —*Paul Helmke, director of the Brady Campaign to Prevent Gun Violence*

Naturally, the two sides—those in favor of more control and those who want less gun control—see politics differently. For example, gun control opponents said they weren't really hurt by the 2006 elections that gave Democrats control of the 2007–2008 Congress. "The Second Amendment has emerged from the biggest Democratic victory since 1974 with relatively little damage," Dave Kopel, research director of the Independence Institute, which opposes gun control, wrote in *National Review*. "One reason is that in races all over the country, Democrats returned to their Jefferson-Jackson roots by running candidates who trust the people to bear arms."

Gun control advocates, in contrast, said the election could be a turning point. "I am grateful to the Brady Campaign to Prevent Gun Violence for their hard work and dedication in my bid for re-election," Illinois governor Rod Blagojevich said. "The issue of gun violence really matters to voters in Illinois, especially when it comes to getting deadly assault weapons off our streets. We have got to do more to fight gun violence, both here in Illinois and across America."

Recent decisions on gun control cases in district and appeals court cases offer few hints about how—or whether—the courts may ultimately decide just what the Second Amendment means. In *Hickman v. Block*, the U.S. Circuit Court of Appeals for the Western states held in 1996 that the Second Amendment does not afford an individual right to gun ownership, rejecting an argument that even minor gun controls could eventually threaten the constitutional right to bear arms. In contrast, the Federal Appeals Court for Texas, Louisiana, and Mississippi ruled three years later in *U.S. v. Emerson* that it was a violation of Second Amendment rights for a court to prohibit someone from owning a gun as part of a marital restraining order.

No overriding political solution seems on the horizon. Gun control advocates have proposed a new Second Amendment that would allow private gun ownership for hunting, sport, collecting, and personal defense, but would allow the government to continue to ban at least some kinds of guns, such as automatic assault weapons, that are not typically used for sport or personal defense of the home.

Consequently, unless and until the Supreme Court begins taking up cases like the above, the legal questions over the Second Amendment and the right to bear arms will linger. But even if the Supreme Court does suddenly decide to take on this controversial issue, which seems unlikely after all these years of ducking it, one thing is certain: Americans will continue to have sharply differing opinions on the effectiveness of gun control.

> **People**
>
> "Gun control? We need bullet control! I think every bullet should cost $5,000!" —Chris Rock, comedian

The Third Amendment: Quartering Troops

"No soldier shall, in time of peace be quartered in any house, without the consent of the owner, nor in time of war, but in a manner to be prescribed by law."

While the Second Amendment is one of the most controversial parts of the Bill of Rights, the Third Amendment is one of the least controversial passages in the entire Constitution. It seems antiquated today, the idea that we need an amendment—part of the Bill of Rights, no less— to keep the U.S. Army from forcing us to take in soldiers and give them room and board. But it wasn't such a crazy idea in 1787, when the framers of the Constitution could remember the English army invading their homes and forcing them to provide food and shelter.

The only significant case law relating to the Third Amendment came in *Engblom v. Carey* in 1982. The case grew out of a strike by New York prison officers in 1979. The guards lived in state housing that was part of their compensation package. But when they went on strike and members of the New York National Guard were called out to replace them in the prisons, New York officials evicted the prison guards and let the National Guard members live in the state housing.

The prison guards who went on strike and then were tossed out of their homes sued in federal court on the Third Amendment grounds. The U.S. District Court threw out their case, and they appealed. The U.S. Court of Appeals for the Second Circuit—the case never made it to the Supreme Court—ruled that the National Guard could be considered soldiers under the Third Amendment, and said the prison guards might actually have a case.

The case went back to the district court, which found for the state (the defendant, Carey, was the governor of New York) again on different grounds. The prison guards appealed again, but this time their appeal was denied, and that was the end of the case.

The Least You Need to Know

- The Second Amendment is the one that says "the right of people to keep and bear arms shall not be infringed."

- The Second Amendment has not kept many gun laws from being implemented and enforced by local, state, and federal governments.

- The debate over gun control balances two issues: the historic right of law-abiding citizens to own guns for hunting or self-defense, and society's desire to keep guns out of the hands of criminals.

- Because the issue is such a political hot potato, it seems unlikely that either a new Second Amendment or a Supreme Court ruling will resolve this controversy any time in the near future.

The Fourth Amendment: Unreasonable Searches and Seizures

In This Chapter

- ◆ Searches and seizures
- ◆ The exclusionary rule
- ◆ Privacy
- ◆ Stop and frisk

The Fourth Amendment is one of the most cherished legal concepts in our democracy. It is a cornerstone of the right of privacy and sets the boundaries for what law enforcement authorities can do in terms of stopping you, entering your home or workplace or motor vehicle, and searching you and your property. The Fourth Amendment is a buffer zone between personal privacy and police power, but the rules that have been handed down by the courts a bit at a time are often controversial and confusing.

Those rules try to balance society's desire for the protection of individual rights against society's desire to make sure that criminals are caught and convicted. Look at it this way: the Fourth Amendment is aimed at protecting all of us, but the only people who directly benefit are those who get away with committing crimes because of procedural errors in the criminal justice system.

This discussion will show you how the courts have interpreted and enforced the Fourth Amendment to strengthen individual rights in society—your rights—but will also show you the limits to your rights both in the courtroom and out on the streets.

The Fourth Amendment

"The right of the people to be secure in the persons, houses, papers and effects, against unreasonable searches and seizures, shall not be violated, and no Warrants shall issue, but upon probable cause, supported by Oath or affirmation, and particularly describing the place to be searched, and the person or things to be seized."

English History

Look at the opening phrase of the Fourth Amendment: "The right of the people to be secure in their persons, houses, papers and effects ...." The Fourth Amendment is all about privacy—your right to privacy. It's an ancient concept, still evolving in many ways, but the basic premise is that governments should leave people alone unless it can prove they're doing something wrong.

Like much of the Constitution, the Fourth Amendment is rooted in English common law, the rules that evolved over the centuries as Europe emerged from the Dark Ages into the Renaissance and toward the Industrial Age. The rights of individuals gradually became more important as kings and queens and their governments recognized that it was easier to keep the rabble somewhat mollified rather than to put down rebellions. Our Fourth Amendment, the part of the Constitution that protects us from illegal searches and seizures by authorities, is rooted in the English principle that "a man's home is his castle."

That actual language was used in a British court case in 1603. A citizen challenged the right of the crown's agents to break into his home and search for evidence that he had not paid his tax bill in full. Up until that time the king's men could do pretty much whatever they wanted to whomever they wanted, no questions asked. In a remarkable departure from the acceptance of the monarch as all-powerful, the court declared that a homeowner does have the right to defend against unlawful entry by the king's agents. It was a huge victory for personal liberty—in theory, at least. In practical terms, the impact was not immediate. The court also said that the king's men still had the right to enter and search, including breaking down doors and smashing locks, to do the king's will. And even if authorities conducted unlawful searches, the evidence that they seized could still be used in court.

A system of *warrants* developed: legal orders, requested by law enforcement authorities and approved by judges, that allowed law officers to search and seize people and property. Originally, these were "general warrants," so named because they were so general, so vague. With a general warrant, a law officer could break into almost anybody's house and look for pretty much anything.

Eventually English law moved toward requiring more specifics in warrants. Law officers seeking warrants had to identify the premises they wanted to enter, who they wanted to search, and what they wanted to seize. Further challenges in English courts laid down another important principle that came to guide our Fourth Amendment: the requirement for *probable cause*. It wasn't enough to apply for a warrant with specific names and addresses.

def•i•ni•tion

A **warrant** is a document that serves as a legal permission slip granted by a judge or magistrate allowing a law enforcement officer to take a legal action—in the case of the Fourth Amendment, to carry out an arrest, search, or seizure.

Probable cause is the legal justification for an arrest, search, or seizure, based on sufficient reason to think a crime has been committed, that a certain person has committed a crime, or that certain property may be evidence of a crime.

If the king's men were going to enter a man's home, whether castle or hovel, they had to have probable cause—a good reason to believe that a crime had been committed, that evidence of the crime was in the house, or that the homeowner had been involved in the crime. In 1886, the United States Supreme Court hailed the concept of probable cause for arrest, search, and seizure as "one of the permanent monuments" of British law, and said it no doubt had inspired the Founding Fathers who framed the Constitution.

In Early America

If England had followed its own common law and court cases in the New World, we might still be living under the Union Jack. The colonists might never have rebelled, and the United States might never have been created. Instead, the British imposed much harsher legal rules on the American colonies than they did on their citizens back home.

As so often happens in history, money was at the heart of the story. The British had an empire to keep afloat. They relied on the people and the vast resources of the American colonies to pay for it all, largely through trade and taxes. For example, to protect their trade deficit, the British required that the colonies buy and import certain raw materials, products, and goods from England instead of making or growing their own more quickly, easily, and cheaply. Plus the British taxed everything coming and going.

Cheating on taxes became a way of life for the colonists, except they called it avoiding unfair taxation without representation. The British called it smuggling, and used general warrants—with no specifics in terms of people, places, or evidence to be searched or seized—to find evidence, send offenders to prison, and confiscate their property in the name of the Crown. These warrants were called "writs of assistance," meaning that colonists were supposed to assist the authorities in their searches and investigations. You could be arrested, for example, if you didn't assist the tax men by snooping on and reporting your neighbor.

If someone broke into your house, you could not appeal to anyone. As the British campaign against tax evaders became more aggressive, with blanket searches of neighborhoods, often door to door, the colonists became more outraged.

In 1775, Americans picked up their rifles and undertook the Revolution with a simple goal: to create a government based on law, not people. They wanted their lives to be regulated by laws that applied to everyone, not by the whims of kings and queens or their appointed sheriffs. In non-democratic nations, a law enforcement official can't break the law, because he *is* the law. In our democratic system, a law enforcement official who oversteps legal boundaries becomes a lawbreaker himself.

> **People**
>
> In 1761, James Otis went to court on behalf of 63 Boston merchants to argue that the writs of assistance, general warrants that allowed the Crown's agents virtually unlimited search and seizure powers, were illegal under England's own law. Otis lost the case, but John Adams later said Otis's argument was the real start of the rebellion against England.

After the Constitutional Convention of 1787, when the framers agreed to amend the original Constitution with a Bill of Rights, James Madison stepped up and took the lead. Madison, a member of the first House of Representatives who was to become the fourth president of the United States, figured the 13 states would be more likely to ratify the amendments in the Bill of Rights if the ideas and language were already familiar to them. His home state, Virginia, already had a provision against illegal searches and seizures written into its constitution, so Madison adapted it as the proposed Fourth Amendment.

Searches and Seizures

Today the American rules for search and seizure are remarkably similar, both in the spirit and in the letter of the law, to the procedures outlined by James Otis in 1761. To get a search warrant, authorities have to go before a neutral judge or magistrate—he or she can't be a district attorney or someone else on the prosecuting side of the criminal justice system—and testify under oath or produce a sworn, written affidavit that lays out the specifics of the proposed search.

The specifics may include the place and the people to be searched, perhaps the time the search will be conducted, and what the authorities are looking for. The search warrant is approved if the judge or magistrate finds probable cause that a crime may have been committed, that the person named in the warrant may have committed the crime, and that there may be evidence on the person or property to be searched.

The search warrant cannot be general, like the old British writs of assistance in the 1700s. If the police have a warrant to search your backyard only, they cannot use it to search your house. If the search warrant says they are looking for stolen TVs, they cannot look in desk drawers to go through your papers.

However, police are allowed to seize contraband or evidence of other crimes. For example, if the warrant says they are searching your house for stolen TVs but they see an AK-47, they can arrest you on weapons charges. Police officers using a warrant can go beyond the scope of the warrant under certain circumstances, such as to protect their own safety or the safety of others, if evidence is in *plain view*, if they need to act quickly to prevent the destruction of evidence, or if the evidence that they've found leads them elsewhere in the house or yard.

The Fourth Amendment also allows searches without warrants. Indeed, most arrests, searches, and seizures occur without warrants. However, those undertaken without warrants must not be "unreasonable," under the Fourth Amendment—and deciding just what is unreasonable has kept our courts busy for many years. That tension between individual rights and protecting society results in an ever-evolving process.

What It Means to You

The cops can break down your door if they're investigating a serious crime, have "clear" probable cause to think someone inside did the crime, and think the suspect might be armed or about to escape.

Time is often a factor in the court's reckoning on whether the police should get a search warrant or just go ahead and do the search. For example, let's say a police officer walked past your window, happened to look in, and saw your hydroponic greenhouse full of thriving young marijuana plants. It doesn't look like those plants, or their still-ripening buds and seeds, are going anywhere soon. So the courts likely would say there's time for the police to go get a search warrant and come back.

The Exclusionary Rule

The Fourth Amendment had little effect for more than a century after it was ratified. Yes, it declared that unreasonable searches and seizures were illegal without warrants and probable cause, but there were no legal definitions to set the boundaries. Furthermore, even if a search or seizure was unreasonable, the evidence could still be used. The Fourth Amendment was, in effect, merely advisory.

In 1914, however, the Supreme Court issued a landmark decision in the Weeks case. Fremont Weeks was convicted on gambling charges after authorities—without warrants—searched his home and business and found lottery tickets in his mail. Weeks appealed, and the Supreme Court unanimously ruled that not only had his Fourth Amendment rights been violated, but that the evidence seized in the illegal searches could not be used against him. With the evidence inadmissible, Weeks's conviction was overturned.

This case created the exclusionary rule, the rule that prohibits courts from considering evidence that has been obtained illegally. The exclusionary rule gave the Fourth Amendment a sharp new spur to keep the police in line: evidence that is illegally obtained must be excluded. The Weeks case gave defense attorneys the power to file a pretrial *motion to suppress* evidence that is illegally obtained. If evidence is ruled inadmissible, prosecutors cannot present it, judges cannot consider it, and juries cannot even see or hear about it.

def•i•ni•tion

A **motion to suppress** is a request made by a defense attorney before a judge, usually before trial, to suppress or declare evidence inadmissible under the exclusionary rule.

The Supreme Court made it clear: the goal of the exclusionary rule was to deter law enforcement authorities from conducting unlawful searches and seizures. The logic was that if the evidence they gathered from unconstitutional action was not allowed in court, and if the convictions they gained by going too far were overturned, the police would be more likely to follow the rules.

For decades the exclusionary rule applied only to federal cases. It was up to the individual states to decide how to handle illegal searches and seizures, and whether to exclude evidence obtained unlawfully. In 1961, however, the Supreme Court extended the exclusionary rule to the states in the Mapp case, described later. The court said that the exclusionary rule now applied to the states in determining whether the police could enter without a warrant, and whether the evidence obtained in a subsequent search was admissible.

The high court held that states do not have to stick strictly to the rules of the Fourth Amendment, but they cannot give their citizens less protection—a lowered expectation of privacy—than the Fourth Amendment. They can give more protection against unlawful searches and seizures, in other words, but not less.

The Fruit of the Poisonous Tree

The courts have ruled that unlawful searches result not only in the exclusion of evidence seized directly, but also of evidence that was discovered later or separately—as long as it was a result of the initial violation of the Fourth Amendment. This kind of evidence is called "the fruit of the poisonous tree." An extension of the exclusionary rule, this doctrine suppresses not only evidence seized in an unlawful search, but also any subsequent evidence that might be uncovered because of the search.

Suppose the police come into your house looking for stolen cell phones, but they don't have a warrant or probable cause. They find some stolen phones, and they see a note scrawled on a blackboard: "Deliver E to Smith." As part of a separate investigation, they go find Smith, gather evidence that you are selling ecstasy, come back with a proper warrant, and arrest you.

A court rules first that the stolen cell phones cannot be used against you because the original search was a violation of the Fourth Amendment. In addition, everything about the ecstasy—Smith's testimony, finding the drugs in your home, and even your confession, if you made one—is inadmissible as fruit of the poisonous tree because the police never would have gone in that direction if they had not violated your rights in the first place.

Naturally, public opinion does not applaud Supreme Court rulings that might let a criminal go free, no matter what individual rights are being protected. On one hand, sure, it is a noble goal to protect individual rights. On the other hand, we want to put the bad guys away. We have a certain amount of sympathy for someone whose rights have been abused by law enforcement authorities, but many of us have even more outrage at the ideas of crooks walking, and even more sympathy for their victims.

The provisions of the Fourth Amendment, particularly the exclusionary rule, have come to fall under the scorned catch-all phrase "legal technicality." When unlawfully obtained evidence is excluded and a suspect gets off, we are told the case has been dismissed "on a technicality." Many of us have come to regard technicalities as loopholes created by the courts and exploited by criminals.

> **What It Means to You**
>
> The courts have held that if a private person, someone not connected to the authorities, seizes evidence and hands it to the police, it is admissible. That includes nosy neighbors and private security officers (who outnumber real police by about three to one, incidentally).

In 1957, a bomb went off on the porch at the home of Don King, a Cleveland numbers racketeer who years later, after time in prison, became the preeminent boxing promoter in the world. Police investigating the bombing went to the home of Dollree Mapp, the ex-wife of a boxer, looking for a suspect. The police showed her a piece of paper that they said was a warrant. She grabbed the piece of paper and stuffed it "down her bosom," as the court so delicately described it. The cops wrestled with her and got the piece of paper back, and proceeded to search the house. They apparently didn't find any evidence of the bombing, but they did find some "lewd and lascivious material"—dirty books and homemade pornography, apparently, including sketches—down in the basement.

The police arrested Mapp on obscenity charges. She appealed the conviction of First Amendment grounds, saying her right to free speech allowed her to have erotica in her own home. The Supreme Court reversed her conviction, but not on First Amendment grounds. Instead, the court said the police had violated her Fourth Amendment rights. The police might have had a stronger case, but they could not produce the warrant and said it had been "lost." Moreover, the court extended the exclusionary rule to the states. The dirty books were out as evidence, and Dollree Mapp was once again a free woman. Moreover, state, county, and local police had to abide by the Fourth Amendment or see their cases thrown out of court.

> **People**
>
> In the Mapp case extending the exclusionary rule to the states, Justice Tom Clark wrote, "Nothing can destroy a government more quickly than its failure to observe its own laws, or worse, its disregard of their charter of its own existence ...."

Privacy

The Fourth Amendment is all about privacy, but it protects you only when you have a reasonable expectation of privacy. You expect to be secure and have privacy in your home, and that's reasonable to the normal person. You may expect some degree of privacy at your workplace, too, perhaps, but probably not as much as at home. The same with your car: there is some expectation of privacy, but not as much as at home. Both at work and out in your car, people are more likely to see you.

There is a presumption against any expectation of privacy in most public places; you can't reasonably claim that you expect privacy in a mosh pit or at midfield in a football stadium or while you're using your laptop at the local coffee hangout. But there are exceptions. The courts have ruled, for example, that yes (thank goodness), there is a reasonable expectation of privacy in a public restroom, and law enforcement authorities cannot hide cameras in there to see just what you're doing and whether it's illegal. Here's one more significant point about privacy: the courts say there is no expectation of privacy in illegal acts, wherever they occur.

A key part of the whole issue of privacy concerns the plain view doctrine. If something is in plain view, the police don't need a warrant to seize it. If you're pulled over for running a stop sign and the police see a bong on the floor of your car, you're probably going to get busted for that, too. If you're sunbathing nude behind a tall fence and nobody can see you, you have a reasonable expectation of privacy. But if you open the gate in the fence so that kids can see you on their way home from kindergarten, you've given up your expectation of privacy and you're fair game for an indecent exposure charge.

The Supreme Court in recent years has broadened its vision, so to speak, in determining just what is in plain view and what isn't. A good example is the 1986 case *California v. Ciraolo,* where the Santa Clara cops got an anonymous tip that a guy was growing marijuana. But they couldn't be sure—not sure enough to have probable cause and get a warrant—because of the tall fences around his garden. So the cops got a small plane, cruised over the pot plot at about 1,000 feet, and got a warrant because they had seen the marijuana. The Supreme Court ruled that the search was legal because it was "nonintrusive" and "took place within public navigable airspace." Chief Justice Warren Burger wrote, "Any member of the public flying in this airspace who glanced down could have seen everything that these officers observed."

A much-cited case on privacy expectations came from California and was decided by the Supreme Court in 1988. The police suspected Billy Greenwood of dealing drugs, but didn't have enough evidence to get a warrant. They couldn't show a judge that they had probable cause to toss his place. So the police waited until garbage day, and went through the garbage Greenwood left out by the curb. Bingo. They found enough evidence of drug use and drug dealing to get a judge to give them a warrant. They searched the house and found drugs.

Greenwood appealed that the search warrant had been improperly issued because his garbage was private. The court said, in a word, rubbish. Greenwood had no reasonable expectation of privacy for trash he had thrown out on the street. Any member of the public could have pawed through his garbage the same way the police did. The decision noted that the bags were "readily accessible to animals, children, scavengers, snoops, and other members of the public"—not to mention narcs.

One of the biggest challenges for law enforcement and the judicial system has been keeping up with technology. In 1928, the Supreme Court ruled that wiretapping was not a violation of the Fourth Amendment's right to privacy—as long as the bug was planted outside the home, not inside.

That changed in 1967, in the case of Charles Katz, a bookie who habitually made gambling-related calls from Los Angeles to Miami and Boston. He did a lot of his business from a phone booth—one of those old glass-and-plastic-and-metal boxes out on the street, with the door that folded shut behind you; you know, from the days before cell phones. Anyway, the feds tapped the outside of the phone booth and nailed Katz. He argued that the phone booth was a "constitutionally protected" area. The court disagreed, but threw out the case against him anyway, citing his expectation of privacy. "The Fourth Amendment protects people, not places," Justice Potter Stewart wrote.

A few recent court decisions, however, make it clear that the Supreme Court intends to keep an eye on how the authorities use new technology. In a case decided in 2001, a federal agent suspected that Danny Kyllo was growing marijuana. But he was apparently growing the herb indoors, and the agent did not have probable cause for a search warrant. To show probable cause, he used thermal imaging to indicate there were high-intensity heat lamps inside, the kind sometimes used to give marijuana plants a growth spurt.

The Supreme Court narrowly ruled that the search was unconstitutional because the heat waves were not in plain view. Justice Antonin Scalia noted that when "the government uses a device that is not in general public use to explore details of the home that would previously have been unknowable without physical intrusion, the surveillance is a 'search' and is presumptively unreasonable without a warrant."

The courts have outlined a number of instances when a warrant may not be needed and the standards for probable cause may be less, including:

◆ When the evidence is in plain view

◆ When someone in authority has given consent

◆ When police are in hot pursuit of a suspect

◆ To prevent destruction of evidence

- In case of emergencies or exigent circumstances
- When they stop and frisk someone
- For airport security
- At sobriety roadblocks
- During work-related drug tests
- For public school students and prisoners
- When police act in good faith even though a warrant is faulty

If a police officer wants to enter your home or business and doesn't have a warrant, you can ask that he or she get a warrant, and you can verbally object. But don't try to physically block the officer's entry. For one thing, the officer may have probable cause that you don't know about. For another, whether or not the officer is entering illegally, you could be charged with interfering with police.

If the police stop you on the street and you push back physically, or if you are disrespectful verbally, you probably will be arrested. Even if you were innocent of whatever they were investigating, the charges for not cooperating may stick. And even if you are released with apologies later, you probably won't be able to sue for damages. So keep your cool around the cops.

What It Means to You

The police can lawfully stop motorists merely for driving through a neighborhood that is known for prostitution, especially if the police notice that a car is moving slowly, repeatedly circling the block, or stopping so that the driver can engage in curbside conversation. It usually doesn't do any good to tell the cops you were just asking for directions.

Consent

A search and subsequent seizure are not an issue if the authorities are operating with consent. If someone in control, maybe a relative or a roommate, says it's okay to come in and search the place, the police don't need a warrant. A spouse who shares a home can give authorities consent to search. A suspect's roommate can allow police inside an apartment to search, but not in the suspect's private bedroom. Under ordinary circumstances, police should have a warrant before getting a landlord or hotel manager to unlock a rented room.

Sometimes we give implied consent merely by moving around in public, and in some cases the courts have said the public's security interests override the need for individual warrants. No warrants are necessarily needed, for example, to search passengers going through airport security, or job applicants who provide evidence for drug tests, or someone on parole, or prisoners in their cells. Government employees have a lower expectation of privacy than private employees, and courts have given government supervisors broad leeway in poking through their staff's offices, desks, and filing cabinets. Students give up some of their privacy rights every time they walk into a public school.

In a 1985 New Jersey case, a 14-year-old freshman girl, "TLO," was caught smoking in the restroom at her public school. She denied that she smoked, but when the assistant principal asked for her purse, he opened it and found marijuana, rolling papers, and a list of students and how much money they owed her. It looked like she was a dealer. The school called her parents and the police.

TLO was suspended from school for 10 days and sentenced to a year's probation for juvenile delinquency. She appealed on the grounds that the search of her purse and seizure of her pot was a violation of the Fourth Amendment. Since it was a New Jersey case, the Supreme Court said, "Fuggedaboutit!" Not really, but almost. The court ruled that authorities, including assistant principals, have a lesser standard for searching students in public schools. Instead of probable cause, they need only a *reasonable suspicion* of a crime to undertake a search, and under that standard TLO's search was legal.

def•i•ni•tion

Reasonable suspicion isn't as stringent as probable cause; this lower standard for conducting searches is allowed in certain cases where the courts have said that it made sense for the authorities to suspect wrongdoing and act without a warrant.

Here's a final point related to consent. While third parties can consent to search areas under their control, third parties cannot object to a search or seek to have evidence excluded on a suspect's behalf.

A passenger in a car or a guest in a home cannot object if the police are otherwise lawfully conducting a search of the vehicle or house.

Good Faith

Just because a warrant is faulty doesn't mean the defendant will get off. The courts in recent years have carved out a "good faith" exception so that evidence is admissible as long as the police officers who found it honestly believe that the warrant was properly issued and they had probable cause.

In a 1984 case, a defendant named Alberto Leon was the target of a drug bust. An informant gave information about him to the police, who did surveillance on him and then went to court and filed an affidavit to show probable cause. They got the search warrant, recovered drugs from Leon, and he was convicted on federal charges. On appeal, the court found that the affidavit supplied by the police was insufficient; the warrant never should have been issued because there was no probable cause. However, the court did not exclude the evidence or overturn the conviction. Justice Byron White wrote, "In such a case where the police were acting in good faith, the exclusion of valid evidence has no deterrent effect and exacts too high a price from society."

The court said that the exclusionary rule is not a right, but rather a remedy to deter illegal police conduct. If it is not deterring illegal police conduct (the police thought they were doing everything above board), then the evidence stays in. Many principles of law are based on a cost-benefit analysis, and in *United States v. Leon* the high court said the cost of the exclusionary rule outweighed the benefit to society.

Jimmy Hoffa, the onetime labor leader with organized crime ties, disappeared mysteriously and was never found. His body is reputedly buried somewhere in the New Jersey Meadowlands, perhaps under Giants Stadium. But Hoffa lives on, in a way, through a Supreme Court decision. During one of his many legal travails, Hoffa was placed in a cell with another man. They chatted, and Hoffa said more than he should have. The cellmate turned out to be an undercover cop, and Hoffa's comments were used against him. Hoffa appealed, but the Supreme Court said he had no expectation that his conversation was private, "however strongly a defendant may trust an apparent colleague."

Stop and Frisk

Obviously, the requirements of the Fourth Amendment have a huge impact on the way police actually do their work out on the streets. In recent years, the courts have been gradually giving back some of the leeway that cops gave up under stricter interpretations of the Fourth Amendment. For example, stop-and-frisk cases have had a lot to do with chipping away at the standards of probable cause in favor of the on-the-street standard of reasonable suspicion.

The courts seem intent on helping the police do the job of policing, in part by sometimes considering not only the circumstances but the experience and judgment of the police officer on the scene. The thinking is that a veteran cop actually may be the best judge of whether someone should be a suspect or not. The courts call it the *totality of circumstances*. Critics on the civil liberties side of the equation might be more likely to call it letting the cops act on their biases. However you look it at, the courts have made a little bit of room under the Fourth Amendment for cops to play hunches.

> **def•i•ni•tion**
>
> **Totality of circumstances** is the concept handed down by the courts allowing them to more deeply review search-and-seizure cases to consider, among other factors, the experience and judgment of the police officers involved.

An important case for stop and frisk is *Ohio v. Terry*, decided by the Supreme Court in 1968. John W. Terry and a couple of other guys were spotted in an area of Cleveland where the police had been having a lot of trouble with pickpockets and shoplifters. A police officer thought maybe they were casing a jewelry store. The police stopped the guys and patted them down, and found they were carrying guns.

Terry was convicted of carrying a concealed weapon and appealed, claiming that the search was unlawful because the cops had no probable cause for stopping him; he hadn't been breaking any laws. And he argued that the search was illegal because he hadn't been arrested yet. Terry probably went to the Supreme Court thinking the chances of having the search declared unconstitutional were pretty good. After all, until then the rule was that until someone was arrested, the police needed probable cause to do a search.

The Supreme Court disagreed, however, and fine-tuned the rules in favor of the police. The high court held that the search was legal because a "reasonably prudent man" would have been warranted in believing Terry "was armed and thus presented a threat to the officer's safety while he was investigating his suspicious behavior." Chief Justice Earl Warren's decision held that the Fourth Amendment allows for sometimes giving the benefit of the doubt to the police officer in order to protect the officer's and the public's safety. "The officer need not be absolutely certain that the individual is armed," Warren wrote. "The issue is whether the reasonably prudent man in the circumstances would be warranted in the belief that his safety or others' was in danger."

Police authority expanded further a few years later in another case, when police patted down a man pulled over on suspicion of driving with a revoked license. The pat-down, ostensibly for weapons, revealed marijuana cigarettes. The Supreme Court upheld the drug conviction.

What It Means to You

If you are pulled over for a traffic offense, you can be ordered to step out of the car and be patted down if the officer is concerned that you might have a weapon. Your passengers can be frisked, too. The police can also search the inside of your car—but not the trunk, not until they impound the car or get a warrant.

To Knock or Not

Ordinarily authorities are required to "knock and announce" before they enter a home. An example of the legal rationale can be seen in a 1995 U.S. Supreme Court case, *Wilson v. Arkansas*, which began when Sharlene Wilson sold drugs to an undercover Arkansas state police officer. The police got warrants to search her house and arrest her. They arrived at the house and found the main door open. There was a screen door, and it was unlocked, so the police walked in, identified themselves, and said they had a warrant. Sharlene Wilson was arrested and convicted on drug charges, and then appealed on the grounds that the police should have knocked before they came in, and should have announced themselves before they came in, not after.

The high court agreed with her, saying yes, the cops should have knocked and announced. "Given the longstanding common-law endorsement of the practice of announcement, and the wealth of founding-era commentaries, constitutional provisions, statutes, and cases espousing or supporting the knock-and-announce principle ... the Amendment's Framers thought that whether officers announced their presence and authority before entering a dwelling was among the factors to be considered in assessing a search's reasonableness." However, the court also emphasized that the way the police officers entered could have been considered legal if they had good reasons for not knocking first.

Authorities can get warrants that specifically allow them to enter without knocking first, but usually only after convincing the judge or magistrate that it's for their own safety, or to prevent a suspect from escaping or destroying evidence. In a 1997 Wisconsin case, police suspected a man named Steiney Richards of dealing cocaine from his hotel room. A policeman knocked on the door and said he was a hotel custodian. Richards started to open the door, but then saw a uniformed police officer and slammed the door shut.

The officers broke down the door and grabbed Richards before he could escape. They also found coke and cash in the bathroom. Richards was convicted, but appealed on the grounds that the officers violated the Fourth Amendment by using deception—the phony identification as a hotel custodian—and then forcing their way into his room. The Supreme Court, however, ruled that the officers could legally break down the door as soon as Richards slammed it in their faces. That was a pretty good indication, the court said, that Richards was trying to escape, flush the evidence, or both.

In a 1998 case, the *United States v. Ramirez*, the police were looking for a dangerous prison escapee named Alan Shelby. A federal agent, acting on a tip from an informant, saw a guy who looked like the escaped prisoner at a home in Boring, Oregon. (Yes, that's the real name of the town, a hamlet of 14,000 in Clackamas County.) Agents got a "no-knock warrant" and came back to the home during the night. They broke a window to get in, and woke up the man sleeping inside—Hernan Ramirez. Startled, Ramirez grabbed a gun and fired it into the ceiling. The police found no Shelby, but they found more guns and arrested Ramirez.

The trial court refused to allow the guns into evidence on the grounds that the agents should have knocked and did not have justification for destroying property—breaking the window—to gain entry. The decision was upheld on appeal, but the Bureau of Alcohol Tobacco and Firearms appealed to the Supreme Court. The high court unanimously overturned the verdict and said the guns were in as evidence. The court said breaking the window was justified because the officers had a "reasonable suspicion" to think that knocking and announcing might be dangerous, futile, or inhibit their investigation.

Chief Justice William Rehnquist said that even if the officers had violated the Fourth Amendment, the evidence was still admissible. "Excessive or unnecessary destruction of property in the course of a search may violate the Fourth Amendment," Rehnquist wrote, "even though the entry itself is lawful and the fruits of the search not subject to suppression."

Here's one more no-knock case: *Brigham City v. Stuart*, decided in the spring of 2006. There probably aren't a lot of really loud all-night parties in Brigham City, Utah, so it makes sense that the police responded promptly when a neighbor called in a complaint around 3 A.M. The officers went to the front door and pounded, but got no answer, apparently because the music and voices inside were so loud.

The officers walked up the driveway, saw juveniles drinking in the backyard, and entered the yard. Looking into the house, they saw a juvenile punch an adult in the face. While the adult was spitting blood into the sink, the police entered the home, shouting to identify themselves. After a period of scuffling and shouting, and angry protests from partygoers, the police finally calmed things down and made a number of arrests, including for providing alcohol to minors.

The defendants argued that their Fourth Amendment rights had been violated. The Supreme Court disagreed. The officers had probable cause to enter the backyard when they saw the juveniles drinking, and seeing the attack inside provided enough of an emergency for them to enter the house without knocking first. Besides, they tried to announce themselves but the music was too loud.

The Least You Need to Know

◆ The police do not necessarily need a warrant to search your home, office, yard, car, garage, or barn.

◆ If the police want to search your home or office, ask to see a warrant—politely and calmly.

◆ Don't resist, physically or verbally.

◆ If you have questions, ask if you may have a lawyer present or check with a lawyer later.

Chapter 7

The Fifth Amendment: Due Process

In This Chapter

- ◆ The Fifth Amendment
- ◆ Grand jury indictments
- ◆ Double jeopardy
- ◆ Self-incrimination
- ◆ Due process of law
- ◆ Eminent domain

The Fifth Amendment is one of the Constitution's bulwarks of individual liberty against the powers of police and prosecutors. It restrains the forces of law and order throughout the criminal process, from the moment an individual is suspected of a crime.

The Fifth Amendment

"No person shall be held to answer for a capital or otherwise infamous crime, unless on a presentment or indictment of a grand jury, except in cases arising in the land or naval forces, or in the militia, when in actual service in time of war or public danger; nor shall any person be subject for the same offense to be twice put in jeopardy of life or limb; nor be deprived of life, liberty, or property, without due process of law; nor shall private property be taken for public use, without just compensation."

The Fifth Amendment is best known for protecting you against giving evidence against yourself via confession. When you "take the Fifth" you are refusing to provide possible evidence against yourself, but the Fifth Amendment also gave us the Miranda ruling we hear on all the TV cop shows: "You have the right to remain silent …."

However, the Fifth Amendment contains several other important provisions for protecting your rights. It is the source of the double jeopardy doctrine, which prevents authorities from trying you twice for the same crime, and it requires that people accused of serious crimes be indicted by a grand jury before they can be prosecuted. The Fifth Amendment also guarantees "due process": that the government will follow the law and procedural rules in taking your freedom or property, and that you'll be fairly compensated if the government condemns and takes it over under eminent domain.

The Fifth Amendment originally applied only to federal law, but most of its requirements now apply to the states, too, under the provisions of the Equal Protection Clause of the Fourteenth Amendment.

Grand Jury Indictments

"No person shall be held to answer for a capital or otherwise infamous crime, unless on a presentment or indictment of a grand jury …"

One of the historic cornerstones of the criminal justice system is the Fifth Amendment's requirement that an indictment be returned by a grand jury before the government can prosecute a defendant on serious criminal charges. In effect, the grand jury decides whether the prosecution has enough evidence to bring a defendant to trial. It is an ancient legal concept, going back to English common law in the twelfth century, to prevent a king or his minions from prosecuting someone for no good reason. Designed to prevent prosecutions born out of political, religious, business, or personal motivations, it was one of the first checks on government power in what has become our system of checks and balances.

After all, throwing a rival in prison or chopping off his head was a good way for a nobleman to take over a rival's land, steal his wife, or get him to stop saying things that the nobleman didn't like. The idea was to give some regular citizens a chance to say, "Hey, wait, this isn't fair!"

Most people are familiar with the kind of jury, traditionally 12 people, that hears the evidence in criminal trials, goes off to deliberate in closed session, and then comes back to the courtroom with a verdict: guilty or not guilty. In legal terms, that type of jury is called a petit jury.

The grand jury is different. Like a regular jury, a grand jury is made up of people from the community who receive a summons to report for jury duty. But a grand jury is larger, usually 23 people. A grand jury may be convened to consider just one case, which is what usually happens when a special prosecutor has been appointed to conduct a complex and often high-level government scandal, such as the Whitewater investigation of the Clintons or the more recent inquiry into possible leaks that revealed the identify of an undercover CIA operative related to the search for weapons of mass destruction before the Iraq war. On a local level, however, a grand jury is more likely to be appointed to serve over a period of several weeks, being called into session to consider not one but several different cases during its terms.

Instead of a judge presiding, a prosecutor, such as a U.S. attorney in federal courts or a district attorney in state courts, leads or directs the proceedings, presenting the case against the defendant to the grand jury.

The Fifth Amendment's requirements for grand jury indictments for serious crimes—generally agreed to be any offense that carries a potential prison sentence—applies to federal crimes only. Unlike many other requirements in the Bill of Rights, the Supreme Court has never

What It Means to You

If you are called to serve, the amount of time you spend on a grand jury depends on where you are and what kind of court it is. State grand jurors typically serve for a matter of weeks, while federal grand jurors often serve for months. In either case, you might be called into session almost daily or only a few times a month, depending on the caseload.

extended the grand jury rules to the state courts. As a practical matter, however, state criminal courts either have their own comparable grand jury requirements or a similar process called a "preliminary hearing." In a preliminary hearing, the prosecutor presents evidence to a judge to decide whether there is enough of a case against an accused person to bring an indictment and go to trial.

Another big difference between grand juries and regular juries is that the strict rules of evidence don't apply in grand jury proceedings as they do in a trial; for example, a prosecutor is allowed to lead a witness or use hearsay as evidence. The accused person may attend a grand jury session, but does not have an attorney present and is not allowed to present evidence or ask questions of witnesses. Unlike trial jurors, who are required to sit quietly and pay attention, grand jurors are allowed to directly ask their own questions of witnesses. And while the Fourth Amendment's exclusionary rule prevents a trial jury from considering or even hearing anything about evidence that was acquired in violation of a defendant's rights, grand jurors can hear and consider evidence that was obtained illegally.

While members of a jury at a criminal trial are instructed to find a defendant not guilty unless they agree that guilt is "beyond reasonable doubt," members of a grand jury have a lower standard. They can indict (or "return an indictment against") an accused person if they find "probable cause" that the accused person committed the crime. The indictment is a formal legal document that gives the prosecution the green light to proceed. When an indictment is returned, an accused person is "bound over" to the criminal courts for trial.

As you might imagine, prosecutors don't like to take a case to a grand jury unless they're pretty certain they will get an indictment. And the great latitude they are allowed—hearsay, illegal evidence, probable cause, and so on—lets prosecutors lead grand juries to almost any indictment they want.

> **People** _____
>
> An old saying around the courthouses of America is that a good prosecutor can get a grand jury to indict a ham sandwich. When a Texas prosecutor indicted former House Republican Leader Tom DeLay on conspiracy charges that led him to resign in 2005, one of his supporters, Florida Congresswoman Ileana Ros-Lehtinen, told reporters, "This is a ham sandwich indictment and we just ask, where's the beef?"

Grand jury proceedings have always been held in secret for a couple of reasons: one, to make sure the authorities, whether the nobleman of yesteryear or the government prosecutors of today, would not seek revenge against the members of the grand jury, and two, to avoid publicity or other repercussions that might be unfair to witnesses or to the accused person.

The secrecy requirements of the grand jury system have become more controversial in recent times. Some states allow the release and publication of grand jury testimony in certain circumstances after a criminal case is completed, but some jurisdictions have imposed harsh penalties against those who spill a grand jury's secrets.

For example, the two San Francisco newspaper reporters who broke the story about baseball player Barry Bonds's links to a steroid drug operation were threatened with jail time for refusing to reveal how they got Bonds's testimony and other transcripts from the grand jury. It was a case of the right to free speech versus the need to protect grand jury secrecy. Charges against the reporters were dropped after a suspected steroid dealer's defense attorney pleaded guilty to releasing the grand jury testimony, but for a time it looked like the reporters might spend more time behind bars than the dealers or users or anyone else connected with the case.

Double Jeopardy

"… nor shall any person be subject for the same offense to be twice put in jeopardy of life or limb …"

Civil rights for $200, Alex. Double jeopardy is not only the second half of a venerable television trivia program. It is also a venerable legal concept that, like the grand jury requirement, is designed to limit government harassment of citizens. The idea is simple: you should not have to stand trial twice for the same offense. If you are found not guilty by a judge or jury, then the government cannot try you again for the same thing. In fact, you cannot be tried a second time even if you were convicted. The government cannot lose a case against you and then bring a new charge for the same crime. Nor can the government get a conviction against you and then bring another charge against you for the same crime in hopes of adding to your punishment.

> **Cases**
>
> **Brown v. Ohio (1977):**
> The defendant was convicted of operating a motor vehicle without the owner's permission. The prosecutor subsequently brought new charges—stealing the car—against the defendant. The defendant was convicted, and appealed. The Supreme Court ruled that both charges were based on the same joyride, and the second conviction was overturned.

The concept of double jeopardy applied only to capital cases—crimes that carried the death penalty—in both English common law and the American colonies. In the United States, it applied only to federal criminal cases until 1969, when the Supreme Court decided that it was one of those rights that applied to state law, too. Instead of applying only to capital crimes, the Fifth Amendment's language concerning any case that would put a defendant "in jeopardy of life or limb" means that double jeopardy now generally applies for any offense that carries a potential prison sentence.

The Supreme Court has offered these reasons for the rules against allowing authorities to try citizens twice for the same act:

◆ By sheer use of its superior legal firepower—time, money, investigators, lawyers—the prosecution can wear down the defense and convict an innocent person.

◆ People can suffer in many ways, from financial to emotional, from having to defend themselves repeatedly.

◆ Public respect for the criminal justice system will wane if prosecutors are allowed to pick on people instead of letting them settle their debts to society once and for all.

◆ Prosecutors could develop too much power, and too much potential for abusing that power, if they can drag people they don't like back into court over and over.

◆ Judges would be able to pile on unduly harsh sentences, one on top of the other, for the same offense.

You can be charged with more than one offense for any particular act, but you cannot be punished for it more than once. Suppose someone kills another person. Depending on the prosecutor's assessment of the case, the defendant might be charged with various levels of the crime: manslaughter, second-degree murder, first-degree murder. A jury hearing the evidence and determining the facts of the case can find the defendant guilty of any one of the charges, but not more than one. If you beat up someone (battery) who then dies (murder) you can be charged with both battery and murder, but can be convicted of only one.

It is possible, however, to be charged for the same act in different jurisdictions. A state court might find a defendant not guilty of murder, but then a separate proceeding could be brought in federal court to convict the person of violating the victim's civil rights—death being the ultimate violation of someone's civil rights. And sometimes a civil case, where the typical standard is "a preponderance of the evidence," may succeed despite the failure of a criminal prosecution, where the standard for conviction is "beyond a reasonable doubt." For example, take the case of former football star O. J. Simpson, who was accused of killing his estranged wife. He was found not guilty at a criminal trial. But his wife's family sued in civil court, and Simpson was found to be responsible for her death and ordered to pay monetary damages.

Cases
Ashe v. Swenson (1970): In this case, a guy who robbed a poker game was charged with robbing only one of the seven players. He was acquitted, so the prosecution brought charges against him for robbing the second player, and he was convicted. The U.S. Supreme Court overturned the conviction on double jeopardy grounds.

Mistrials are not covered by double jeopardy, nor are most convictions overturned on appeal. If a judge declares a mistrial because of a hung jury or because of juror misconduct, the prosecution can bring the case against you again. Same thing if you are convicted, you appeal, and the appeals court overturns the conviction. You don't necessarily walk; you're probably going to be retried.

It is important to remember that double jeopardy does not apply to cases in civil rights. You can be sued in civil court, win, and then the same person can sue you all over again for the same thing in the same court. And if you were acquitted in criminal court, you can still be sued in civil court for the consequences of your action. You won't be going to prison, but you can be ordered to pay damages to a plaintiff who claims he or she was wronged and suffered financial losses because of it.

> **People**
>
> The glove didn't fit, so the jury did acquit. But when O. J. Simp-son got off after being charged with two murders, double jeopardy didn't keep him from being sued in civil court by the Brown and Goldman families. A civil court jury found that Simpson had killed Nicole Brown Simpson and Ronald Goldman, and ordered him to pay the families $33.5 million.

Self-Incrimination

"... nor shall any person ... be deprived of life, liberty, or property, without due process of law ..."

The Fifth Amendment is best known for guaranteeing the right to silence—you cannot be forced to give evidence against yourself. The right against self-incrimination, however, is a relatively new one in legal history. Originally, any confession, no matter how the authorities got it—even by torture—was admissible in court.

Confessions

An important case against self-incrimination was brought by John Lilburne in England in 1637. A Puritan activist put on trial for smuggling anti-government pamphlets into the country, he refused to answer questions by the Star Chamber, a notoriously harsh court. He was whipped for his stubbornness, but the case led Parliament to abolish the Star Chamber and agreed that citizens should not be forced to give evidence against themselves.

Even in colonial America, the Puritan settlers in Massachusetts, who faced the same sort of oppression from authorities on the other side of the Atlantic, permitted torture as a means of extracting confessions from the accused. Not until the eighteenth century did English common law, in Great Britain and subsequently in the colonies, embrace the notion that it might be a good thing to disallow confessions obtained by coercion, extortion, or trickery.

As a practical matter, of course, police in America had a long history of pushing that particular envelope. The "rubber hose treatment"—rubber hoses supposedly left fewer marks, and less evidence of police conduct—was a cliché for a reason. So was giving a suspect "the third degree" to gain a confession, or "sweating it out of him."

What It Means to You

If you think something about yourself— something you know, something you've done— could conceivably be used against you in a criminal proceeding, you do not have to divulge that information.

Gradually, the federal courts led the way in forcing the police not to abuse suspects, primarily by reversing the convictions in cases when the police stepped over the line. In a 1936 case in Mississippi, three black men were accused of killing a white plantation owner, and the police readily confirmed that the men had been whipped to encourage them to confess. The United States Supreme Court overturned the convictions on Fifth Amendment grounds. The high court also reversed a conviction in a 1940 Florida case where a defendant finally confessed after being interrogated for five days. The same thing happened in a 1944 case in Tennessee, where a defendant confessed after being grilled pretty much nonstop under hot lights for 36 hours.

In those and other cases, the court reasoned that a prolonged interrogation made a confession inadmissible because it was unreliable: defendants would say whatever the authorities wanted them to say just to get the questions to stop, or get a slice of pizza, or get that blazing hot and incredibly bright light out of their face.

The Self-Incrimination Clause of the Fifth Amendment forces prosecutors to come up with independent evidence, something other than the accused person's confession, to secure a conviction. Make no mistake, the Fifth Amendment does not diminish the weight of a voluntary confession, and in fact the willing confession is still the biggest single piece of evidence in many if not most criminal prosecutions. Once an accused person has signed that confession, a plea bargain—pleading guilty to a slightly lesser charge or in exchange for a more lenient sentence—which avoids the time and expense of a trial is often a perfunctory matter.

> ### Cases
>
> **Hiibel v. Sixth Judicial District Court of Nevada (2004):** In this case, the U.S. Supreme Court ruled that you have to give the police your name if they ask. Neither the right to free speech under the First Amendment nor the right to silence under the Fifth Amendment applies. It's reasonable for the authorities to ask you your name, and simply giving your name is not necessarily regarded as incriminating.

Taking the Fifth

The Fifth Amendment's protections against self-incrimination apply in state or federal court and anywhere else you have to testify under oath, including in civil proceedings. That's why, back in the 1950s, when the House Committee on Un-American Activities was handing out subpoenas to anyone and everyone rumored to have any links to Communists or communism, those Hollywood celebrities took the Fifth:

Q: "Are you now or have you ever been a member of the Communist party?"

A: "On the advice of counsel, I respectfully refuse to answer on the grounds that my answer might incriminate me."

Whether they are hearings on organized crime or the Enron collapse, it's become a familiar scene: the witness in the hot seat ducking the question. Intellectually we know that the witness is exercising a constitutional right that we all share, but it doesn't exactly inspire confidence in someone's integrity or innocence—even when a witness such as

Enron's late chairman, Ken Lay, tried to convince a congressional hearing that he really would like to answer all those pesky questions and clear everything up, but his doggone lawyers just won't let him, darn it.

Taking the Fifth in a civil proceeding beats outright lying for one simple reason: lying under oath is perjury, and that's criminal. You might not go to jail for whatever it is that you have to testify about, but if you lie about it, you might go to jail for committing perjury. For example, former Bush administration aide Lewis "Scooter" Libby was implicated in the scandal over the outing of Valerie Plame as a CIA agent. But he was never charged with the crime of revealing her name. Instead, he was charged with and convicted of lying to a grand jury about what he told reporters about Plame. Going further back, President Bill Clinton initially denied having relations with Monica Lewinsky, but later admitted it rather than lie under oath and face perjury charges.

What It Means to You

It is a well-established principle: a jury is not supposed to draw an inference of guilt if a defendant has exercised the right to silence. But what about you? What do you think of a person who takes the Fifth? Do you think, "Hmm, that person is exercising an inalienable right"? Or do you think, "Hmm, that's somebody who's been doing something wrong"?

Immunity

If you agree to testify against someone in exchange for immunity from prosecution, you give up your right to silence. There are two kinds of immunity, *transactional* and *use immunity:*

- In **transactional immunity** you cannot be prosecuted for anything relating to your testimony.

- In **use immunity** you can still be prosecuted, but the testimony you provided in exchange for immunity cannot be used against you.

The Miranda Warning

No doubt the most far-reaching aspect of the Fifth Amendment's protection against self-incrimination—even more than taking the Fifth—is the right to remain silent, and the requirement that police inform a suspect of that right at the time of arrest. We are talking, of course, about the rights outlined in the well-known Miranda warning:

- ◆ You have the right to remain silent.

- ◆ You have the right to consult an attorney before and during questioning.

- ◆ If you cannot afford an attorney, the court will appoint one for you for free.

- ◆ Any statements you make to the police can and will be used as evidence against you in a court of law.

Ernesto Miranda was a guy who'd been in a lot of trouble when he was picked up by the police for robbery, kidnapping, and rape in Arizona in 1963. He confessed, signed a statement admitting his guilt, and was convicted, but appealed. The appeal made it before the U.S. Supreme Court in 1966, and became the best-known of a series of controversial cases decided by the court under Chief Justice Earl Warren. Critics said the Warren court was tipping the scales of justice too far in favor of the accused and endangering society by making it harder for the police to do their job. Supporters, notably the American Civil Liberties Union, welcomed constitutional interpretations that aimed to protect individual rights.

Chief Justice Warren, himself a former prosecutor, wrote the Miranda decision himself. He said Miranda's Fifth Amendment right against self-incrimination had been violated, and spelled out the warning word for word. He rejected, however, the ACLU's suggestion that every police station have a lawyer either on duty or nearby, so that every suspect brought in could see a lawyer immediately.

What It Means to You

Legal authorities are virtually unanimous: a suspect has little or nothing to gain by making any comment to police before consulting with an attorney.

Studies show that despite the mandatory Miranda warnings, many suspects still talk with the police before consulting an attorney. And the warning has survived a number of challenges in recent years, including one in 2000 when Chief Justice William Rehnquist, a notably conservative jurist, voted to uphold the warning and noted that Miranda warnings "have become part of our national culture." But critics, including Justice Antonin Scalia, maintain that the Warren Court overstepped its authority in 1966 and that the Constitution doesn't require such a warning. They hold out hope that the Miranda decision may someday be reversed.

Confessions obtained without a proper Miranda warning cannot be used as evidence under the exclusionary rule. But an inadmissible confession doesn't prohibit the prosecution from using other evidence. In fact, that's what happened to Ernesto Miranda. On appeal, the Supreme Court overturned his conviction on the grounds of an inadmissible confession and sent the case back for retrial. Prosecutors in Arizona then retried Miranda and convicted him using other evidence.

People

Ernesto Miranda served several years for rape and kidnapping. After his release, he made pocket change selling autographed copies of the Miranda warning. He was stabbed to death in a bar fight in Phoenix in 1976.

One of the keys to the Miranda ruling and the admissibility of confessions is whether a suspect has been arrested or taken into custody. To ask questions in what the courts call a "custodial interrogation," the police must administer the Miranda warning first. The Supreme Court has said "by custodial interrogation, we mean questioning initiated by law enforcement officers after a person has been taken into custody or otherwise deprived of his freedom of action in any significant way."

A number of cases have tried to define exactly when a suspect is in custody. Simply being in a police station—taking a ride downtown, as they say on the cop shows—is not necessarily being in custody. If you can leave, you're not in custody. Sometimes, of course, a suspect is not sure whether he can leave or not. The police don't necessarily need to declare that you're under arrest. If you cannot leave, or if it's reasonable for you to believe you cannot leave, you're in custody.

What It Means to You

You don't need to be in custody, and the police don't need to be asking you questions, for anything you say to be used against you. Sometimes two police officers will discuss a case in front of a suspect in the hopes that the suspect will just have to interject something. It's not deception, and the evidence is admissible.

The information you provide on your federal income tax returns can be used against you. In a 1927 case, the Supreme Court ruled that a taxpayer could not plead the Fifth Amendment's protections against self-incrimination when the information on his tax return—he said he was a professional gambler—was used against him at his trial for trying to fix sporting events. "If the form of return provided called for answer that the defendant was privileged from making," the court held, "he could have raised the objection in the return, but could not on that account refuse to make any return at all. We are not called on to decide what, if anything, he might have withheld."

Companies cannot claim the Fifth Amendment to withhold records from the authorities. The courts have ruled that the right against self-incrimination protects only "natural persons"—real human beings, in other words.

What It Means to You

You cannot be forced to testify against your spouse, and your spouse cannot be forced to testify against you. But the rules are less well defined, from case to case and especially from state to state, over when and whether you can *prevent* your spouse from testifying against you. Someone who truly wants to put his or her spouse away often gets the chance in court.

Even if a confession is inadmissible on Fifth Amendment grounds, it can still end up being used against a defendant under certain circumstances. For example, let's say a defendant is on trial; his confession is inadmissible, but there is other evidence. If the defendant takes the stand to deny committing the crime, he opens the door to what he did or said, and the prosecution can then use the confession to impeach that testimony.

Due Process of Law

"... nor be deprived of life, liberty, or property, without due process of law ..."

Due process of law is hard to define, but it's a powerful legal doctrine. It's an all-encompassing concept that means you cannot be harmed by loss of freedom or property unless the rules of the justice system have been followed and your rights have not been violated.

The principle was expressed in the Magna Carta this way: "No free man shall be seized, or imprisoned, or disseised, or outlawed, or exiled, or injured in any way ... except by the lawful judgment of his peers, or by the law of the land." That last phrase, "the law of the land," was the due process part. When a government sets up rules, the rules have to be reasonable, and it has to follow them.

In many ways, due process honors the rule of law. Society insists that the government play by the rules and treat everyone fairly. Due process also goes to entitlement: we have inalienable rights and we're entitled to them all the time, not just when it's convenient for the government to respect them. Society, and society's customs, have a lot to do with determining what is fair, what we're entitled to—and what due process means.

Due process originally applied only to the federal government under the Fifth Amendment, but the Fourteenth Amendment extended its protections to the states, too. Legal scholars make a distinction between procedural and substantive due process.

Procedural due process is the "how" of the law: How was a law approved? How is it applied? How does it affect the public? If the answer to any of those "how" questions is not acceptable—if there are violations of our rights—the law may be unconstitutional.

Substantive due process is the "why" of the law: Why was the law passed? Why does it make sense? Why is it fair? If the answer to any of those "why" questions is not acceptable—if there are violations of our rights—the law may be unconstitutional.

In practical terms, though, most of us don't need to know the difference between substantive and procedural due process. We merely need to know that laws have to be fair, and they have to be enforced fairly.

Here are just a few examples of the many types of cases pertaining to individual rights that can hinge on whether due process was followed in enacting or administering a law:

◆ Death penalty cases

◆ Affirmative action cases

◆ Privacy cases

◆ Voting rights cases

Eminent Domain

"… nor shall private property be taken for public use, without just compensation."

The concept of eminent domain—that the government can take away a person's private property for public use—is another principle that has evolved through the ages from English common law. Back in the day, the Crown could take away a landowner's property without compensation, but the Fifth Amendment requires "just compensation."

Eminent domain played a big role in the building of American society dating back to colonial times. If a new road or bridge was needed to help open up the frontier for economic development, it didn't make sense to go miles out of the way to build around someone's private property. It made more sense to declare eminent domain over the needed property—condemn it, in other words—and then appropriate it for public use.

During the Revolutionary War, both sides seized property—land and supplies—from citizens, against their will and without compensation. After independence, some states seized the property of loyalists who had supported Britain in the war, and some states had few qualms about taking over property inside their borders that was owned by residents of other states.

The Eminent Domain Clause is one of the Constitution's classic balancing acts: what's good for society versus what's good for the individual. On one hand, it makes sense to allow the government to take possession of private property—usually land, but it can be personal property, too—if it will benefit the general public. On the other hand, if and when that happens, the property owner should be fairly compensated for the loss.

As with any balancing of different interests, there are bound to be tensions. In America we've been arguing for a long time—and continue to argue—over exactly just what is in the public interest, and exactly what is fair compensation.

The general agreement on the Fifth Amendment's provisions, which have been applied by the Supreme Court to the states, too, is that "just compensation" usually means fair market value—what a property owner could get for the property by selling it on the open market. In theory, it should be pretty easy to figure out what property is worth: simply have it appraised. But what if the property is worth more to its current owner than the appraised value? What if the property owner has plans for the property that will make it more valuable? What if the property has sentimental value, such as a family homestead or a historic site?

Sometimes an eminent domain case can cause problems not only for the owner whose property has been seized, but for other people, too. Suppose the county decides a new highway has to come through your neighbor's backyard, and pays him to pull up and move out. What about you? You may not technically be eligible for compensation—it wasn't your property that was taken away—but your peaceful little haven in the country may not be worth as much if it's across from an on-ramp. If zoning laws change and you're suddenly under the flight pattern for a new airport, should you be compensated? Probably. Maybe. But not necessarily. And how much? The courts will decide based on the particular facts you present when you sue.

The definition of "for public use" also remains contentious. The courts always have left it to Congress to decide, and there's usually little debate if eminent domain is used by the government for a purpose that directly benefits the public and provides open access to the public. Anybody can use a highway or an airport or a school or a park, for instance; those are examples of private property being turned into public property.

But eminent domain also has been used to seize property that will not actually be public. The courts have said only that there must be a benefit to the public, even if that benefit seems to be indirect and it seems to directly benefit certain individuals. In a 2005 case from

Connecticut, *Kelo v. City of New London*, the U.S. Supreme Court held, in a controversial 5–4 decision, that it was permissible for the city to take over property from one private owner so that it could be used for private development, including a resort, hotel, conference center, shops, restaurants, offices, and apartments. Justice Paul Stevens, delivering the majority opinion in the Kelo case, wrote, "The city has carefully formulated a development plan that it believes will provide appreciable benefits to the community, including, but not limited to, new jobs and increased tax revenue."

Dissenting, Justice Sandra Day O'Connor warned that the danger was that rich people would be able to benefit from eminent domain as governments took away land from poor people: "Any property may not be taken for the benefit of another private party, but the fallout from this decision will not be random. The beneficiaries are likely to be those citizens with disproportionate influence and power in the political process, including large corporations and development firms." She urged the court, futilely, to stick to a strict interpretation of "for the public use" in the Fifth Amendment.

Not long after that decision, a libertarian activist asked the town council in Weare, New Hampshire, to use eminent domain to take over the home of David Souter, who was one of the five justices in the majority in the Supreme Court decision. The activist said he would turn the property into a hotel—the Lost Liberty Hotel, no less—and it would have the same benefits, including new jobs and local tax payments, as the property development in the New London case. At last report, the town council had no plans to turn the justice's home into a hotel.

The Least You Need to Know

◆ You cannot be forced to give any evidence against yourself, and neither can your spouse.

◆ You have the right to remain silent—and if you're ever in the position, you probably should use it.

◆ Grand jury testimony is secret, and the rules are different from a regular trial.

◆ If the government does something that affects the value of your property, you may have a case for compensation.

Chapter 8

The Sixth and Seventh Amendments: Fair Trials

In This Chapter

- A public and speedy trial
- An impartial jury
- Witnesses for and against
- The right to counsel
- Juries in civil trials

The Sixth Amendment guarantees criminal defendants the right to a fair trial. It ensures that defendants are brought to trial soon after they are charged, that their trials are held in public, that they have a fair and impartial jury, that they can confront the witnesses against them, and that they can compel potentially helpful witnesses to appear and testify. The Seventh Amendment extends many of the same rights to litigants in civil cases.

The Sixth Amendment: Juries in Criminal Trials

"In all criminal prosecutions, the accused shall enjoy the right to a speedy and public trial, by an impartial jury of the State and district wherein the crime shall have been committed, which district shall have been previously ascertained, to be confronted with the witnesses against him, to have compulsory process for obtaining witnesses in his favor, and to have the assistance of counsel for his defense."

The Sixth Amendment's provisions for fair trials in criminal cases are part of the bedrock of individual rights. Its provisions aim to protect individuals, but they also strengthen society. The concept of the speedy trial goes back to the Magna Carta, the concept of an impartial jury goes back even farther, and the concept of a public trial goes back to the Bible. Fair trials prevent governments from persecuting individuals or classes of people, but also assure everybody that they won't be persecuted. Fair trials give people confidence in their judicial system and their government.

The Speedy Trial Clause

It's not fair for the government to charge you with a crime and then not give you a chance to clear your name as soon as possible. The longer an accusation hangs over your head, the more it hurts you, the more people believe you did it, and the more it hurts your ability to defend yourself.

By the same token, there are also reasons that the government wants speedy trials. Defendants who really are crooks can commit more crimes instead of being locked away where they cannot hurt anyone else. Long delays increase the chances they will jump bail. And if they might be reformed or rehabilitated, long delays may keep them from getting treatment that might help. In the big picture, citizens are never happy with a government that locks up people without giving them a chance to tell their side of the story.

In the United States, the speedy trial became an issue as caseloads grew with the rise in crime in the 1960s. As dockets became more clogged, lawyers began filing and winning appeals on behalf of defendants who had to wait too long to go to trial. Few hard-and-fast rules have emerged amid the ensuing court decisions and legislation, however, so even today it is often difficult to say exactly how long is too long.

In general, the clock starts running at the time of arrest. But the Supreme Court has ruled that there are no specific time limits, and how long is too long depends on a number of factors. As usual, there is a balancing act: the defendant's constitutional right to a fair trial versus factors such as the reason for delay, the length of the delay, whether the defendant pushed for a speedy trial, and whether delays affected the outcome of the trial.

On one hand, the mere fact of a delay does not necessarily overcome the public's interest in seeing justice done. On the other hand, a defendant whose trial has been delayed doesn't necessarily need to show any harm from the delay. But one thing is pretty clear: when the courts do find that a defendant has been denied the right to a speedy trial, the charges are dropped or the conviction is overturned.

No matter what deadlines apply, many exceptions waive those deadlines without objection from defendants. Indeed, the defendants typically are responsible for many of the delays, largely through filing motions that let them find and gather witnesses and do research that will help their defense. In practical terms, defendants often don't want a speedy trial because it can close the window of opportunity for a plea bargain; the longer the delay, the longer the attorneys have a chance to work out a deal.

What It Means to You

The federal Speedy Trial Act of 1974 sets forth a timetable. There must be an indictment within 30 days of arrest, an arraignment within 10 days of indictment, and a trial within 60 days of arraignment. Many states have comparable rules, but the state deadlines are usually less stringent, providing more time for grinding the various legal gears.

In addition, judges and lawyers routinely accommodate each other's schedules, including for personal reasons. For example, if a prosecuting attorney asks to put off a trial for a week because of a long-scheduled family vacation, the judge will ordinarily agree and the defense attorney ordinarily will not object.

The Public Trial Clause

Our form of democracy is deeply rooted in the concept that government should be conducted in the open—including public trials. Historically, public trials have been seen as a safeguard against a government using secret trials to persecute individuals or groups of people. The Spanish Inquisition and England's Star Chamber are notorious examples of judicial proceedings that were conducted out of the public view. The original 13 states either had their own legal guarantees for public trials by the time the Sixth Amendment was ratified in 1791, or enacted them soon after.

A trial that is open to the public is more likely to be fair. It discourages perjury, makes judges or lawyers less likely to bend the rules or do anything inappropriate, and reduces the chances that decisions will be made arbitrarily or as a result of prejudice. The public trial is also a First Amendment issue; the press should be able to attend and report on government proceedings, particularly if those proceedings might take away someone's liberty or property.

The right to a public trial in criminal cases is not absolute, but because it is such an ingrained concept in our system, the Supreme Court has not been asked to consider many cases on public trials. The courts have ruled that the Sixth Amendment does not extend to the right to televise a trial, though individual jurisdictions can set their own rules for when and whether trials may be broadcast. Juveniles are not guaranteed the right to a public trial, and neither are defendants in the military justice system.

Despite the presumption that all trials should be public, judges can close court proceedings for a number of reasons, including when witnesses or jurors might be afraid to be identified—as in cases involving organized crime or terrorism—or in cases involving victims of sex crimes or juveniles who might be unduly harmed if their identities became public. Judges can decide on a case-by-case basis and consider intimidation, trauma, embarrassment, common decency, and other factors. Those same factors can lead a judge not to close a trial but to impose a gag order that keeps the participants—and sometimes the media—from identifying victims, defendants, or witnesses.

Sometimes a judge may close part of a court proceeding, but not the whole thing. In the 1984 case *Waller v. Georgia*, police used legal wiretaps to gather evidence on illegal gambling. The defendants filed a motion to suppress the wiretap evidence. Since a number of people not on trial were mentioned on the wiretaps, including suspects who might have been tipped off about the possible evidence against them, the court barred the public from the suppression hearing.

On appeal, the Supreme Court noted that the suppression hearings were closed for seven days, but the evidence from the wiretaps against other people took up only two hours. In a unanimous decision, the high court said that the Sixth Amendment right to a public trial is "no less pressing in a hearing to suppress wrongfully seized evidence." The justices agreed that there could be instances when trials and hearings can be closed to the public, but only in specific cases when there is no alternative.

Either the prosecution or the defense can ask a judge to close a trial or hearing. In either case, the judge must consider whether the defendant's right to a fair trial would be endangered in open court, and whether there are any reasonable alternatives to closing the courtroom to the public. If a judge does decide to close a trial, the press can object—and so can the public—on First Amendment grounds.

The Impartial Jury Clause

This clause shores up the Constitution's Article III guarantees for jury trials, and can be traced back to the Magna Carta, when the noblemen wanted to make sure that, if King John's government charged them with crimes, they would be tried before a jury of their peers—other noblemen, presumably, who might be sympathetic.

The framers of the Constitution viewed the impartial jury as a way to protect citizens against overly aggressive prosecutors or incompetent judges. The participation of ordinary citizens brought checks and balances to the everyday working of the judicial system and kept prosecutors and judges from having too much authority.

Historically in English common law, jurors were chosen for their wisdom and good judgment, and often because they knew a lot about the case at hand. Who better to understand what the case was about and render a fair decision than someone who knew the defendant, the prosecutor, and the particulars of the alleged crime?

In contrast, today's juries often seem to be selected for their lack of knowledge about the case. The less they know, in theory, the more able they are to make an impartial judgment. Ironically, some lawyers who want jurors who know nothing about a case then complain after they lose that the jurors were too dim to understand their erudite arguments.

In terms of what a jury is supposed to do under the Sixth Amendment, it's important to note that the jury is not expected to know anything about the law. In a jury trial, the judge administers the law and the jury determines the facts. That's why a jury, for example, is not asked to determine whether a confession is admissible and why, if a confession is ruled inadmissible, a jury is not even told about it.

A jury's decisions about the facts of a case—who, what, when, where, why, and how—are not carved in stone, but almost. When a conviction is appealed, the appeals court typically looks only at whether the law was carried about properly and fairly. Appeals courts do not ordinarily consider whether the jury decided the facts properly. Let's say you are accused of stealing your neighbor's garden gnome. You claim it's a case of mistaken identity—another neighbor, not you, stole the garden gnome—but the jury finds you guilty. You appeal your conviction. The appeals court cannot even consider whether it really was a case of mistaken identity, but the court can overturn the conviction if authorities did not follow proper procedures for the lineup that identified you as the gnome-napper.

What It Means to You

If you have been a victim of a similar crime, and you tell the judge and lawyers during the jury selection process that it would keep you from considering the case fairly, there is almost no chance you will end up on the jury. But don't make up anything or exaggerate: you're under oath, and lying is perjury.

To meet the Sixth Amendment's requirements for a fair trial and an impartial jury, the courts have developed a system of jury selection. Just as the noblemen who pushed the Magna Carta on King John wanted to have a jury that might give them a break, today's *voir dire* process, from the French "to see, to speak," allows the prosecution, the defense lawyers, and the judge to question prospective jurors and exclude them if there is a chance they might be biased.

Prospective jurors can be dismissed "for cause" for knowing too much about the case, for knowing people involved, or for having opinions or experiences that might color their judgment. The opposing attorneys also may have a set number of "peremptory" challenges that allow them to reject jurors for any reason or no reason. It is okay for a juror to have opinions, as long as the judge believes the juror can still consider the case fairly. Typically, prospective jurors are required to show that they can ...

- Put aside whatever they have read or heard about the case.
- Listen to evidence with an open mind.
- Deliver an impartial verdict.

Naturally, opposing lawyers try to gauge which prospective jurors will be more sympathetic to their case. Lawyers may ask jurors about personal prejudice in a civil rights case, or how they feel about the death penalty in a capital case. In a 1968 case, *Witherspoon v. Illinois*, the Supreme Court held that a defendant's right to an impartial jury was violated during the jury selection process when prospective jurors were rejected if they said they were against the death penalty. The high court said a jury cannot be "organized to return a verdict of death," and said that the jurors who oppose the death penalty also should have been asked if they could nonetheless follow the law and impose the death penalty if it was applicable in that particular case.

The Sixth Amendment does not specify that a jury must have 12 members. Indeed, the Supreme Court has said in a number of cases over the years that having 12-member juries appears to be an "accident of history" dating back to feudal times. Rather than any specific number, a jury is supposed to be large enough to ...

◆ Foster group deliberations.

◆ Resist outside intimidation.

◆ Represent the community at large.

In a 1970 case, *Williams v. Florida,* the Supreme Court said a jury does not have to be 12 members. Justice Byron White wrote, "In short, neither currently available evidence nor theory suggests that the 12-man jury is necessarily more advantageous to the defendant than a jury composed of fewer members." The courts have held that six-member juries do not necessarily violate the Sixth Amendment, but have shown a preference for larger juries in more serious cases.

Jury decisions need not be unanimous, but the courts have frowned on anything less than unanimous decisions for six-member juries. In general, the more serious the charge, the more the courts prefer larger juries and more unanimity. The Supreme Court has overturned a conviction on a 5–1 verdict that carried a prison term, and upheld another conviction on a 9–3 verdict.

Cases

Taylor v. Louisiana (1975): A defendant convicted of kidnapping said he did not get a fair trial because Louisiana required women to register to serve on juries. If they didn't sign up, they weren't called. The Supreme Court reversed the conviction, noting, "It can no longer be held that women as a class may be excluded from jury service or given automatic exemptions based solely on sex ...."

A jury is supposed to be a reasonable cross-section of the community, and has been found to be impartial if it excludes any specific group or class of people within the community. But it is not easy for a defendant to get a conviction overturned by claiming that a jury was impartial because of bias in the selection process. The defendant must prove that a distinctive group in the community was excluded, that the exclusion was not fair and reasonable, and that the exclusion was systematic.

Pretrial publicity can also prejudice a jury. Trials ordinarily are to be held in the district where the alleged crime was committed, but if the courts find that publicity tainted the jury pool so that it is impossible to empanel an impartial jury in a specific area, the trial can be moved—a change of venue—to an area where prospective jurors are less likely to have heard or read about the case and formed an opinion.

A jury can also be biased by what happens once the trial starts—by the actions of the judge, lawyers, defendant, witnesses, or even other jurors. When that happens, jurors can be instructed to ignore whatever they saw or heard that might keep them from deliberating fairly. If whatever they saw or heard is nonetheless likely to influence their deliberations, the judge will declare a mistrial.

Cases

Sheppard v. Maxwell (1966): The Supreme Court reversed the conviction of Sam Sheppard, a Cleveland physician accused of murdering his wife, Marilyn. The court cited pretrial publicity, including news stories calling Sheppard a liar, for depriving him of his Sixth Amendment right to a fair trial. The case inspired the television series *The Fugitive* and later the movie of the same name.

In December 2006, the U.S. Supreme Court ruled that a federal appeals court erred in granting a new trial to an accused murderer after the victim's relatives came to court every day wearing badges with a photo of the dead man. The appeals court said the badges prejudiced the jury, and ordered a new trial. The Supreme Court disagreed and reinstated the conviction, but on technical grounds rather than specifically because of the badges. The unanimous opinion by Justice Clarence Thomas said the question of whether the badges were prejudicial remains "an open question in our jurisprudence," to be decided in the future.

In general, a defendant has the right to a jury trial for any offense that carries a potential penalty of more than six months in jail. That does not apply, however, if a defendant is charged with a series of offenses with penalties that would extend to more than six months if convicted on all counts; there must be at least one charge that carries a potential sentence of six months or more.

Like other principal aspects of the Sixth Amendment, the impartial jury clause applies to states through the Fourteenth Amendment. The Supreme Court extended this protection in 1968 in *Duncan v. Louisiana*, a case that began two years earlier when a young black man named Duncan was driving down a Louisiana highway and noticed two of his cousins with a group of young white men alongside the road. Fearful that his cousins were being harassed because they had recently complained about racial bias in local schools, the young man pulled his car over and asked his cousins to get into his car and leave with him.

The white youths said Duncan slapped one of them. Duncan and his cousins denied it, but Duncan was arrested and charged with battery—a misdemeanor in Louisiana, but punishable by up to two years in prison. Duncan was convicted by a judge and sentenced to 60 days in jail, but appealed on the grounds that he was denied right to a jury trial. The Supreme Court agreed, overturning the conviction on the grounds that the Sixth Amendment applies to state law, too.

There is no constitutional right to a trial before a judge only—a bench trial, it's called—but courts routinely allow defendants to waive the right to a jury trial. The rule of thumb is that you ask for a bench trial only if you think a judge might be more sympathetic to your case than a jury of your peers—for example, if your case is particularly complex or if you are particularly unpopular in the community.

The Confrontation Clause

The Sixth Amendment guarantees defendants in criminal proceedings the right to confront the witnesses against them, to look them in the eye and ask them questions. The Confrontation Clause is aimed to prevent defendants from being convicted on the basis of *ex parte* statements, affidavits, or depositions that were made outside court. The history of this principle supposedly dates back to Sir Walter Raleigh, the Elizabethan-era adventurer who supposedly took off his cloak and threw it in the mud so that Good Queen Bess would not soil the royal shoes. Once the queen died and Sir Walter no longer had her protection, his legal troubles began. His enemies and rivals made statements about him, including allegations of conspiracy. Those statements were taken into evidence at Sir Walter's trial, even though the accusers were not required to appear and testify in person. He spent years in the Tower of London, and finally was beheaded in 1618.

As part of the Confrontation Clause, defendants are entitled—but not required—to attend their own trials. However, defendants can be removed from the courtroom or restrained for disrupting court proceedings. For example, Bobby Seale's outbursts led him to be shackled and gagged at the trial of the Chicago Eight (which became the Chicago Seven when Seale's trial was separated). More recently, Saddam Hussein was removed from portions of his trials in Baghdad.

> **People**
>
> One of America's best-known legal scholars, Professor John Henry Wigmore, called the right to cross-examine "the greatest legal engine ever invented for the discovery of truth."

The Confrontation Clause gives defendants the right to cross-examine witnesses—to test their credibility in front of the judge and jury, to hear what they have to say and how they say it, to view their demeanor, and to consider their body language. That makes sense in our judicial system, an adversarial process that pits the prosecution and defense against each other in a competition.

Other criminal justice systems, such as those in France and Spain and Italy, rely less on competition—which side has the better legal team—and more on a prosecutor who is, in theory at least, less interested in winning convictions than in seeking truth and fairness. Our system, with its emphasis on individual rights, prefers the adversarial contest to putting more trust in the government to do what is right.

As a result, lawyers in our system try to get jurors to disbelieve or distrust or at least dislike prosecution witnesses. They use strategies to bother opposing witnesses: they move around the courtroom, they change the pace or tone of questioning, they look for contradictions and inconsistencies, they try to get witnesses to misspeak or get flustered. Sometimes they attack the character of witnesses; even if a witness isn't lying, a lawyer may make points with a jury by pointing out that the witnesses might have reason to lie. The O. J. Simpson trial, remember, turned out to hinge on the prosecution witnesses. The jury didn't like the witnesses, and Simpson was acquitted. If you're a law student or lawyer who wants to see a masterful cross-examination, look up David Boies's cross-examination of Bill Gates and other Microsoft executives in their antitrust trial.

This part of the Sixth Amendment is where hearsay is a factor. Unlike the accusations against Sir Walter Raleigh, statements made outside of court proceedings today are usually inadmissible. You're allowed the right to confront the witnesses against you, but you cannot confront them if they are not in court. It is worth noting, however, that the hearsay rule is not universal.

Hearsay can be admissible in civil cases, and even in criminal cases there are exceptions. In a 1980 landmark case, *Ohio v. Roberts*, the Supreme Court set forth conditions for allowing hearsay. One, the prosecution must show that it has tried to produce the witness and show good reason why the witness will not appear. Two, if a witness cannot appear, the prosecution must show that the hearsay is reliable and trustworthy.

The "dying declaration" is a widely accepted exception to the hearsay rule, under the theory that people who think they are dying—they don't actually have to die—are probably going to tell the truth. In addition, forensic expert testimony is sometimes allowed in response to hypothetical questions. Some states allow dying declarations to be admitted as evidence in all or most trials, but in federal courts the dying declaration is admissible only in civil cases and homicide cases.

> **People** _____
>
> In American courts, the dying declaration goes back to 1770, at the murder trial of British soldiers accused of shooting down colonial citizens in the Boston Massacre. One of the victims, Patrick Carr, told authorities with his dying gasp that the crowd had provoked the soldiers. His testimony helped the defense attorney, John Adams, get charges reduced or dismissed against the soldiers.

There are also exceptions to the way cross-examinations can be conducted; they don't always have to be face to face in front of the judge and jury, especially if the witness would be traumatized by the presence of the defendant. The Supreme Court has ruled, for instance, that children testifying in sexual abuse cases do not necessarily have to face the defendants. The kids can testify behind a screen or via closed-circuit TV or videoconference. Even if there is no face-to-face confrontation with the defendant, however, the judge and jury still get to see the witness, and the defendant still has the right to cross-examine.

The Sixth Amendment has been at the heart of recent controversy over how the United States should prosecute suspected terrorists, and the Supreme Court gave mixed results to the George W. Bush administration. The Supreme Court refused to consider a case that challenged the administration policy of withholding names and other information about people taken into custody after the September 11, 2001, attacks on the World Trade Center and the Pentagon.

In the summer of 2006, however, the Supreme Court struck down the administration's plans for prosecuting suspected terrorists held at Guantanamo Bay. The 5–3 decision did not say that the military tribunals were necessarily unconstitutional, but said some of the aspects of the administration's plans for the tribunals were violations of the Sixth Amendment. The administration classified suspected terrorists as "enemy combatants" and planned to prosecute them in military tribunals—exempt from the Sixth Amendment's requirements for trial by jury. Plans for the tribunals included allowing hearsay evidence, and in some cases the defendants would not be able to cross-examine witnesses, have legal counsel, protest their incarceration in federal court, see the evidence against them, or even attend their own trials. Congress reacted quickly, and in the autumn of 2006 sent President Bush legislation aimed at legalizing the military tribunals.

That Supreme Court decision on the military tribunals could turn out to be a significant constitutional footnote regarding the separation of powers and the system of checks and balances. The Bush administration argued that the Supreme Court did not even have the power to consider whether the tribunals were legal. The administration also said that the sweeping anti-terrorism authority Congress granted the president after the 2001 attacks gave Bush—and subsequent presidents—broad powers that were beyond review by the courts. The Supreme Court disagreed, obviously.

The Compulsory Process Clause

The Sixth Amendment not only guarantees the right to cross-examine witnesses who testify against you, but also gives you the power to call witnesses who might testify in your favor—and to force them to appear in court even if they are reluctant.

This right also extends to state courts, thanks to the Supreme Court's 1967 decision in *Washington v. Texas.* In that case, a defendant charged with murder wanted to call a defense witness who had already been convicted of participating in the same murder. Texas authorities said no, citing a state law that prohibited people charged in connection with the same crime from testifying on each other's behalf. Without the testimony, the defendant was convicted but then appealed. The Supreme Court reversed the conviction, saying the defendant's Sixth Amendment right to call witnesses had been violated.

What It Means to You

You might not be involved and you might not want to get involved, but if you are served with a subpoena to testify, you have to appear and testify. You have a legal right to challenge the subpoena, but don't expect to get out of it. The best policy is to show up, take the oath, and then tell the truth.

The clerk of the court issues a subpoena, and then it's served on the witness by a law enforcement officer or process server. There's no charge to the defendant. Defendants can compel almost anyone to testify, as long as they can show that the testimony will be material to the case and favorable to their arguments. A judge will reject the request for a subpoena if it seems like the witnesses are being called merely to prolong the proceedings. If a judge decides that the testimony is redundant, the witness is out.

Witnesses can also be disallowed if the side calling them didn't give the other side notice that those witnesses would be called. Court rules do not ordinarily permit surprise witnesses or any sort of surprise evidence, and both the prosecution and the defense normally are required to show each other pretty much their entire case before the trial begins. This helps ensure a fair trial, but as a practical matter it also speeds up the judicial process by encouraging plea bargaining. If you know the other side has the smoking gun, you're probably going to want to make a deal for a lesser charge if you can.

Witnesses can also be disallowed if they are too important to testify. From George Washington to Richard Nixon to Bill Clinton to George W. Bush, American presidents have claimed that their jobs make them exempt from testifying, supplying evidence, or otherwise responding to subpoenas. Executive privilege, it's called.

People

The first president to claim executive privilege was George Washington, who rejected a House demand in 1796 that he turn over papers relating to the Jay Treaty with England. Washington ducked a constitutional confrontation by agreeing to turn the documents over to the Senate, the chamber that ratifies treaties.

During the Watergate investigations, John Dean and other aides to President Richard Nixon offered conflicting testimony before Congress. Someone was committing perjury. Another aide revealed that Nixon had been taping conversations in the Oval Office, so the Watergate special prosecutor subpoenaed the tapes. Nixon refused, citing executive privilege, and the case went to the Supreme Court in the summer of 1974. The high court ruled that executive privilege was a legitimate claim by the president even though it was not specifically mentioned in the Constitution. However, in a unanimous decision that cited several constitutional grounds, including the Sixth Amendment, the Supreme Court ordered Nixon to turn over the Oval Office tapes.

Here's an interesting historical question: What if Nixon had refused to comply with the Supreme Court's decision? What if he had burned the tapes in a bonfire on the South Lawn? What if he had called out the troops to surround the White House and prevent anyone from coming and getting the tapes or presenting him with articles of impeachment? Two weeks after the Supreme Court's decision, he turned over the tapes. Four days later he resigned rather than face impeachment and possible removal from office. But the hypothetical—what if he hadn't?—shows just how tenuous our democracy can be, and how it hinges on a society's willingness to follow the rule of law.

More recently, Dick Cheney claimed that executive privilege applies to vice president, too. In 2002, Congress's Government Accounting Office asked him for more information on his National Energy Policy Development Group as part of an inquiry into the oil industry's influence on government policies, but Dick Cheney's office refused on the grounds that executive privilege applies to vice presidents, too.

Assistance of Counsel

The Fifth Amendment's Miranda warning requires authorities to tell people who are being arrested that they have the right to an attorney, but the actual right to an attorney comes from the Sixth Amendment. You don't have to accept an attorney's help; you can represent yourself. But courts can deny a defendant the right to represent himself if it seems like the defendant will be incompetent or disruptive.

The landmark case, from the height of the Great Depression, is officially in the law books as *Powell v. Alabama*, but it is more widely known as the Scottsboro Boys case. In March 1931, when it was common for jobless young men to strike out from home and ride the rails, a group of black hoboes got into a fight aboard a freight train passing through Alabama. The black hoboes won the fight, and tossed most of the white guys off the train outside the town of Stevenson. The white hoboes told the stationmaster at Stevenson what had happened, and the stationmaster messaged ahead to Scottsboro. The sheriff organized a posse that stopped the train and pulled off the nine black guys on board. Two white women were on the train, and they told the authorities, apparently under prodding, that they had been gang-raped.

The men were taken to the Scottsboro jail, and the National Guard was called out to maintain order and prevent a lynching as word of the alleged rapes spread. The men were charged with rape, a crime that carried the death penalty, but none of them was allowed to have an attorney or even to contact relatives, all of whom lived in other states. They still did not have an attorney on the day of the trial, when the judge finally appointed two local lawyers to represent them, but the lawyers had no chance to prepare a case or even talk with the young men.

Doctors who examined the women testified there was no evidence of rape, but all nine men were convicted, and eight of the nine were sentenced to death. The state courts in Alabama rejected their appeals, and the case went to the U.S. Supreme Court.

The high court overturned the convictions and ordered new trials on the grounds of the Sixth Amendment. The court's 7–2 opinion held: "No attempt was made to investigate …. Defendants were immediately hurried to trial …. [A] defendant, charged with a serious crime, must not be stripped of his right to have sufficient time to advise with counsel and prepare his defense." The court ruled that the right to counsel was part of the "fundamental principles of liberty and justice which lie at the base of all our civil and political institutions." The Scottsboro decision was the first in a string of Supreme Court cases over the ensuing decades that guaranteed the right to counsel at no expense to the defendant, not only in capital cases but in all serious criminal cases.

The Seventh Amendment: Juries in Civil Trials

"In Suits at common law, where the value in controversy shall exceed twenty dollars, the right of trial by jury shall be preserved, and no fact tried by a jury shall be otherwise re-examined in any Court of the United States, other than according to the rules of the common law."

The framers considered extending Article III's guarantees of a jury trial to civil cases as well as criminal cases. But it didn't come up until late in the Constitutional Convention, after a long hot summer of hard work, and it may have been voted down simply because the men were all eager to go home. There was widespread support for the idea, however, including among the states. Congress approved the proposed Seventh Amendment without debate, and the right to a jury trial in civil cases became part of the Bill of Rights.

The Constitution does not extend the right to a jury trial in civil cases to the states, but as a practical matter the states have comparable rules with varying requirements for the nature of the lawsuit and the amount of money damages at stake. In general, the Seventh Amendment has been interpreted to hold that the right to a jury does not include an "equity" lawsuit—an action seeking not money damages but nonmonetary relief, such as an injunction or some other type of "performance" order in which a court tells someone they must or must not do something.

The Least You Need to Know

◆ You have the right to a jury trial in serious criminal cases.

◆ You have the right to a jury trial in many civil cases.

◆ You have the right to defend yourself in court.

◆ You have the right to cross-examine hostile witnesses.

◆ You have the right to subpoena witnesses at no expense to you.

Chapter 9

The Eighth Amendment: Bail and Punishment

In This Chapter

◆ The Eighth Amendment

◆ Excessive bail and fines

◆ Cruel and unusual punishment

"Excessive bail shall not be required, nor excessive fines imposed, nor cruel and unusual punishments inflicted."

The Eighth Amendment's vague language has led to confusing and conflicting court rulings over the years, especially with shifts in society's standards and the makeup of the Supreme Court. What does "excessive" mean? What does "cruel and unusual" mean? In particular, there's been a lot of uncertainty over the death penalty: most of us don't like it but many of us think it is necessary and all of us think it should be administered fairly. Society's attitudes have been reflected in the convoluted and sometimes contradictory Supreme Court rulings.

Excessive Bail and Fines

In Olde England, the same sheriff who arrested you had the right to decide whether you should be released on bail, and the king could have you arrested and confined without bail. The unfairness was obvious, and Parliament nicked away at the power to withhold bail until 1689, when the English Bill of Rights declared that if bail was granted, it could not be excessive.

Our Eighth Amendment says pretty much the same thing. There is no right to be granted bail and released pending trial, but if bail is granted, the amount cannot be unreasonable for meeting the purpose of granting bail. The primary purpose of granting bail is to make sure the defendant shows up in court to face the charges. You're less likely to skip town if it means you're going to take a serious financial hit.

In considering bail, judges are supposed to balance the amount of bail—or whether to grant bail—against the severity of the crime. In a 1987 case, *U.S. v. Salerno*, the Supreme Court held that denying bail and keeping a defendant in jail prior to trial is not necessarily a violation of the Eighth Amendment. However, the court said the government must prove that the defendant might be a danger to the community. Chief Justice William Rehnquist's opinion said the rule for bail is that "the government's proposed conditions of release or detention not be 'excessive' in light of the perceived evil."

In many cases, particularly for less serious crimes, or when a defendant has an otherwise relatively clean criminal record and strong ties to the community, pretrial release is granted "on recognizance," without any financial commitment. The defendant is released after promising to appear at the trial or the next scheduled hearing. When charges are serious, however, especially for any sort of homicide, or when the defendant is considered a "flight risk," the judge often requires bail in the form of a financial bond. A defense attorney ordinarily wants the sum to be as low as possible, of course, while the prosecutor may seek higher bail. Since the primary purpose of the bail is to guarantee appearance, the judge may set the bond much higher for a rich person, though the Supreme Court has held that judges do not necessarily need to consider a defendant's financial status.

What It Means to You

If bail is set at $100,000, the court may require only a percentage, often 10 percent, to be put down in cash. If the defendant does not show up, however, the entire amount is forfeited and a warrant is issued for the defendant as a fugitive. If you put up your assets to guarantee someone's bail, you could lose your house if he or she doesn't show up for trial.

When a crime is particularly serious and the defendant is a flight risk likely to skip town, the judge may deny bail altogether. Besides guaranteeing appearance, a prosecutor can also argue that the defendant should be kept in custody as a matter of preventive detention—to keep him or her from committing further crimes. This is a tricky area since our judicial system is based on the presumption of innocence, and on penalizing people not for what they might do but only for what they actually have done. Someone has to be a pretty bad actor for a judge to deny bail on the grounds that society is safer if he or she remains behind bars while awaiting trial. Sometimes, besides money, judges will set conditions for bail, such as requiring a defendant to stay away from victims or witnesses or the scene of the crime.

Cruel and Unusual Punishment

One person's idea of cruel might be another person's idea of tough love. It's the same dilemma whether raising kids or punishing society's wrongdoers. And while strict constructionists think the Constitution should be interpreted as closely as possible to the original intentions of the framers in 1787, the Eighth Amendment is an example of how the Constitution is flexible, bending to changes in society. After all, pretty much everyone agrees that society's views on punishment have changed. As the Supreme Court ruled in one case, the standard for cruel and unusual "must draw its meaning from the evolving standards of decency that mark the progress of a maturing society."

One literal interpretation has not changed much over the years, however. The "and" is important in the phrase "cruel and unusual punishment." The courts have ruled, to varying degrees, that punishment can be cruel. Punishment can also be unusual. But it's not supposed to be both.

Supreme Court rulings in the nineteenth century made it clear that some forms of punishment would always be unconstitutional as cruel and unusual, including drawing and quartering, beheading, burning alive, and disemboweling. Death by hanging and by firing squad were permissible, however, in part because those were the common ways that states executed criminals; even if it was cruel, it wasn't unusual.

One of the decisions that reflected changing views in society came in a 1962 case, *Robinson v. California.* A 90-day sentence for being a drug addict was determined to be cruel and unusual punishment by the Supreme Court because drug addiction "is apparently an illness," and authorities were trying to punish the defendant for an illness rather than for a specific criminal act. It's important to remember that sentences are supposed to meet the acceptable goals of punishment—retribution and deterrence—and that punishment is excessive if it does not fulfill those purposes, or if it's out of proportion to the severity of the crime.

Three Strikes and You're Out

The "three strikes and you're out" laws that many states have enacted in recent years have prompted a range of court rulings. The Supreme Court upheld a mandatory life sentence for a three-time loser even though his three nonviolent felonies netted him barely $200. In another case, however, the court overturned the conviction of a guy who wrote a $100 bad check. Under state recidivism laws, he received a mandatory life sentence without the chance for parole. The court said it was cruel and unusual he had no chance for parole, while the defendant in the previous case at least had a chance at parole after 12 years in prison. In a third case, the Supreme Court said that a life sentence without the possibility of parole for a repeat offender is not necessarily cruel and unusual, particularly since that offender had a long record of violent crime and the most recent conviction was for possession of more than 600 grams of cocaine.

In a 1983 case, *Solem v. Helm*, the Supreme Court for the first time said the length of a sentence in and of itself could be cruel and unusual if it was "disproportionate" to the severity of the crime. The court has waxed and waned on this "proportionality" test over the years, but often seems to come back to three factors:

- The gravity of the offense and the harshness of the penalty

- Sentences imposed on other criminals in the same jurisdiction

- Sentences imposed for the same crime in other jurisdictions

Lower courts, both state and federal, have held on numerous occasions that conditions in certain prisons or entire prison systems violate prisoners' protections against cruel and unusual punishment. The Supreme Court in general has endorsed the power of the courts to step in, but at the same time has indicated that courts need to proceed with caution when coming in conflict with the states or the federal executive branch over how prisons are run.

Cases

Trop v. Dulles (1958): In this case, the Supreme Court ruled that punishing a citizen by taking away citizenship is a cruel and unusual punishment. The high court called it worse than torture, "total destruction of the individual's status in organized society," and "a fate forbidden by the principle of civilized treatment guaranteed by the Eighth Amendment."

The Death Penalty

Capital punishment has always been part of the American criminal justice system, even as much of the rest of the world has moved away from the death penalty. The American Civil Liberties Union, long an opponent of the death penalty, says the vast majority of the court-imposed executions in the world today occur in four countries: China, Iran, Saudi Arabia, and the United States.

The Supreme Court has had many opportunities to declare the death penalty unconstitutional, and has overturned a number of convictions based on the way death sentences were handed down. But the court has never said that capital punishment itself is cruel and unusual.

"Whatever the arguments may be against capital punishment," the court held in a case in the 1950s, "the death penalty has been employed throughout our history and, in a day when it is still widely accepted, it cannot be said to violate the constitutional concept of cruelty."

Concern about the death penalty led many states to suspend executions in the 1960s, and there was a period, from 1967 to 1976, when there were no court-ordered executions in the United States. In a 1972 landmark case, *Furman v. Georgia*, a narrowly divided court effectively struck down every existing state death penalty. The 5–4 majority was divided over whether the death penalty was always unconstitutional as cruel and unusual, and whether it could be legal if the states could come up with capital punishment procedures that were not random and capricious and did not discriminate against blacks and poor people.

In the Furman decision, the Supreme Court laid down restrictions on punishment, declaring that any form of punishment is unconstitutional if it is ...

◆ Degrading to human dignity—as in torture.

◆ A severe punishment obviously inflicted in a wholly arbitrary fashion.

◆ A severe punishment that is clearly and totally rejected throughout society.

◆ A severe punishment that is patently unnecessary.

> **People**
>
> In the Furman case, Justice Potter Stewart criticized the random application of capital punishment in America this way: "These death sentences are cruel and unusual in the same way that being struck by lightning is cruel and unusual."

The criticisms and guidelines laid down by the high court in the Furman decision gave the states a road map for rewriting their capital punishment laws. Starting with Florida, in the following months 35 states passed new death penalty laws that aimed to remove the arbitrary and irrational aspects of their old laws.

One of the key aspects was the two-part trial: first a jury would decide whether the defendant was guilty of the crime, and then it would decide whether the defendant should be sentenced to death. Relying on suggestions from court decisions, the new procedure made sure that judges and juries considered a defendant individually and personally, and weighed any mitigating factors. Since death is a unique punishment, the court ruled, the death penalty needs to be considered on a case-by-case basis, with consideration of each defendant's individual circumstances and the particular details of each case.

Before any more executions took place, the Supreme Court reconsidered a series of cases based on new death penalty laws passed by several states. The justices have remained mindful that the reasons for any penalty, including a death sentence, are retribution and deterrence, and that it may be preferable for state legislatures to lay out the particulars. As a result, the Supreme Court issued a series of opinions in 1976, including *Gregg v. Georgia*, that opened the door for executions to resume. Today each state's death penalty process includes …

◆ Standards for the sentencing authority, whether judge or jury, to evaluate both the circumstances of the offense and the character of the accused.

◆ A two-part trial for considering first guilt and second the sentence.

◆ Automatic appeal of both the conviction and the sentence to the state supreme court.

Subsequent Supreme Court decisions have narrowed the range of crimes that carry the death penalty, and expanded the range of reasons for sentencing defendants to life in prison instead of execution. For example, rape was a capital crime in many states, but a 1977 Supreme Court case, *Coker v. Georgia*, said that the death sentence was cruel and unusual punishment for the rape of an adult female. The court seemed to be saying that the death

> **Cases**
>
> The ACLU says that 455 men were executed for rape in the United States between 1930 and 1967, and 405 of them—almost 90 percent— were black.

penalty may be imposed only for the intentional killing of another person, but in recent years there have been proposals in some states to execute repeat child molesters. The courts have also become more attuned to racial bias in the way the death penalty has been applied, and to the quality of legal representation.

Three cases before the Supreme Court in 2002 looked at the quality of representation provided to defendants who were charged with capital crimes but could not afford their own attorneys. In two cases, the high court rejected appeals from death row, once holding that a defendant's rights were not violated when his lawyer skipped the closing argument to the jury, and another time when a defendant was assigned a lawyer who had represented the victim in an earlier case. However, the Supreme Court did overturn the Texas murder conviction of a gay man whose court-appointed lawyer slept through parts of the trial. The prosecution, which had argued in favor of the death penalty on the grounds that prison was not such a severe punishment for a gay man, futilely claimed that the defense lawyer snoozed only in unimportant parts of the trial.

Other recent Supreme Court cases have determined that the states cannot impose an automatic death penalty for certain crimes, such as the murder of a police officer or for prison inmates who are already serving life sentences without the chance of parole. The Supreme Court has also made it more difficult for states to impose the death penalty on defendants accused of felony murder—for example, when they participate in a crime in which someone is killed, but they don't actually pull the trigger themselves.

Other rulings have said the insane and the mentally retarded can no longer be executed, and a 2005 case, *Roper v. Simmons*, prohibits states from executing defendants whose crimes were committed before turning 18 years old. For a time it appeared that the Supreme Court was moving away from "victim impact statements," but recent decisions have opened the door for judges and juries to consider the character of victims as well as defendants.

As this book went to press during the Supreme Court's 2006–2007 session, the high court had not yet ruled on whether execution by lethal injection is cruel and unusual punishment. During the previous session, the court accepted a case, *Hill v. McDonough*, that sought to challenge Florida's process of execution by lethal injection, but did not rule directly on the issue. The high court agreed in the spring of 2006 that the death row defendant, Clarence Hill, had a proper civil rights claim to challenge lethal injection. However, the court ruled that Hill should have made the challenge as part of an earlier appeal against his death sentence. Since that earlier appeal had been rejected, the court said, it was too late to bring the new appeal. Hill's execution was rescheduled, and he asked for a stay to pursue the appeal against lethal injection. The Supreme Court denied a stay of execution by a 5–4 vote and Hill was put to death by lethal injection on September 20, 2006.

The Least You Need to Know

- If you are arrested and brought before a judge, you have the right to be released on bail.

- Sentences are supposed to match the crime.

- The Supreme Court has never ruled that the death penalty is cruel and unusual punishment.

- The Supreme Court has, however, been concerned about making sure the death penalty is carried out as fairly as possible.

- The Supreme Court has yet to rule on whether execution by lethal injection is cruel and unusual.

10

The Ninth Through Twelfth Amendments: The Political System

In This Chapter

◆ The Ninth Amendment: unenumerated rights

◆ The Tenth Amendment: states' rights

◆ The Eleventh Amendment: suing states

◆ The Twelfth Amendment: picking the president

The last two amendments of the Bill of Rights—the Ninth and Tenth—were aimed at providing flexibility in the Constitution. The framers did not want future American leaders, legislators, or judges to say, "You don't have the right to do that because it isn't mentioned in the Constitution."

Instead, the Ninth Amendment said that just because a particular right is not mentioned does not mean that it doesn't apply, or that the government can abridge that right. The Tenth Amendment said that any authority not granted to the federal government in the Constitution is reserved to the people or the states. The Eleventh Amendment protects states' sovereignty by prohibiting them from being sued in federal court. The Twelfth Amendment separated the campaigns for president and vice president, while keeping the same qualifications for both offices.

The Ninth Amendment: Unenumerated Rights

"The enumeration in the Constitution, of certain rights, shall not be constructed to deny or disparage others retained by the people."

Other parts of the Constitution, and especially the Bill of Rights, specify or "enumerate" particular rights, such as free speech and fair trial. But the framers of the Constitution did not think they had all the answers. In effect, this amendment says, "In case someone raises a right we didn't list, it can still be valid. The government cannot take away a right from the people just because we didn't mention it."

The seeds of the amendment were planted in the Constitutional Convention, when anti-federalists argued for a Bill of Rights to limit national government. The federalists did not want a written Bill of Rights included in the Constitution, and for the same reason: to limit the power of the central government. They were afraid that if the Constitution included a written list of individual rights that the government cannot abridge, then anything not on the list might be considered fair game for government limits or controls.

James Madison, leading the Federalist movement, put it this way: "It has been objected also against a bill of rights, that, by enumerating particular exceptions to the grant of power, it would disparage those rights which were not placed in the enumeration; and it might follow by implication, that those rights which were not singled out, were intended to be assigned into the hands of the General Government, and were consequently insecure."

The anti-federalists got their promise of a Bill of Rights, of course, in part as a compromise to gather support for the Constitution from the states during the ratification process. As part of the compromise, the Ninth Amendment was created. Imagine that individuals have a big basket of rights. The Bill of Rights plucked out a few of those rights—free speech, fair trial, and so on—and held them up: these are shiny examples of the kinds of inherent, inalienable, individual rights that the new government cannot limit.

The Ninth Amendment says there are other rights in the basket, too, beyond the ones plucked out for the Bill of Rights. They are just as inalienable, and just as valid, even if they are not specifically mentioned anywhere in the Constitution, including the Bill of Rights.

The Ninth Amendment was an afterthought in the development of constitutional law for most of the United States' first two centuries, but it has had some flurries of controversy in recent years. Today some say it is meaningless, while others say it is crucial to democracy. Some say it grants many rights; others say it is merely a guide for how to read the Constitution. Some say it defends fundamental rights; others say it allows activist judges to reach any decision they want for social, political, or even personal reasons.

Much of the controversy centers around the right to privacy. The right to privacy is not specifically mentioned anywhere in the Constitution, but few people would say there is no such thing. We all have the right to be left alone, especially from government interference in our personal lives. Court rulings have found the parts of the First, Third, Fourth, and Fifth Amendments—the right to speak our minds, for example, and the right not to give evidence against ourselves—pertain to the right of privacy.

The Ninth Amendment stepped to the forefront in a 1965 case, *Griswold v. Connecticut*, after the director of Planned Parenthood in Connecticut teamed up with a Yale medical professor to open a birth control clinic in New Haven. They were arrested, tried, and fined $100 under Connecticut's 1879 law banning contraceptives. They appealed, the state courts rejected their appeal, and they took their case to the Supreme Court.

The Supreme Court overturned the convictions and declared the law unconstitutional, along with similar anti-contraceptive laws in other states, on the grounds that it violated the marital right to privacy.

The majority opinion cited "zones of privacy" guaranteed by the Constitution, including the Ninth Amendment, while a concurring opinion by Justice Arthur Goldberg flatly said that since privacy was not covered elsewhere in the Constitution, it was an individual right protected by the Ninth Amendment.

People

Justice Goldberg's often-quoted concurring opinion in *Griswold v. Connecticut* said in part: "To hold that a right so basic and fundamental and so deep-rooted in our society as the right of privacy in marriage may be infringed because that right is not guaranteed in so many words by the first eight amendments to the Constitution is to ignore the Ninth Amendment and to give it no effect whatsoever."

Most of the subsequent Supreme Court decisions on privacy have confirmed that there is a right to privacy, but have shied away from finding it in the Ninth Amendment. In a 1972 case, *Eisenstadt v. Baird*, the Supreme Court ruled that unmarried couples could legally use contraceptives, too. In *Roe v. Wade*, the case that set the parameters for legal abortions in 1973, the Supreme Court rejected a lower court's reasoning that said reproductive rights were part of the privacy protections of the Ninth Amendment. Instead, the Supreme Court said a woman's right to abortion is protected by due process.

Here's the specific court language on privacy from the majority opinion in the *Roe* case: "This right of privacy, whether it be founded in the Fourteenth Amendment's concept of personal liberty and restrictions upon state action, as we feel it is, or, as the district court determined, in the Ninth Amendment's reservation of rights to the people, is broad enough to encompass a women's decision whether or not to terminate her pregnancy."

Another case that looked at privacy, *Planned Parenthood v. Casey* in 1992, narrowly upheld *Roe v. Wade* but allowed Pennsylvania to impose restrictions, such as a 24-hour waiting period and parental consent for minors. Again, that case found the right to privacy in the Fourteenth Amendment rather than the Ninth.

Other significant privacy cases in recent years include *Lawrence v. Texas*. Police, acting on a call from a neighbor who reported a man with a gun, entered a home, found two men having anal sex, and arrested them for violating Texas's anti-sodomy law. After being fined $200 each, they appealed. The Supreme Court overturned their conviction in 2003 and tossed out the Texas law along with the remaining handful of anti-sodomy laws in other states. Incidentally, the neighbor who had called the cops with the fake weapons report was arrested and spent 15 days in jail.

> **People**
>
> Arguing to uphold the Texas anti-sodomy law, Justice Antonin Scalia dissented: "Let me be clear that I have nothing against homosexuals, or any other group, promoting their agenda through normal democratic means. Social perceptions of sexual and other morality change over time, and every group has the right to persuade its fellow citizens that its view of such matters is the best ...."

The privacy cases brought it onto the constitutional stage briefly, but the Ninth Amendment now seems to be back in the wings again, not playing a major part. Some constitutional scholars believe the Ninth Amendment may become a factor in the development of American law in the future, but perhaps only if and when the courts stop thinking about it in terms of preserving individual liberty instead of particular individual rights.

The Tenth Amendment: States' Rights

"The powers not delegated to the United States by the Constitution, nor prohibited by it to the States, are reserved for the States respectively, or to the people."

Just as the Ninth Amendment sought to preserve individual rights, the Tenth Amendment preserves state rights not specifically mentioned in the Constitution. Consequently, some describe this amendment as the essence of federalism: the national government has certain powers listed in the Constitution, and that's it; everything else can and should be up to the states.

The Tenth Amendment, growing out of the original states' unease about having another out-of-touch, faraway government replace British rule, was requested by the states to protect their own self-identity and self-rule at a time when it was much more meaningful to say you were a Virginian or a New Yorker than it was to say you were an American. It is often called the "states' rights" amendment and is cited by those who believe that the federal government's primary—and perhaps only—role is to defend the shores and deliver the mail.

> **People**
>
> Thomas Jefferson summed up the spirit of the Tenth Amendment this way: "The States should be left to do whatever they can do as well as the federal government."

The Tenth Amendment was viewed as being very important when the nation was new, and was seen as a brake on growing federal power—particularly taxing power and police power—but has become less significant over time. Tension between the Tenth Amendment and the Constitution's Commerce Clause generally has evolved in favor of the Commerce Clause, giving the government broad authority to oversee and regulate all manner of activity among citizens, whether across state lines or not.

In the first half of the twentieth century, there was still enough life left in the Tenth Amendment for the Supreme Court to strike down a range of congressional controls on the states, including the imposition of taxes on products from factories that relied on child labor, coal, poultry, grain futures, and other agricultural products. Other court rulings, however, upheld the federal government's authority to regulate interstate transportation of lottery tickets and transporting women across state lines for immoral purposes.

The Tenth Amendment was the rationale for a 1918 Supreme Court decision that gave the states "nullification" authority over congressional legislation that violated state authority. But that decision was overturned in a 1941 case, *United States v. Darby*, that all but dumped the Tenth Amendment into the constitutional wastebasket:

"The amendment states but a truism that all is retained which has not been surrendered. There is nothing in the history of its adoption to suggest that it was more than declaratory of the relationship between the national and state governments as it had been established by the Constitution before the amendment or that its purpose was other than to allay fears that the new national government might seek to exercise powers not granted, and that the states might not be able to exercise fully their reserved powers."

The Darby decision also made it clear that the Commerce Clause, giving the federal government broad authority over anything it defines as commerce, is the one that matters in modern law: "The power of Congress over interstate commerce is complete in itself, may be exercised to the utmost extent, and acknowledges no limitations other than are prescribed by the Constitution."

The concept of "states' rights" also fell into disfavor during the second half of the twentieth century when it became a rallying cry among foes of the civil rights movement in Southern states, who argued that the individual states should be allowed to require that African Americans, among other things, sit in the back of the bus.

The concept of states' rights had a brief revival in a 1976 case before the Supreme Court, *National League of Cities v. Usery*. The court ruled against the federal government's attempts to set requirements for working hours and wages for certain local and state employees, but did not specifically mention the Tenth Amendment. In any event, the ruling was overturned in a 1985 case, *Garcia v. San Antonio Metropolitan Transit Authority*, which said states retain their sovereignty only to the extent they have not given up their powers and transferred them to the federal government via the Constitution. Some interpret this ruling as saying that merely by being part of the United States, the individual states have ceded their authority to the federal government.

One line of reasoning in that case said that any states' rights challenge should be a political rather than a judicial issue. The rationale: the Tenth Amendment prohibits Congress from passing laws that are a burden on the states, but the people have given Congress the authority to make laws, so if a law is burdensome it is up to the people to elect members of Congress who will change it.

In a 1992 case, *New York v. United States*, the Supreme Court threw out federal regulations that required the states to clean up low-level radioactive waste that failed to meet federal standards. The court said the U.S. government cannot force a state to administer federal regulations. Similarly, another Supreme Court opinion in 1997, *Printz v. United States*, threw out the Brady Handgun Violence Prevention Act's requirements that state and local officials conduct background searches on people who are buying handguns.

In general, however, the federal government has become more and more dominant in our everyday lives, and the differences between being a Virginian and a New Yorker are not as meaningful as the similarities in being American. States are in theory still free to buck federal laws, but there is often a high price. For example, Congress in effect mandated lower speed limits for the entire nation and a national minimum drinking age of 21 by threatening to withhold highway funds for any state that did not fall in line.

The Tenth Amendment isn't what it used to be, but it still could be a factor in future decisions balancing state and federal powers, particularly in terms of anti-terrorist programs. For example: can the federal government require the states to enforce new federal immigration procedures?

The Eleventh Amendment: Suing States

"The Judicial power of the United States shall not be construed to extend to any suit in law or equity, commenced or prosecuted against one of the United States by Citizens of another State, or by Citizens or Subjects of any Foreign State."

This amendment, like the Tenth, reflected the independence and autonomy that the original states enjoyed and wanted to preserve in the new union. In effect, it was aimed at giving them a measure of sovereign immunity, a phrase that dates back to the English principle that the king had to agree to any lawsuit filed against him. If he didn't agree, there could not be a lawsuit. The Eleventh Amendment was aimed at providing a similar insulation from lawsuits for the individual states.

The amendment was proposed, approved by Congress, and ratified by the states in quick sequence as a result of a 1793 Supreme Court case.

In that case, *Chisholm v. Georgia,* two residents of South Carolina said they were owed money by the State of Georgia under a contract for supplies during the Revolutionary War. Georgia said it could not be sued by residents of another state, but the Supreme Court disagreed. Georgia's leaders were angry; the state legislature passed a law saying anyone who came to Georgia to collect the debt could be hanged. The leaders of other states were afraid that the same thing could happen to them: they could be sued by residents of other states, and the federal courts would end up deciding the cases. The Eleventh Amendment was passed to overcome the court decision and bar lawsuits against states by nonresidents. In an 1890 case, *Hans v. Louisiana,* the Supreme Court launched a series of decisions holding that not only are nonresident citizens barred from suing states, but resident citizens are barred from suing their own states in federal court.

The Eleventh Amendment is generally viewed as barring cases brought *in law,* seeking monetary damages, but case law has established that the federal courts can take cases against the states *in equity,* seeking nonmonetary relief or "performance" such as injunctions ordering someone to do something or not to do something. The courts have done some legal tap dancing in some opinions. For example, there is the line of reasoning that says suing a state official is not the same as suing the state, because if a state official is violating the law then he or she is not acting on behalf of the state.

def•i•ni•tion

The Eleventh Amendment bars suits against states "in law or equity." In legal language, a suit **in law** is one that seeks monetary damages. In contrast, a suit **in equity** seeks a court order, such as injunction, that orders a specific action to be taken, or sometimes bars a specific action from being taken.

Cases in recent years have yielded mixed results. One said there can be Fourteenth Amendment grounds for limiting state sovereign immunity and another said that Article I's Bankruptcy Clause can, too. But other recent cases have bolstered states' immunity, including one that said states do not have to respond to private complaints filed with federal agencies.

The Twelfth Amendment: Picking the President

"The Electors shall meet in their respective states, and vote by ballot for President and Vice-President, one of whom, at least, shall not be an inhabitant of the same state with themselves; they shall name in their ballots the person voted for as President, and in distinct ballots the person voted for as Vice-President, and they shall make distinct lists of all persons voted for as President, and of all persons voted for as Vice-President, and of the number of votes for each, which lists they shall sign and certify, and transmit sealed to the seat of the government of the United States, directed to the President of the Senate;

"The President of the Senate shall, in the presence of the Senate and House of Representatives, open all the certificates and the votes shall then be counted; The person having the greatest number of votes for President, shall be the President, if such number be a majority of the whole number of Electors appointed; and if no person have such majority, then from the persons having the highest numbers not exceeding three on the list of those voted for as President, the House of Representatives shall choose immediately, by ballot, the President. But in choosing the President, the votes shall be taken by states, the representation from each state having one vote; a quorum for this purpose shall consist of a member or members from two-thirds of the states, and a majority of all the states shall be necessary to a choice. And if the House of Representatives shall not choose a President whenever the right of choice shall devolve upon them, before the fourth day of March next following, then the Vice-President shall act as the President, as in the case of the death or other constitutional disability of the President.

"The person having the greatest number of votes as Vice-President, shall be the Vice-President, if such number be a majority of the whole number of Electors appointed, and if no person have a majority, then from the two highest numbers on the list, the Senate shall choose the Vice-President; a quorum for the purpose shall consist of two-thirds of the whole number of Senators, and a majority of the whole number shall be necessary to a choice. But no person constitutionally ineligible to the office of President shall be eligible to that of Vice-President of the United States."

The Twelfth Amendment was drafted to replace the part of Article II (Clause 3 of Section 1) that laid out the process for selecting the president and vice president. Originally, that clause called for members of the Electoral College to vote for their top two choices for president. The majority winner would be president and the second-place finisher would be vice president. This resulted in a president from one party and a vice president from another in the election of 1796, but it was the following election, in 1800, that led to amending Article II.

A majority of the Electoral College expected to elect Thomas Jefferson as president and Aaron Burr as vice president in 1800. A deal was worked out: all the Jefferson-Burr supporters would vote for both men, but one elector would leave Burr off the ballot so that he would finish second. The plan went awry, however, and Jefferson and Burr ended up with the same number of votes. That threw the election to the House of Representatives, where each state had one vote. The House was deadlocked for a week before Jefferson finally was declared president, in large part thanks to Alexander Hamilton's tireless campaigning against Burr.

> **People**
>
> Aaron Burr was furious at the scurrilous things Alexander Hamilton said about him in 1800 when Burr wanted to be president and again in 1804 when Burr lost a campaign for governor of New York. After the 1804 loss, Burr challenged Hamilton to a duel. Hamilton fired first and missed. Burr's shot hit Hamilton in the abdomen, and he died the next day.

The Twelfth Amendment changed the Electoral College procedure so that instead of submitting one ballot with two names, electors now each submit two ballots, one for president and one for vice president. The candidate with a majority of the vote is elected. If no candidate for president gets a majority in the Electoral College, the election is thrown to the House. The House then votes by state among the top three vote-getters. If no candidate for vice president gets a majority, the Senate votes by state from the top two vote-getters. If the House cannot declare a winner of the presidential race by inauguration day—March 4 when the Twelfth Amendment was ratified, or January 20 now—the newly elected vice president serves as acting president until the election is resolved.

The Twelfth Amendment also requires the vice president to have the same qualifications as the president: 35 years old, natural-born citizen, and a resident of the United States for at least 14 years.

The Twelfth Amendment does not prohibit a president and a vice president from being elected from the same state, but voters in the Electoral College cannot vote for two candidates from their own states. In other words, an elector from Ohio can vote for either a presidential candidate or a vice presidential candidate from Ohio—but only one of them, not both. In 2000, Republican nominee George W. Bush, then the governor of Texas, chose Dick Cheney, then a Texas businessman, as his running mate. Cheney changed his residence to Wyoming, where he grew up and was elected to Congress, to make sure that Texas electors would be able to vote for both him and Bush.

> **People**
>
> In the 1824 presidential race, Andrew Jackson had 99 of the 131 Electoral College votes needed for a majority. John Quincy Adams had 84 votes, and two other candidates combined for 78 votes. Jackson expected to be elected by the House, but Adams got the support of 13 of the 23 states and became president.

The Least You Need to Know

◆ The Ninth Amendment protects individual rights not specifically mentioned elsewhere in the Constitution, including—maybe—the right to privacy.

◆ If no presidential candidate wins a majority in the Electoral College, the election is thrown to the House of Representatives.

◆ The vice president must meet the same qualifications for office as the president, including being 35 years old and a natural-born citizen.

◆ The president and vice president can be from the same state. But if they are, Electoral College voters from that state can vote for only one of them.

11

The Thirteenth Through Fifteenth Amendments: Civil Rights

In This Chapter

- The Thirteenth Amendment: abolishing slavery
- The Fourteenth Amendment: due process and equal protection
- The Fifteenth Amendment: voting rights

The three amendments that combine to form a constitutional bulwark for civil rights were ratified in the years following the Civil War and are known as the Reconstruction Amendments.

The Thirteenth Amendment formalized President Lincoln's Emancipation Proclamation, making slavery illegal as part of the law of the land. The Fourteenth Amend-ment aimed to make sure that every citizen is treated the same under the law, no matter what race or economic standing, and has turned out to be one of the most far-reaching parts of the Constitution for protecting the individual regardless of race or creed. The Fifteenth Amendment not only guaranteed the right to vote, but banned authorities from putting up obstacles such as registration requirements that might be discriminatory against minorities and the poor or uneducated.

The Thirteenth Amendment: Abolishing Slavery

"Neither slavery nor involuntary servitude, except as a punishment for crime whereof the party shall have been duly convicted, shall exist within the United States, or any place subject to their jurisdiction.

"Congress shall have power to enforce this article by appropriate legislation."

Massachusetts in 1641 became the first of the American colonies to legalize slavery. By July 4, 1776, slavery was legal in all 13 original states. In one of its most infamous decisions, the Supreme Court in 1857 held that slavery was legal. The Dred Scott decision, formally *Scott v. Sandford*, came in the case of a lifelong slave claiming his freedom. Historically and legally, if a runaway slave could make it to a free state or territory, he or she was free. Dred Scott argued that since his owner had taken him to a jurisdiction where slavery was outlawed, he was free.

The Supreme Court, in a blatantly political decision that was designed to head off a confrontation between slave and free states, rejected Scott's argument. The court not only held that slavery was legal, but reversed longstanding legal precedent and said Scott was still a slave even in a free state. The reasoning behind the case was due process: setting a slave free would be to deprive an owner of his property. Even worse, the Supreme Court ruled that people of African descent, whether slave or not, could not be American citizens because they were inferior.

territories

Protesting the Dred Scott decision, abolitionist leader Frederick Douglass pointed out that the Constitution said "We the people," not "We the white people." He added: "Slavery lives in this country not because of any paper Constitution, but in the moral blindness of the American people, who persuade themselves that they are safe, though the rights of others may be struck down."

People

The Supreme Court decision that said Dred Scott was still a slave was handed down in March 1857. Two months later, the sons of his first owner purchased the freedom of Scott and his family. Scott died the following year, apparently of tuberculosis.

The Civil War

The Supreme Court apparently hoped that the Dred Scott decision would defuse tensions between slave owners and abolitionists, between slave states and free states. It didn't. In fact, it fanned the flames that led to the Civil War. The year following the decision, in 1858, Abraham Lincoln, in one of the debates with Stephen Douglas for a U.S. Senate seat from Illinois, made the speech—"A house divided against itself cannot stand"—that helped turn him into a national figure. Lincoln lost that race, but won the Republican presidential nomination and then the election in 1860.

Lincoln was against slavery, and the Confederate states, comparing themselves to the American colonies less than a century earlier, declared independence. Lincoln took pains to make war against the Confederacy not on the grounds of slavery—it had been ruled legal by the Supreme Court, after all—but because the rebel states had violated our constitutional form of government by seceding. To Lincoln, it was ostensibly not a war of slavery but of secession. In August 1862, Lincoln defined the war this way: "My paramount object in this struggle is to save the Union, and it is not either to save or destroy slavery. If I could save the Union without freeing any slave, I would do it; and if I could save it by freeing some and leaving others alone I would also do that."

The war began in 1861, and it was not until January 1, 1863, that Lincoln's Emancipation Proclamation, based on his assumption of war powers, went into effect. It may be worth noting that the Emancipation Proclamation actually freed relatively few slaves—those in the Union states, or who had escaped to Union states.

Reconstruction

Even before the Civil War ended, when it became clear that the Union would prevail, Lincoln and his advisers agreed that a constitutional amendment was needed to overturn the Dred Scott decision and prevent any state—or the federal government—from again legalizing slavery. Lincoln also saw the proposed Thirteenth Amendment as a political move to demoralize the South in the last throes of the war. Amid pitched battles in Congress—the Republicans were for it, the Democrats against it—the Thirteenth Amendment was approved in February 1865. The war formally ended with the signing of the treaty at Appomattox in April, and the amendment was ratified later in the year. A number of states refused to ratify the amendment in 1865. The last state to ratify it was Mississippi in 1995.

In an 1873 case, the Supreme Court, by then made up of a roster considerably different than the justices who came up with the Dred Scott decision 16 years earlier, ruled that the Thirteenth Amendment prohibited all types of involuntary servitude, not solely the slavery of people of African descent. "If Mexican *peonage* or the Chinese coolie labor system shall develop slavery of the Mexican or Chinese race within our territory, this amendment may safely be trusted to make it void," the court held.

def•i•ni•tion

Not quite slavery, **peonage** is enforced servitude that forces a person to work against his or her will to pay off a debt or some other obligation. A key factor, even if there is no real legal obligation, is whether the person in servitude has been led to believe the debt must be worked off.

The nation and the Supreme Court took a broad view of civil rights in the years immediately after the Civil War, during the period known as Reconstruction, when the South was in effect ruled by Northern occupying forces. At first, the courts seemed to be moving toward identifying and eliminating symbols and manifestations—"badges and incidents"—of slavery, including many different types of discrimination against blacks.

For example, there was concerted effort to keep former slave owners from keeping their former slaves working for them in conditions comparable to slavery, including sharecropper arrangements. Under these arrangements, a former slave might be granted property—40 acres and a mule was typical—but then would be charged exorbitant fees for rent, seeds, food, furniture, and equipment. Every year the sharecropper would fall farther behind and deeper into servitude—a form of post–Civil War slavery that carried the threat of jail for nonpayment. But the advances against involuntary servitude slowed when the federal forces withdrew from the South in 1877, and many areas began institutionalizing discrimination in the form of so-called Black Codes and Jim Crow laws.

Another notorious Supreme Court case came in 1896: *Plessy v. Ferguson*, which ushered in the "separate but equal" doctrine, holding that under the Thirteenth and Fourteenth amendments (see the following section, "The Fourteenth Amendment: Due Process and Equal Protection") the states had to make sure that blacks and whites had the same benefits in society; however, they did not need to ensure that blacks and whites enjoyed those benefits shoulder to shoulder, or had access to them together. It was not until 1968 that the Supreme Court made it clear that a black family had the right to move in next door to a white family: "At the very least, the freedom that Congress is empowered to secure under the Thirteenth Amendment includes the freedom to buy whatever a white man can buy, the right to live wherever a white man can live."

What It Means to You

The courts will not order "specific performance"—requiring you to do what you agreed to do—if you violate a personal services employment contract. For example, athletes who sign a contract but refuse to play for their teams can be liable for money damages but cannot be forced to play. In addition, mandatory military service is not considered involuntary servitude under the Thirteenth Amendment.

The Fourteenth Amendment: Due Process and Equal Protection

"All persons born or naturalized in the United States, and subject to the jurisdiction thereof, are citizens of the United States and of the State wherein they reside. No State shall make or enforce any law which shall abridge the privileges or immunities of citizens of the United States; nor shall any State deprive any person of life, liberty, or property, without due process of law; nor deny to any person within its jurisdiction the equal protection of the laws.

"Representatives shall be apportioned among the several States according to their respective numbers, counting the whole number of persons in each State, excluding Indians not taxed. But when the right to vote at any election for the choice of electors for President and Vice-President of the United States, Representatives in Congress, the Executive and Judicial officers of a State, or the members of the Legislature thereof, is denied to any of the male inhabitants of such State, being twenty-one years of age, and citizens of the United States, or in any way abridged, except for participation in rebellion, or other crime, the basis of representation therein shall be reduced in the proportion which the number of such male citizens shall bear to the whole number of male citizens twenty-one years of age in such State.

"No person shall be a Senator or Representative in Congress, or elector of President and Vice-President, or hold any office, civil or military, under the United States, or under any State, who, having previously taken an oath, as a member of Congress, or as an officer of the United States, or as a member of any State legislature, or as an executive or judicial officer of any State, to support the Constitution of the United States, shall have engaged in insurrection or rebellion against the same, or given aid or comfort to the enemies thereof. But Congress may by a vote of two-thirds of each House, remove such disability.

"The validity of the public debt of the United States, authorized by law, including debts incurred for payment of pensions and bounties for services in suppressing insurrection or rebellion, shall not be questioned. But neither the United States nor any State shall assume or pay any debt or obligation incurred in aid of insurrection or rebellion against the United States, or any claim for the loss or emancipation of any slave; but all such debts, obligations and claims shall be held illegal and void.

"The Congress shall have the power to enforce, by appropriate legislation, the provisions of this article."

In 1868, three years after the Thirteenth Amendment outlawed slavery, the Fourteenth Amendment was ratified to help wipe out the inequality and discrimination that lingered after slavery. The Fourteenth Amendment also struck down the part of the original Constitution that counted a slave as three fifths of a person for allocating seats for the House of Representatives and members of the Electoral College, and blocked the former Confederate states and their citizens from filing lawsuits seeking compensation for damage to their property during the Civil War, including claims that their freed slaves represented property losses.

Citizenship

Beyond those historical artifacts, the continuing impact of the Fourteenth Amendment comes from that brief opening paragraph, which begins: "All persons born or naturalized in the United States ... are citizens of the United States."

The Constitution does not define citizenship, but has been interpreted to give the same rights to both natural-born and naturalized citizens—people from other countries who become American citizens. Natural-born citizens include children born within the United States and children born outside the United States but whose parents are U.S. citizens. Neither the Constitution nor the Supreme Court has said so explicitly, but the longtime practice has been to regard any baby born in the United States—including those whose parents are in the country illegally—as a natural-born citizen. There have been and no doubt will continue to be proposals in Congress to require at least one parent to be an American citizen for a baby to be a citizen from birth, but wholesale changes in the rules of citizenship seem unlikely in the foreseeable future. As a nation of immigrants, our culture, tradition, and laws have always held a bias toward making it easier rather than harder for newcomers to become citizens.

What It Means to You

Many people think that Americans who are born with dual citizenship with another country "have to choose" at age 18 or at some other point. Not true. Some countries do prohibit dual citizenship, but the United States is not one of them.

The second part of the opening paragraph, dealing with civil rights, is the one that has sent so many ripples through American society: "No State shall make or enforce any law which shall abridge the privileges or immunities of citizens of the United States ..." or deny any due process of law or equal protection of the laws.

In practical terms, the Fourteenth Amendment allowed the federal courts to extend many of the provisions of the Bill of Rights to the states, too. Free speech, fair trial, the right not to give evidence against yourself—none of those rights in the first 10 amendments applied to the states until the Supreme Court extended them, literally on a case-by-case basis, under the Incorporation Doctrine. This doctrine holds that many of the liberties in the Bill of Rights are so fundamental to our system of justice that they should be incorporated into the Fourteenth Amendment's Due Process Clause. A prime example is the Sixth Amendment. The right to legal counsel originally covered only federal defendants, but the Supreme Court extended it to state defendants in capital cases in the Scottsboro case in 1932 and in noncapital felonies in *Gideon v. Wainwright* in 1963. (See Chapter 8, under "Assistance of Counsel.")

Civil Rights

Due process is, in a word, fairness. It might be procedural fairness: you should get a hearing, your day in court, your chance to tell your side of the story, and for a decision to be made fairly, according to an established process and set of rules. If you lose your government job or your kid gets kicked out of college or your property taxes go up, you might want to make sure the proper procedures have been followed. Due process might also be substantive, which covers every other aspect of fairness and protects specific rights, even if they are not mentioned specifically in the Constitution. For example, the courts have relied on substantive due process to tell the government to keep its nose out of our bedrooms.

The Equal Protection Clause is the authority behind the "one man, one vote" principle, along with many other aspects of fairness in our society. If one person or group of people is allowed to do something, we should all be allowed to do it. However, the concept of equal protection under the Constitution is misunderstood in the sense that it does not really require that all people be treated equally, either as individuals or groups or classes. The Fourteenth Amendment requires only that the laws be applied equally to individuals and groups. The day-to-day real-world effects of a law or regulation may turn out to be more detrimental to certain people, but it might be permissible anyway as long as there is a good reason for the law or regulation and it was not enacted for the purpose of discrimination.

In other words, there can be a legal justification for lumping certain people into classifications and then prohibiting them from doing something that everybody else is allowed to do. Over time, the Fourteenth Amendment's equal protection provisions have been applied not only to racial discrimination, but to women, gays, and other groups claiming discrimination. As with so many other aspects of constitutional law, perhaps the best way to figure out what it means today is to look at how the law evolved through the Supreme Court cases over the years.

An 1886 Supreme Court case, *Yick Wo v. Hopkins,* showed how a law can discriminate legally, and at the same time how a law can be administered in a discriminatory fashion. San Francisco had many Chinese immigrants at the time. Because of discrimination, the only work opportunities for many of them were in laundries. San Francisco passed an ordinance requiring a permit to operate a laundry in a wooden building. Since most laundries were in wooden buildings and most laundries were owned and operated by Chinese people, this ordinance presented an economic hardship to the Chinese community. The laundries had to either close down or get a permit.

The Supreme Court ruled that the ordinance was not unconstitutional because it had a legitimate purpose: there was a high danger of fires in laundries, and the chances of the fire spreading and causing more harm was greater if the laundry was in a wooden building. A permit allowed authorities to inspect laundries and determine if they were being run safely. The fact that Chinese suffered more than the rest of the population was an unfortunate and unintended side effect. The ordinance itself was not unconstitutional.

However, the court found that the law was being enforced unfairly: permits were routinely approved for non-Chinese laundries and rejected for Chinese laundries. The court struck down the law not because it was discriminatory, but because it was administered in a discriminatory way. Incidentally, there was one other important point made in that case. The court said that the Chinese deserved equal protection under the Fourteenth Amendment because equal protection applies not only to citizens but to "any person" under a state's jurisdiction.

A series of cases in 1873 produced what have become known as the Supreme Court's Slaughterhouse decisions. The cases grew out of a New Orleans ordinance that granted a monopoly for slaughterhouses. Would-be competitors sued on Fourteenth Amendment grounds, claiming economic discrimination. They said that the monopoly had been granted as patronage in return for political favors. The Supreme Court upheld the monopoly, citing the city's justifiable reasons for it: to keep slaughterhouses from dumping offal into the city's waterways.

What It Means to You

In general, equal protection applies to government action only. Private individuals and organizations can discriminate—which is why country clubs, for example, can exclude women or certain racial or ethnic minorities from membership.

In an 1880 decision, the Supreme Court held that a state ban on blacks serving on juries did not violate the prospective black jurors' rights, but did violate the rights of black defendants under the Equal Protection Clause. A series of cases in 1883 known as the Civil Rights cases held that the Constitution does not prohibit racial discrimination by private individuals or organizations.

The 1896 Supreme Court decision in *Plessy v. Ferguson* (see "The Thirteenth Amendment: Abolishing Slavery") overturned the Civil Rights Act of 1875, which was enacted in the hopes of bringing equality or at least legal equilibrium between blacks and whites in the former slave-owning states. Amid a raft of Jim Crow laws that denied black people the use of various public facilities, from toilets to schools, Louisiana in 1890 passed a law that required blacks and whites to ride in separate railroad cars. The "white" cars were considerably more well appointed. Homer Plessy, who was one eighth black—an "octoroon" in the parlance of the day—bought a first-class ticket for the white part of a train, pointed out to a conductor that he was black, and was arrested. He was fined $25 and appealed the conviction all the way to the Supreme Court, which decided by a 7–1 vote that he was not a victim of discrimination prohibited by either the Thirteenth or Fourteenth amendments. Justice John Marshall Harlan, himself a former slave owner, filed a memorable dissent, warning about the United States developing a "caste" system. But for half a century, until *Brown v. Board of Education* in 1954, the "separate but equal" doctrine remained the law of the land.

From the end of the nineteenth century through the first part of the twentieth, the Supreme Court went through a long period that emphasized a business-oriented view of the Fourteenth Amendment and due process. The court, reflecting a predominant attitude at the time, took a laissez-faire stance in a number of cases. The focus of due process was not on personal, individual liberties, but rather on property. The court had a market-oriented approach with echoes of social Darwinism, a theory of the era that suggested that the haves in society should make the rules for the have-nots.

One of the defining cases was *Lochner v. New York* in 1905, when the Supreme Court overturned a law prohibiting bakers from working more than 10 hours a day or 60 hours a week. The reasoning: the bakery owner would make less profit, and that was a violation of his right to due process. The court did recognize some measure of "police power" that allowed states to set some health and safety rules—for working in mines, for instance—but other rulings came down squarely on the side of employers and owners, including one that struck down minimum wage requirements.

The courts gradually came to recognize that due process protected not only economic rights, but also personal rights, and became more likely to presume that there were valid reasons behind a state law, and that those reasons were not necessarily outweighed by business interests. "We do not sit as a superlegislature to weigh the wisdom of legislation or to decide whether the policy which it expresses offends the public welfare," the Supreme Court mused in one case.

In 1908, in *Berea College v. Kentucky*, the Supreme Court upheld a Kentucky law that prohibited black and white students from *and Catholic*

attending the same college. In a 1925 case, *Pierce v. Society of Sisters,* one of the first privacy cases extending parental rights, the court upheld a Ku Klux Klan lawsuit allowing KKK parents to have their own private schools rather than send their kids to public schools.

During World War II, the federal government forced tens of thousands of Japanese and Americans of Japanese descent—including U.S. citizens whose families had been Americans for generations—to surrender their liberty and move to internment camps. A young Japanese American, Fred Korematsu, was thrown in prison when he refused to turn himself in and live in a camp. He appealed his conviction, and in 1944, in *Korematsu v. United States,* the Supreme Court upheld the internment program. Yes, it was a violation of the Japanese Americans' individual rights, but the high court said it was justified because of concerns about espionage—national security, in other words.

When the Japanese Americans were finally freed, each was given $25 for train fare, or $50 for a family. A commission appointed by President Jimmy Carter in 1980 subsequently found that the Japanese Americans had been subjected to "race prejudice, war hysteria, and a failure of political leadership." The government granted $20,000 payments to each internment camp survivor still alive more than four decades later, including Fred Korematsu. Some believe the compensation to the internment camp survivors sets a precedent that could pave the way to reparations for slavery to African Americans today, but others say it is unlikely there will ever be an American reparations program so long after slavery ended.

> **People**
>
> In 1984, a federal judge overturned Fred Korematsu's original conviction, saying he did not get a fair trial. Korematsu remained politically active, and filed a "friend of the court" brief in the 2004 lawsuit challenging President George W. Bush's program detaining enemy combatants at Guantanamo. Korematsu died in 2005 at age 86.

In a pair of 1948 cases, black families in Missouri and Michigan challenged racially discriminatory restrictive covenants—legal restrictions that some owners put on their property to keep it from being sold to blacks. The cases were consolidated into one decision, *Shelley v. Kramer,* and the Supreme Court ruled that restrictive covenants that discriminate are not necessarily unlawful, at least as long as the people buying and selling voluntarily abide by them. The court held, however, that the covenants in the Shelley case were unconstitutional because the neighbors, by filing a lawsuit against their new black neighbors, tried to get the state to enforce the discrimination.

One of the most famous Fourteenth Amendment cases was *Brown v. Board of Education*, handed down in 1954. Oliver Brown, a black man who worked as a welder in Topeka, Kansas, filed the suit because his daughter Linda was not allowed to go to the neighborhood schools with her white friends. Instead, she had to walk to a bus stop and take a bus to a black school. The Supreme Court consolidated the Topeka case with several similar cases from South Carolina, Virginia, Delaware, and Washington, D.C. Thurgood Marshall, who later became the first black justice of the Supreme Court, was the lead attorney for the NAACP, in charge of a legal team that included some of the top lawyers from some of the biggest—and whitest—law firms in the country.

The Supreme Court's 9–0 decision struck down the last vestiges of the "separate but equal" doctrine and sent out shock waves still being felt. Chief Justice Earl Warren wrote, "Today, education is perhaps the most important function of state and local governments …. Such an opportunity, where the state has undertaken to provide it, is a right which must be available to all on equal terms." Change was not immediate, of course, and there were many more court decisions and wrenching local controversies as schools integrated, sometimes with forced busing not only of black students to previously white schools but also white students to previously black schools.

The Fourteenth Amendment and its "one man, one vote" principle led the federal courts to get involved in reapportionment of congressional voting districts, which prevented states from redrawing or maintaining district boundaries that discriminated against black voters. These court rulings helped lead to the Civil Rights Act of 1964 and the Voting Rights Act of 1964, and to further advances in education and other equal opportunities for minorities.

One of the best-known—and most controversial—extensions of constitutional rights through the Fourteenth Amendment came in a series of cases beginning in the 1960s involving contraception, abortion, and

1965

homosexual acts. The cases cited due process, and took steps toward recognizing a fundamental right to privacy—a right not specifically mentioned anywhere in the Constitution. The Griswold case in 1965 struck down Connecticut's anti-contraceptive law, the Roe case legalized abortion in 1973, and the Lawrence case prohibited states from criminalizing consenting adult homosexual acts. (See Chapter 10.)

Miscegenation laws were not uncommon through much of U.S. history, but the last laws barring interracial marriage were struck down by the Supreme Court in a 1967 case, *Loving v. Virginia*. In that case, a white husband and his part-black, part–Native American wife were each sentenced to a year of prison for being married to each other. The decision overturning the law was unanimous.

In *Washington v. Lee*, a 1968 case, the Supreme Court struck down Alabama's laws requiring that black and white prisoners be housed separately in state prisons, and in 1970 the high court ruled in *Goldberg v. Kelly* that the due process provision of the Fourteenth Amendment requires that a hearing be held and evidence presented before certain benefits can be taken away by regulators or administrators, including welfare benefits, pensions, and licenses. Welfare benefits are a type of property, the high court reasoned, and property cannot be taken away without due process. In 1971, in *Reed v. Reed*, the court ruled that state law cannot give preference to men over women to serve as executors of estates, thereby ruling for the first time that gender-based laws can violate the Equal Protection Clause.

> **Cases**
>
> **Washington v. Glucksberg (1997):** The Supreme Court turned down a challenge to Washington's state law prohibiting physician-assisted suicide. The court said, in effect, that American law does not include the right to die.

In a 2000 "states' rights" case, *United States v. Morrison*, a female college student who said she had been raped by two members of the school's football team sued the men for damages under the federal Violence Against Women Act of 1994. The Supreme Court, in a 5–4 ruling, held that the part of the law allowing female victims of violence to collect damages in federal court was unconstitutional because it exceeded the authority of the Fourteenth Amendment. The court noted that the law was designed to help women who did not get justice in state courts, but said under the Commerce Clause it was up to the states, not the federal government, to provide remedies for private wrongs.

The Fifteenth Amendment: Voting Rights

"The right of citizens of the United States to vote shall not be denied or abridged by the United States or by any State on account of race, color, or previous condition of servitude.

"The Congress shall have the power to enforce this article by appropriate legislation."

The Fourteenth Amendment was drafted with the goal of creating no new rights; instead, it was supposedly to merely extend existing rights to the states. Specifically, the Fourteenth Amendment did not give freed slaves the right to vote. It was still up to the states to decide who would vote and who wouldn't. Congress approved the Fifteenth Amendment to counter any state laws that would deny the vote to blacks. Ratified in 1870, the third and last of the so-called Reconstruction Amendments said that the states cannot use race, color, or status as a former slave as a reason for denying someone the right to vote.

As in so many other cases, the actual language of the Fifteenth Amendment was a compromise. Some people wanted no constitutional rules on voting eligibility; they wanted to let the states continue to set their own rules. Others wanted universal suffrage—or rather universal male suffrage, since women did not generally have the right to vote, and didn't get it until a half-century later. The Fifteenth Amendment as ratified staked out a middle ground: states could still set their own rules for voting eligibility, but those rules could not bar a potential voter because of race. Consequently, the Supreme Court ultimately made it clear that the amendment did not confer the right to vote on anyone.

When the newly elected President Rutherford B. Hayes withdrew federal troops from the South in 1877, the idea was to heal the nation's wounds and ease political dissent in the South, where many people felt like they were an occupied country within a country. With less federal oversight, however, a number of states brought in voter-qualification laws that seemed nondiscriminatory but had the practical effect of preventing blacks from voting. Poll taxes, for example, kept poor people from voting, and blacks were more likely to be poor. Literacy tests kept many blacks from registering, especially when administered by clerks who sometimes rejected black voters who could actually read and write more proficiently than white voters who were approved. Sometimes strict registration procedures were instituted that were not publicized in the black community and presented opportunities for clerks to reject black voters for minor technical missteps in the process.

In *Guinn v. United States,* the Supreme Court in 1915 overturned the "grandfather" clauses that a number of states had instituted, which said that you were automatically eligible to vote if you were a descendant of someone who had voted earlier or been eligible to vote earlier—such as before blacks had the right to vote. This kept whites from having to take literary tests or meet other registration requirements, while giving clerks more opportunities to reject black voters. In a 1939 case, *Lane v. Wilson,* the Supreme Court struck down an Oklahoma law that said people who had voted earlier did not have to reregister, while others had a 121-day window to register—or be ineligible to ever vote. And in 1944, the high court struck down a Texas law that said you had to be a member of one of the major political parties to vote in a primary election; the parties' respective central committees decided who was a member of the party and who wasn't, and not many black people were welcomed to membership back then.

In reality, many black voters suffered discrimination for many years, until the Voting Rights Act of 1965 spelled out equal voting rights for all.

The Least You Need to Know

◆ The Thirteenth, Fourteenth, and Fifteenth amendments are known as the Reconstruction Amendments.

◆ The Thirteenth Amendment banned slavery and involuntary servitude.

◆ The Fourteenth Amendment, including the Due Process Clause and the Equal Protection Clause, extended many Bill of Rights protections, including free speech and fair trial, to state as well as federal laws.

◆ The Fifteenth Amendment prohibited states from establishing voting laws based on race or color.

12

The Sixteenth and Seventeenth Amendments: Taxes and Senators

In This Chapter

◆ The Sixteenth Amendment: income taxes

◆ The federal income tax law

◆ Tax protests

◆ The Seventeenth Amendment: election of senators

After the Fifteenth Amendment was ratified in 1870, no amendments were added to the constitution for more than four decades. In 1913, however, two amendments were ratified: the Sixteenth, allowing Congress to enact the federal income tax system we have today, and the Seventeenth, providing for the direct election of senators.

The Sixteenth Amendment has always been controversial. Critics from the 1800s and from today have contended that both the amendment and the income tax are illegal. Despite losing challenge after challenge, the tax protest movement today may be stronger than ever, thanks to the Internet and the willingness of some Americans to grasp any notion—and particularly any conspiracy theory—that justifies not sending Uncle Sam some of their hard-earned cash every April 15.

The Seventeenth Amendment changed the way senators are elected. Originally, the Constitution left it up to each state, and specifically up to each state's legislature, to send two senators to Washington. A number of problems in the selection system developed, however, and the public began asking: why can't we vote for our senators directly, the same way we vote for members of the House of Representatives? The Seventeenth Amendment scrapped the old system and provided for direct election of senators.

The Sixteenth Amendment

"The Congress shall have power to lay and collect taxes on incomes, from whatever sources derived, without apportionment among the several States, and without regard to any census or enumeration."

Article I of the Constitution set strict limits on how Congress could levy taxes, requiring that any "direct" tax on the people had to be proportionate to the population of each state. In other words, if Pennsylvania accounted for 15 percent of the population, then the people of Pennsylvania would be required to pay no more than 15 percent of the direct taxes collected by the government. Direct taxes were generally considered to be taxes on property—what you owned, rather than income from your labor. Article I exempted indirect or *excise tax* from the proportional requirement.

def•i•ni•tion

An **excise tax,** as it relates to the Constitution, is a tax paid not on property that you own, but on some "event" in which you participate—buying or selling something, getting a license. Customs, duties, tolls, and sales tax are all examples.

This system worked fine for most of the century after the Constitution was approved in 1789. The federal government paid for itself through a range of excise taxes, customs, duties, and tariffs. After all, the federal government didn't do a lot—nowhere near what it does today, anyway—and it didn't cost much to run. Things changed when the Civil War broke out. Wars are expensive, and this one cost the federal government up to $2 million a day, an astronomical sum in the 1860s. Congress passed the Revenue Act of 1861, which raised excise taxes and included a personal income tax: 3 percent on all incomes above $800 a year. You were doing pretty well if you made $800 a year in those days, so most Americans were not affected. Congress tweaked the new income tax in 1862, imposing a 5 percent tax rate on those with incomes over $10,000 a year, which included a relative handful of the superwealthy.

The first national income tax faded away after the Civil War, and the federal government happily subsisted on excise taxes, customs, duties, and tariffs until the late 1800s. Gradually, however, it became clear that the rapid growth of the country required government growth. In 1894, Congress passed the Wilson-Gorman Tariff, which put a 2 percent tax on incomes over $3,000—the equivalent of more than $70,000 today, by Consumer Price Index estimates.

Opponents challenged the new law on the grounds that it violated Article I of the Constitution. Their argument was that the income tax was a direct tax, and therefore was unconstitutional unless Congress could figure out how to make sure that the people of every state contributed no more than their share, according to population. In practical terms, that was an impossible administrative task. Besides, it would have meant that the tax rate would be different for every state, depending not only on population but on average income levels.

The issue came before the U.S. Supreme Court in 1895 in the case *Pollock v. Farmers' Loan & Trust Co.* Now, there are many good things about our system of checks and balances, and the way that the federal courts, and particularly the Supreme Court, can review legislation and overturn it if it violates the Constitution. But one bad thing about our system is that if the Supreme Court makes a mistake, it can be difficult to undo, and the aftereffects can ripple throughout society for a long time.

In the Pollock case, the Supreme Court declared the federal income tax law unconstitutional. The court, in a narrow 5–4 decision, held that the previous view was wrong. An income tax was not always indirect. Instead, the court ruled, the income tax was a direct tax if the income was generated by property—as in the case of rent collected for land, for example. In that case, the court ruled, the income tax had to be apportioned among the states. The income tax law as set up by Congress was null and void.

So the federal government went back to paying its way through excise taxes. The government sold bonds, started collecting fees for the use of land for recreational purposes, and raised a number of sales and use taxes, especially on beer and tobacco, to help pay for the Spanish-American War in 1899. It became clear that a national tax was needed, a way for the government to routinely and reliably raise the money it needed to run the country. It also became clear that the apportionment provisions of Article I were not fair. If every state's contribution to the national coffers had to match its percentage of the national population, the residents of the richer, more populous states in the Northeast would have to pay less than people in the South and West.

Let's look at how it would work today if our modern income tax was subject to the apportionment provisions of Article I. New Jersey is a state with about 9 million people, or about 3 percent of the U.S. population, while Mississippi is a state with a population of about 3 million people, or about 1 percent of the U.S. population. Under the apportionment provisions of Article I, New Jersey residents would contribute 3 percent of the taxes collected by the federal government, and Mississippi would contribute 1 percent. But the average household income in New Jersey is in excess of $60,000, while the typical household in Mississippi earns about half that. So taxpayers in New Jersey would have to pay only about half the percentage of taxes that taxpayers in Mississippi would have to pay.

The Supreme Court apparently realized the inequities of the Pollock decision and began backpedaling in subsequent decisions. At the same time, Congress wrestled with how to get around it. When the judicial branch of government interprets the law in a way that the legislative branch doesn't like, the alternative is for the legislative branch to change the law—even if it is the supreme law of the land. And that's what Congress proposed by approving an amendment to allow an income tax and sending it to the states in 1909 for ratification.

>) **People** _____
>
> Even some of the sponsors of the Sixteenth Amendment held their nose when it came before Congress. One of the sponsors, Sereno E. Payne, a Republican congressman from New York, said, "As to the general policy of an income tax, I am utterly opposed to it. I believe with Gladstone that it tends to make a nation of liars."

The Federal Income Tax Law

Arizona became the forty-eighth state in 1912, so 36 states needed to ratify. In February 1913, Secretary of State Philander Knox announced that 38 states had ratified the Sixteenth Amendment. If you live in one of the six states that did not ratify, none of the rest of us can blame you: Virginia, Pennsylvania, Rhode Island, Connecticut, Florida, and Utah.

Eight months later, in October 1913, Congress enacted a new federal income tax law. The new tax rates began at 1 percent and went all the way up to 7 percent for those earning more than $500,000 a year—the equivalent of more than $10 million today. Because of exemptions, though, only a small percentage—less than 1 percent—of Americans were required to pay any tax at all in those early years.

It sounds simple now, and probably was, but even back then, when Congress was debating how to set up the income tax system in 1913, people were complaining about how complex it is. In 1913, during the debate on the first income tax act under the Sixteenth Amendment, Senator Elihu Root commiserated with those who said they didn't understand how the new income tax system would work:

> I guess you will have to go to jail. If that is the result of not understanding the Income Tax Law I shall meet you there. We shall have a merry, merry time, for all of our friends will be there. It will be an intellectual center, for no one understands the Income Tax Law except persons who have not sufficient intelligence to understand the questions that arise under it.

March 1, incidentally, was the original tax day. The official annual filing date was changed to March 15 in 1918, and did not become the current April 15 until 1954. The 1040 form was introduced from the beginning, though of course it has changed many times and in many ways over the years.

The original law allowed Congress to tax "lawful income," but the word lawful was dropped in 1916 just to make it clear that illegal income was not tax-exempt. The court agreed in subsequent decisions, including one in which Justice Oliver Wendell Holmes wrote, "We see no reason ... why the fact that a business is unlawful should exempt it from paying the taxes that if lawful it would have to pay." This gave federal law enforcement authorities another arrow in their quiver: even if they couldn't convict crooks for their criminal acts, they could still send them up the river for failing to declare and pay taxes on their ill-gotten gains. That's how many a Prohibition-era bootlegger was sent to prison, including Al Capone.

def•i•ni•tion

The courts say a question or issue is **moot** when it doesn't matter, when it is irrelevant or of academic interest only. A more relevant law or court ruling or other events can make an issue become moot.

Meanwhile, the Supreme Court continued to distance itself from the Pollock decision, including in a series of cases that have taken a broad view of what is income, and it seemed as if the court would have reversed the decision outright if it had not become *moot* with the enactment of the Sixteenth Amendment.

Tax Protests

A small but busy and mostly underground industry has developed in response to the Sixteenth Amendment, the tax laws, and the court decisions interpreting the laws. Anti-tax entrepreneurs sell various packages, both in print and online, that challenge the legality of both the amendment and the income tax. The promoters of these schemes often end up paying not only their original tax bills, but interest and penalties, too. Sometimes they end up in jail, but the IRS likes to point out that a fair number of the charlatans who sell anti-tax packages actually do pay their own taxes. Let's look at some of the most frequent claims by those who say the income tax is illegal.

One argument is that the Sixteenth Amendment was never approved because a number of states "amended" it before ratification. The courts agreed that the versions of the Sixteenth Amendment sent back to Congress after ratification are not identical to the wording that Congress sent out to the states. However, the courts have held that these are not substantive amendments but "errors of diction, capitalization, punctuation, and spelling." The courts have noted that Philander Knox, who as secretary of state was in charge of determining whether the amendment was ratified, actually considered and rejected the argument that the amendment was invalid because of the changes by some states.

Another argument by the tax protestors is that the Sixteenth Amendment is invalid because it is in conflict with state laws prohibiting income taxes. The Supreme Court shot that one down in 1922, ruling that national income taxes are a proper federal function that cannot be taken away by the states. Another is that the Constitution never properly defines "income," but the courts have pointed out that the Constitution has lots of significant words and phrases that are never defined, such as "free speech" and "due process" and "fair trial." The Supreme Court ruled in 1935 that for legal purposes the word "income" is used in the Constitution "as used in common speech."

The protestors also claim the Sixteenth Amendment is not legal because it didn't repeal anything. But most of the amendments did not repeal anything; the Bill of Rights did not repeal anything. Some would say the only amendment that formally repealed another part of the Constitution was the Twenty-First, which explicitly wiped the Eighteenth Amendment off the books to end Prohibition.

Another argument that has gotten nowhere is that the Sixteenth Amendment violates other parts of the Constitution, including the Fourth Amendment's privacy protections, the Fifth Amendment's guarantees against giving evidence against yourself, and the Fourteenth Amendment's right to due process. T. Coleman Andrews, after serving as commissioner of the IRS from 1953 until 1955, cited these arguments when he resigned because he was unhappy over the income tax:

> The income tax is bad because it has robbed you and me of the guarantee of privacy and the respect for our property that were given to us in Article IV of the Bill of Rights. This invasion is

absolute and complete as far as the amount of tax that can be assessed is concerned. Please remember that under the Sixteenth Amendment, Congress can take 100 percent of our income anytime it wants to.

According to the courts, he was correct only about the last part of that statement.

What It Means to You

The tax protesters have all sorts of theories and strategies for arguing that the Constitution does not allow the income tax. But the Sixteenth Amendment language specifically says Congress has the "power to lay and collect taxes on income." The bottom line: no matter how much you detest paying taxes, it is illegal not to file a return and pay the taxes you owe.

The Seventeenth Amendment

"The Senate of the United States shall be composed of two Senators from each State, elected by the people thereof, for six years; and each Senator shall have one vote. The electors in each State shall have the qualifications requisite for electors of the most numerous branch of the State legislatures.

"When vacancies happen in the representation of any State in the Senate, the executive authority of each State shall issue writs of election to fill such vacancies: Provided That the legislature of any State may empower the executive thereof to make temporary appointments until the people fill the vacancies by election as the legislature may direct.

"This amendment shall not be so construed as to affect the election or term of any Senator chosen before it becomes valid as part of the Constitution."

Article I of the Constitution specified different ways for electing members of the House and Senate. Representatives were elected directly by the people, but the two senators for each state were selected by that state's legislature. Apparently, the rule for letting the legislatures choose senators was part of an effort by the Constitutional Convention to persuade the states to support the draft Constitution. The framers reckoned that if the state legislatures had more power, they would be more likely to ratify the Constitution. In addition, the framers liked the idea that one chamber of Congress could be above the fray of street politics. Senators chosen by legislatures rather than by citizens directly would be able to do what's right in office rather than what they needed to do to get re-elected.

Problems soon developed. Unlike members of the House of Representatives, senators were not beholden to the public. A representative who didn't do a good job would be voted out of office; a senator could do a lousy job and then merely persuade a few friends in the state legislature to return him to office. In addition, frequent political spats within states often resulted in stalemates, and some senate seats remained vacant for long periods. In the very first congress, New York did not have one of its senators for three months. Later, Indiana and Delaware each went years with a Senate vacancy.

Corruption became rampant. Senators bribed their way into office, and special interests realized that if they couldn't get their own senator into office, they could block unfriendly legislation merely by keeping someone else from getting their senator into office. The process of selecting senators was driven underground, literally into smoke-filled rooms. A number of senators, including a wealthy Montana silver miner who paid state legislators $140,000 in bribes for his seat, ended up being kicked out of Congress or resigning in disgrace.

Naturally, the public was dissatisfied. Many of the states began having their own primary elections for the Senate, with the understanding that their legislatures would appoint the winners. Progressives such as Wisconsin Republican Gov. Robert La Follette led the call for a constitutional amendment, and the movement gathered momentum as the media highlighted the corruption.

People

An early investigative reporter, David Graham Phillips, published an article, "The Treason of the Senate," in 1906 in *Cosmopolitan* magazine that exposed the corruption over Senate seats and crystallized public opinion behind the Seventeenth Amendment.

The Seventeenth Amendment was readily approved by Congress in 1912 and sailed through the ratification process, becoming effective a year later. The amendment has not been totally without controversy, however. A number of conservative politicians over the years, including former Senator Zell Miller and former House Majority Leader Tom DeLay, have called for repealing the Seventeenth Amendment on the grounds that it violates the system of checks and balances. Critics say the states should still have the authority to appoint—and remove—senators. By taking power from the states, critics say, the Seventeenth Amendment led to an imbalance of power in favor of the federal government, and resulted in myriad woes, including federal budget deficits. One of the more disingenuous arguments, given that the amendment was approved because of bribery to buy Senate seats, is that repealing the Seventeenth Amendment would be a type of campaign finance reform: if there's no campaign, there can't be any campaign finance.

The Least You Need to Know

◆ The Sixteenth Amendment specifically authorized the federal income tax in 1913.

◆ Tax protesters have many theories for why the income tax is illegal. No courts have ever recognized any of those theories.

◆ No matter what the protestors say, if you don't pay your taxes you could go to jail.

◆ Senators originally were chosen by state legislatures, but corruption led to direct election by the public.

13

The Eighteenth and Twenty-First Amendments: Prohibition and Repeal

In This Chapter

- ◆ The Eighteenth Amendment: Prohibition
- ◆ America and alcohol
- ◆ The Volstead Act
- ◆ The downside of dry
- ◆ The Twenty-First Amendment: repeal

It's difficult today to imagine a United States of America where drinking alcohol would be so widely criticized that the federal government would try to outlaw it entirely. But that's what happened in the early part of the twentieth century—with disastrous results and a classic lesson in what happens when a government tries to go too far in regulating personal behavior in a democracy founded on individual liberty.

The Eighteenth Amendment: Prohibition

"After one year from the ratification of this article the manufacture, sale, or transportation of intoxicating liquors within, the importation thereof into, or the exportation thereof from the United States and all territory subject to the jurisdiction thereof for beverage purposes is hereby prohibited.

"The Congress and the several States shall have concurrent power to enforce this article by appropriate legislation.

"This article shall be inoperative unless it shall have been ratified as an amendment to the Constitution by the legislatures of the several States, as provided in the Constitution, within seven years from the date of the submission thereof to the States by the Congress."

America and Alcohol

Perhaps there has never been a nation with so many enthusiastic drinkers and so many aggressive anti-drinkers. The earliest European settlers depended on alcoholic beverages, particularly beer, because it was cleaner and healthier than water. Parents and children alike drank beer or wine with the majority of their meals—even the Puritans. At the time the Constitution was being written and ratified, George Washington and other leaders were lamenting the way that drinking, often to excess, had become such a part of daily life. For example, many workers routinely took a late-morning break—"elevenses," they called it—for a stiff whisky or two.

Temperance groups that campaigned against alcohol—some against drinking too much, some against drinking at all—began rising in influence in the early 1800s. A religious revival that disparaged alcohol use swept across the country in the 1820s and 1830s, led by prominent Methodists. In 1846, Maine became the first state to prohibit alcohol. President Lincoln, pressed for federal funding before there was an income tax, resorted to higher taxes on liquor and beer to defray the costs of the Civil War. After the war, however, the temperance movement grew through the Prohibition Party, the Women's Christian Temperance Union, and the Anti-Saloon League.

The WCTU reflected the growing political influence of women in American society; they could not yet vote, but they could influence public policy by marching and speaking out against the harm that alcohol abuse wreaked on marriages and families. The problems were heightened by industrialization and urbanization as more men began working in factories and drinking in nearby bars before and after their shifts. And established society came to see drinking as an immigrant problem, with the Irish and Germans devoted to their beer and the Italians to their wine. Many Protestants saw use of alcohol as a Catholic frailty. The Anti-Saloon League, formed in 1893, fought against the growing power of big-city political machines that were based on cronyism that stretched from the neighborhood tavern to city hall and beyond.

By the turn of the century, temperance education—classes where students were taught the evils of Demon Rum—were standard in schools across the country. Support for a total ban on alcohol across the country grew, particularly as anti-German sentiment swelled in World War I, when there was a temporary period of Prohibition to preserve grain for food supplies. Even many drinkers favored a ban on public alcohol sales, including wealthy and upper-middle-class people who believed they would be able to continue to enjoy their decent wines in their homes while the unwashed masses would be better off without their cheap beer, gin, and whisky. Some reasoned that less alcohol would increase productivity in the factories, and besides, the lower classes simply didn't have the self-control to handle their liquor.

As Congress was considering the constitutional amendment to impose Prohibition nationally, Republican Senator Warren Harding proposed the first time limit for ratification: if the states did not ratify within seven years, the amendment was dead. Harding, who was elected president not long after Prohibition went into effect, was known to enjoy his whisky but his home state, Ohio, was a hotbed of temperance. The time limit was challenged, but the Supreme Court upheld it in *Dillon v. Gloss* in 1921.

> **People** _____
> Republican strategists pushed Warren G. Harding to head the
> ticket in 1920 because he looked presidential, and he won easily.
> A critic said his cliché-ridden speeches were like "an army of pompous
> phrases moving over the landscape in search of an idea," and his brief,
> scandal-ridden administration ended when he died of a heart attack in
> San Francisco in 1923.

The Volstead Act

Congress approved the Eighteenth Amendment and sent it to the states
in January 1918. Many of the state legislatures were dominated by
rural lawmakers who were generally more anti-alcohol than city politicians, and the amendment was ratified a year later. Scholars say that
the Eighteenth Amendment was one of only two amendments—the
Thirteenth, banning slavery, is the other—that specifically outlawed
personal behavior. Subsequent challenges, all futile, argued that the
amendment was illegal because it amounted to legislation, while the
Constitution was supposed to offer only general guidance and principles, and that amendments were not supposed to break new ground but
rather only clarify or rectify pre-existing portions of the Constitution.

By 1919, the year the Eighteenth Amendment went into effect, 26
of the 46 states had their own Prohibition laws. Congress enacted
the Volstead Act, which gave enforcement teeth to the amendment.
However, like the Eighteenth Amendment itself, it did not define
intoxicating liquor or prohibit the purchase, possession, or consumption of alcoholic beverages. The act, named after Andrew Volstead, the
Minnesota Republican congressman who introduced it, also allowed
small quantities of wine for personal consumption, and slightly alcoholic drinks, such as near beer, that were no more than .5 percent
alcohol. The Volstead Act allowed people to keep and enjoy alcoholic
beverages they had purchased before the amendment was ratified. The
penalties for selling liquor—brandy, whisky, rum, beer, gin, ale, porter,
wine—ranged from 30 days in jail to 5 years in prison and fines of $500
to $10,000.

> **People** _____
>
> Andrew Volstead, a lawyer, was the mayor of Granite Falls,
> Minnesota, before being elected to Congress in 1903. One of
> the few congressmen who favored a federal law against lynching, he
> was typical of the progressives who thought Prohibition would be good
> for the country's morals and morale. As public opinion turned against
> Prohibition, he was defeated in his 1922 re-election bid.

The most ardent temperance leaders exulted in Prohibition. Evangelist
Billy Sunday held mock funerals for John Barleycorn and announced,
"The slums will soon be only a memory. We will turn our prisons into
factories and our jails into storehouses and corncribs." Indeed, absen-
teeism at factories declined and the welfare rolls shrank. Police received
fewer calls for domestic disturbances, delinquency, disorderly conduct,
vagrancy, assault, and other crimes.

The Downside of Dry

But the general public soon became disenchanted. The idea of a dry
nation was more palatable than actually going without a drink. And
instead of giving up booze, Americans were simply doing it more sur-
reptitiously, and paying more for it. California's vineyards expanded
during Prohibition, and retailers legally sold "blocks" or "bricks" of
dehydrated "grape juice" that carried wine names. One set of instructions read: "After dissolving the brick in a gallon of water, do not
place the liquid in a jug away in the cupboard for 20 days, because
then it would turn into wine." Another set of instructions reminded
customers that it was legal to drink wine in their own homes, but not
to transport it.

Illegal booze was readily available at parties where so-called gin was
made in bathtubs; in the tens of thousands of speakeasies that popped
up everywhere, including in private homes; and through the untold
numbers of rumrunners and moonshiners and gangsters who found a
new way to make a living. Much of the money for illegal booze went
to smugglers such as Al Capone, who earned tens of millions annu-
ally for several years from his Chicago headquarters. Some believe that
Prohibition was the breeding ground for organized crime in the United
States.

Enforcement was a problem. Both the state and federal authorities had enforcement authority, but neither seemed to want it very much. With their own laws, some states were more strict than others, but enforcement also varied from city to city, judge to judge, prosecutor to prosecutor, and even cop to cop. Awash in money, the gangsters could bribe entire police departments. One magistrate in Philadelphia collected $88,000 in bribes in less than a year on the bench, and in South Jacksonville, Florida, virtually the entire city administration, including the mayor, chief of police, president of the city council, and even the fire chief, were indicted for corruption by a federal grand jury. One study reports that from 1921 to 1923 there were 7,000 Prohibition-related arrests in New York City, but only 27 convictions. In Chicago, the Untouchables, the famous crime fighters led by Eliot Ness, were celebrated as much for not taking bribes as for the arrests they made.

> **People**
>
> Alcohol was not illegal in Canada during Prohibition, and great quantities of quality, brand-name liquor—as opposed to the often dubious homemade stuff—were smuggled across the border. One of the most notorious smugglers was Bill McCoy, and speakeasy operators would assure customers that their drinks were the real McCoy.

As the gangsters fostered violence and corruption, the bodies and the bribes both led to public disregard for government and the law. President Harding noted that Prohibition had become a divisive class issue: "Many citizens, not teetotalers in their habits, lawfully acquired stores of private stocks in anticipation of Prohibition ... so there are literally American millions who resent the lawful possessions of the few, the lawless practices of a few more, and rebel against the denial to the vast majority."

It soon became clear that Prohibition was a failure, an expensive mistake. Even the industrialist John D. Rockefeller, a teetotaler who had donated hundreds of thousands of dollars to the temperance movement, called for an end to Prohibition. President Herbert Hoover called it "the great social and economic experiment, noble in motive and far reaching in purpose," but agreed that it had failed. In 1932, the Democratic Party made repeal a plank in its national campaign platform, and when the Democrats swept into office the street bands blared, "Happy Days Are Here Again."

The Twenty-First Amendment: Repeal

"The eighteenth article of amendment to the Constitution of the United States is hereby repealed.

"The transportation into any State, Territory, or possession of the United States for delivery or use therein of intoxicating liquors, in violation of the laws, thereof, is hereby prohibited.

"This article shall be inoperative unless it shall have been ratified as an amendment to the Constitution by conventions in the several States, as provided in the Constitution, within seven years from the date of the submission hereof to the States by the Congress."

After President Franklin Delano Roosevelt took office, one of the first acts of the new Congress was to approve the Twenty-First Amendment. A few months later Utah became the thirty-sixth and final state needed for ratification, and Prohibition ended. The Eighteenth Amendment became the only one ever repealed by another amendment, and the Twenty-First was the only one approved by state conventions rather than by legislatures; Congress had stipulated state conventions out of fear that rural-dominated legislatures would vote to keep Prohibition.

The Ontario (Calif.) *Daily Report* newspaper noted: "A lot of factors went into the decision to do away with Prohibition. None, however, was quite as important as the nation's desire to get out from under the speakeasy and the rumrunner. They were a load too heavy to be carried any farther. We have dropped them." The Supreme Court ruled that the Twenty-First Amendment made the Volstead Act invalid, but a number of states retained Prohibition. Mississippi was the last state, in 1966, to lift its complete ban on alcoholic beverages.

> **People**
>
> In his 1934 State of the Union speech, FDR said: "The adoption of the Twenty-First Amendment should give material aid to the elimination of those new forms of crime which came from the illegal traffic of liquor."

If you look at the Twenty-First Amendment, you'll note that repeal is taken care of succinctly in the 15-word opening clause. The third and final clause deals with the seven-year time limit for ratification, which was not a factor since the states voted for repeal so quickly. However, the second phrase of the amendment, prohibiting transportation or possession into any state "in violation of the laws, thereof," would appear to give broad powers to the states to regulate alcohol. That's certainly the way the Supreme Court has interpreted it.

There have been tensions and potential conflicts with other parts of the Constitution, including free speech and interstate commerce, and the Supreme Court has indicated there must be a balancing act on a case-by-case basis. But for the most part states have wide latitude in regulating alcohol sales and distribution. An exception was a 2005 case, *Granholm v. Heald*, which looked at Michigan and New York laws allowing in-state wineries to ship wine directly to in-state residents, but prohibiting out-of-state wineries from shipping directly to their respective resident customers. The two states maintained that the second clause of the Twenty-First Amendment gave them unlimited authority to regulate wine sales and distribution in their states, but the Supreme Court disagreed. In a 5–4 decision, the high court said the laws were unconstitutional because they violated the Constitution's protections for interstate commerce.

Cases

Barnes v. Glen Theatre, Inc. (1991): Two bars, claiming that dancing nude represents freedom of expression, challenged an Indiana state law requiring dancers to wear at least a G-string and pasties. The Supreme Court turned down the appeal and held that "the enforcement of Indiana's public indecency law to prevent totally nude dancing does not violate the First Amendment's guarantee of freedom of expression."

A number of Supreme Court rulings relating to the Twenty-First Amendment have dealt with topless or nude dancing, porno movies, and sexual activities in bars and taverns. In *California v. LaRue* in 1972, *New York State Liquor Authority v. Bellanca* in 1981, and *City of Newport v. Iacobucci* in 1986, the Supreme Court said the states can ban or regulate nude or partly nude dancing as part of the power to regulate alcoholic beverages under the Twenty-First Amendment.

In other cases, the Supreme Court has said that performers may be enjoying their First Amendment rights of expression, but made a distinction between dancing topless in a bar where drinks are served and appearing nude in a serious theater presentation. In *44 Liquormart v. Rhode Island* in 1996, the Supreme Court said, "Entirely apart from the Twenty-First Amendment, the state has ample power to prohibit the sale of alcoholic beverages in inappropriate locations" and "to restrict the kind of 'bacchanalian revelries' described in the LaRue opinion regardless of whether alcoholic beverages are involved." Subsequently, however, the Supreme Court put some limits on state and local regulation of topless and nude dancing, sometimes requiring proof that the dancing would have harmful effects on the community.

The Least You Need to Know

◆ Prohibition was the result of a complicated combination of social, cultural, and economic factors.

◆ Prohibition, as enforced by the Volstead Act, lasted from 1920 until 1933.

◆ It was illegal to sell and transport alcoholic beverages, but it was not illegal to drink them in your own home.

◆ Prohibition had little impact on American alcohol consumption except to drive it underground and put it in the hands of gangsters.

Chapter 14

The Nineteenth Amendment: Women's Suffrage

In This Chapter

- ◆ The Nineteenth Amendment
- ◆ The birth of a movement
- ◆ Winning the vote
- ◆ Ratification

American woman were first allowed to vote less than a century ago. It was a long and difficult campaign spanning decades, and many of the leaders of the movement did not live to see the Nineteenth Amendment become part of the Constitution in 1920 and give them the right to vote.

"The right of the citizens of the United States to vote shall not be denied or abridged by the United States or by any State on account of sex.

"Congress shall have the power, by appropriate legislation, to enforce the provisions of this article."

The Birth of a Movement

Before independence, some of the colonies allowed women to vote, and some didn't. During the Revolutionary War, Abigail Adams wrote to her husband, John, insisting that the Founding Fathers should make room for some founding mothers, too. "If women are not represented in this new republic," she warned, "there will be another revolution." New Jersey allowed all its citizens to vote in 1776, as long as they had a certain amount of money, but the state took the vote away from women in 1807.

def•i•ni•tion

Suffrage means the right to vote. During the long campaign to win the vote, most women preferred to be called **suffragists,** a neutral term that covered both men and women and the range of the political spectrum. The term suffragette, used by some newspapers and by opponents of the women's vote, referred to women only and carried connotations of political and social radicalism.

The attitude of the day among traditionalists who opposed women's *suffrage*—both men and women— was summed up in a nineteenth-century Supreme Court case upholding an Illinois law that banned women from becoming lawyers. A concurring opinion in that case said in part: "It is true that many women are unmarried and not affected by any of the duties, complications and incapacities arising out of the married state, but these are exceptions to the general rule. The paramount destiny and mission of woman are to fulfill the noble and benign offices of wife and mother."

Women were regarded by some as too flighty or not smart enough or too concerned with taking care of their homes and families. *Suffragists* were derided for abandoning their femininity, and a popular joke in the 1800s suggested that the best way to deal with demands for the women's vote was to allow it for women over age 30. The problem would disappear, the joke went, because no woman wanted to admit to being over 30.

Many point to the start of the women's movement as the two-day women's rights convention held in Seneca Falls, New York, in July 1848. Organized by Lucretia Mott and Elizabeth Cady Stanton, the convention concluded with a Declaration of Sentiments that objected to the unfair treatment of women politically, culturally, and economically. It was also the first large-scale public demand for women to have the vote.

Women promoted their cause through marches, letters, pamphlets and books, lobbying, silent vigils, and hunger strikes. But they did not always agree on tactics and strategy. For example, there was a debate within the early suffragist movement over whether to fight for equal suffrage (women having the same voting rights as men) or universal suffrage (equal voting rights for everyone, including women and racial minorities). Before the Civil War, the cause lagged in the South in part because many suffragists were also abolitionists. Some suffragists feared that they might hurt their cause by linking it to voting rights for blacks, but it turned out that the Fifteenth Amendment gave black men the right to vote decades before women.

Susan B. Anthony did not become active until she was in her thirties, in the 1850s, when she was bowled over by a speech given by suffragist leader Lucy Stone, the first woman in America to keep her own name after marriage. Anthony was swept up in the cause, and her tireless work soon made her one of the movement's national leaders. She believed that the Fourteenth Amendment gave women the right to vote, and believed that if the right case came up the Supreme Court would agree. In the autumn of 1872, she organized a group of women in her hometown, Rochester, New York, to register to vote in the upcoming presidential election. When election officials refused, she browbeat and intimidated then, threatening both criminal charges and lawsuits seeking damages, until they let her register. The day before the election, the local newspaper huffed, "Citizenship no more carries the right to vote than it carries the power to fly to the moon."

> **People**
>
> Lucy Stone attended Oberlin College in Ohio, the first college in the United States to admit women. It was also the first college in the United States to admit blacks.

On November 5, shortly after the polls opened at the West End News Depot in Rochester, Susan B. Anthony voted. "Well I have been & gone & done it!" she exulted in a letter to Elizabeth Cady Stanton as soon as she got home. Incidentally, she voted a straight Republican ticket—the party of Lincoln—largely because Republicans were generally more open than the Democratic Party to at least listening to the argument for women's suffrage. Indeed, it was a Democratic poll watcher who filed the complaint that led to criminal charges against Anthony for illegal voting.

It took several days for reluctant local authorities to come to her home and arrest her, and once in custody she refused bail. She figured that a writ of habeas corpus was the fast track to the Supreme Court. Her lawyer, however, posted her bail, and tried to console the dismayed Anthony by saying that he could not bear to see her behind bars. After months of exhaustive speaking and writing, she finally came to trial in June 1873, facing up to three years in prison and a $500 fine. She wanted to take the stand, but the judge upheld a prosecution objection that she was not competent as a witness on her own behalf. As soon as the testimony was complete, the judge pulled a statement from his pocket that apparently had been written before the trial started. He ruled that the Fourteenth Amendment did not give women the vote, and that Anthony had voted illegally. He directed the jury to return a guilty verdict, and then fined her $100. Anthony refused to pay the fine. The authorities could have pursued her and taken action to collect the fine or throw her in jail, but instead they did nothing. With the case in legal limbo, Anthony was never able to appeal.

The United States Supreme Court did take up women's suffrage the following year, in 1874, when a would-be voter named Virginia Minor sued a local election official in Missouri for refusing to let her register. Just as Anthony had envisioned, Minor based her appeal on the Fourteenth Amendment, on the grounds that denying women the vote abridges the privileges of citizenship. In its decision in the case, *Minor v. Happersett*, the Supreme Court conceded, "There is no doubt that women are citizens," and that the Fourteenth Amendment aims to protect the privileges of all citizens.

However, in a long and sometimes meandering discussion of what it means to be a citizen, the high court finally concluded that voting is not one of the rights guaranteed to citizens by the Constitution: "The Constitution does not define the privileges and immunities of citizens." Instead, the court said, it is up to the individual states to determine who can and cannot vote. If the framers had wanted women to have the right to vote, the court reasoned, they would have included that right in the original Constitution. If the right to vote was universal, the court asked, why was the Fifteenth Amendment needed to prevent the states from denying the right to vote because of race? The court held that women's suffrage was a political issue, and threw it back into the laps of the women themselves. "If the law is wrong, it ought to be changed," the opinion said. "But the power for that is not with us."

Winning the Vote

Susan B. Anthony, her close ally Elizabeth Cady Stanton, and other suffragist leaders developed a two-pronged attack, state and federal, seeking both an amendment to the U.S. Constitution and state-by-state changes in voting laws. In 1875, Anthony drafted the wording of the amendment that was eventually approved. It was first introduced in Congress in 1878, and was introduced every session after that until it was ratified. The amendment never even made it out of committee, however, until 1887, when it was slapped down in the Senate by a vote of 34 to 16. The amendment did not make it back to the floor of either house for 27 years.

> **People**
>
> Though Susan B. Anthony gets more space in history books—and on dollar coins—her dear friend and colleague Elizabeth Cady Stanton was equally influential in the suffragist movement. Stanton often preferred to stay home and take care of her seven children, but she was the writer who composed many of Anthony's most stirring public utterances.

Publicly, members of Congress were concerned not only about whether women were suited to shoulder the responsibility of voting, but also about the changes that women voters might bring about. For instance, women were known to be concerned—maybe overly concerned—about health, safety, education, and working conditions, especially for child labor. Newspapers fulminated about the impact an eight-hour workday for women would have on industries such as canning and millinery, and bemoaned that restrictions on night work for women would backfire by putting "elevator girls" and theater ticket-takers out of work.

Privately, the men serving in Congress did not want to change the formula that got them into office and kept them there. They knew how to campaign for men's votes. If they gave women the vote, they'd risk re-election even if they changed the way they campaigned. The reaction in Congress was similar when the Seventeenth Amendment was proposed to provide for the direct election of senators; it took a national ground-swell of public opinion to get the amendment through Congress, and in the late 1800s there was no national groundswell for women's suffrage.

There were local and regional groundswells, though, and the suffragists made better progress in trying to change state laws. Wyoming granted women suffrage as a territory, and in 1890, when it became a state, it was the first state where women could vote equally with men. Other Western states followed, including Colorado in 1893, Utah in 1895, and Idaho in 1896.

In 1890, two of the leading suffragist organizations merged to form the National American Woman Suffrage Association, but the movement seemed to sag around the turn of the century as its longtime leaders faded from the scene. Lucretia Mott died in 1880, Lucy Stone in 1893, Elizabeth Cady Stanton in 1902, and Susan B. Anthony in 1906. The cause was soon reinvigorated, however, in part by a surprise victory in Washington State in 1910 and another narrow victory in California the following year. By 1912, women could vote in nine Western states, and momentum was building across the country.

In 1913, one of the new generation of suffragist leaders, Alice Paul, led a march of several thousand women through Washington on President Woodrow Wilson's inauguration day. More than 250,000 spectators lined the parade route, not all of them friendly. Marchers were harassed and skirmished with taunting onlookers, and dozens of women were hospitalized with injuries. More marches and demonstrations followed. A group of women drove—they actually drove the cars themselves, which was unusual at that time—cross-country gathering signatures, and presented a petition for women's suffrage to the White House signed by half a million people. In 1916, women voted for president in 11 states, and suffragist leaders claimed that women were responsible for re-electing President Wilson. The president did not disagree even though he opposed women's suffrage.

In 1917, for Wilson's second inaugural, Alice Paul led another march, this time around the White House. That same year, New York gave women the right to vote and Montana elected Jeannette Rankin the first female congresswoman. The suffragist marches, demonstrations, speeches, and lobbying intensified, and a group of women took up positions outside the White House, vowing to stand as silent sentinels until they had the right to vote. In the states, women stepped up their campaigns, working to elect pro-suffragist men running against congressmen and state lawmakers who opposed women's right to vote.

People

After losing a Senate race in 1919, largely because she had voted against the United States entering World War I, Jeannette Rankin had a long career as a social activist before again winning election to Congress in 1940. The following year, after the attack on Pearl Harbor, she was the only member of Congress to vote against declaring war on Japan. She did not run for re-election.

Ratification

Looking ahead to the 1920 elections, at least 15 states were going to allow women to vote in all races, and women would be voting for president in at least 15 other states. President Wilson changed his position, and spoke ardently in favor of granting women the right to vote via the proposed Nineteenth Amendment. The proposed amendment passed the House by the necessary two thirds by a single vote in 1918, but fell two votes short in the Senate later that year, and one vote short when the Senate took it up again in early 1919. In May 1919, the amendment was approved in the House by 14 votes more than needed. It came up for a vote in the Senate for a fifth time, and the third time in less than a year, all unsuccessful. A senator from Alabama proposed that the amendment be considered by state constitutional conventions rather than the state legislatures, but that was defeated. So was a proposal by a Louisiana senator to change the amendment so that it would be enforced by the states individually rather than by the federal government.

The Senate approved the amendment by a vote of 56 to 25, two more than necessary to send the amendment to the states for ratification. When the vote was announced, the suffragists thronged in the galleries "broke into deafening applause," newspapers reported. "For two minutes the demonstration went on ...."

> ### People
>
> Charlotte Woodward, only 19 when she attended the convention in Seneca Falls in 1848, was the sole surviving signer of the Declaration of Sentiments when the Nineteenth Amendment was ratified. Many historical references today assume that she voted at age 91 in the 1920 election, but government archives say she stayed home ill that day, and died before she ever actually cast a ballot.

Arizona became the forty-eighth state in 1912, so 36 states needed to ratify the Nineteenth Amendment for it to become part of the Constitution. Nine Southern states were vehemently opposed, so suffragists needed ratification from all but three of the other 39 states. Illinois, Wisconsin, and Michigan were the first to ratify, and 32 other states followed in the ensuing months. By August 1920, only one more state was needed. The vote was coming up in Tennessee, but it appeared that the amendment was going to fall a single vote short of ratification in the state legislature. Then a lawmaker named Harry Burn, only 24 and until then an outspoken opponent of women's suffrage, changed his vote. Tennessee ratified the amendment, and the results were certified in Washington a few days later, on August 26, which is why that date is celebrated as Women's Equality Day by presidential proclamation in the United States every year. After he cast his vote, according to the story, Burn revealed a note he had been carrying in his pocket. "Don't forget to be a good boy," the note read. "Vote for suffrage." It was from his mother.

A case came before the Supreme Court in 1922, *Leser v. Garnett*, that challenged the Nineteenth Amendment, but the justices dismissed it quickly, briefly, and unanimously.

The Least You Need to Know

◆ The Nineteenth Amendment gave women the right to vote in 1920.

◆ The suffragist movement had many leaders, but the two foremost were Susan B. Anthony and Elizabeth Cady Stanton.

◆ The unofficial beginning of the women's movement in America was the convention in Seneca Falls, New York, in 1848.

Chapter 15

The Twentieth and Twenty-Second Through Twenty-Seventh Amendments

In This Chapter

While not as well known as other amendments that are more commonly discussed by the Supreme Court or the subject of news headlines, the most recent amendments to the Constitution are significant for a number of reasons. Among other things, these amendments: set rules for presidential succession, including the two-term limit; provide for District of Columbia residents to vote for president; allow citizens to vote at age 18; prohibit states from charging voters' fees; and prevent Congress from voting itself immediate pay raises.

The Twentieth Amendment: Lame Ducks

"The terms of the President and the Vice President shall end at noon on the 20th day of January, and the terms of Senators and Representatives at noon on the 3d day of January, of the years in which such terms would have ended if this article had not been ratified; and the terms of their successors shall then begin.

"The Congress shall assemble at least once in every year, and such meeting shall begin at noon on the 3d day of January, unless they shall by law appoint a different day.

"If, at the time fixed for the beginning of the term of the President, the President elect shall have died, the Vice President elect shall become President. If a President shall not have been chosen before the time fixed for the beginning of his term, or if the President elect shall have failed to qualify, then the Vice President elect shall act as President until a President shall have qualified; and the Congress may by law provide for the case wherein neither a President elect nor a Vice President shall have qualified, declaring who shall then act as President, or the manner in which one who is to act shall be selected, and such person shall act accordingly until a President or Vice President shall have qualified.

"The Congress may by law provide for the case of the death of any of the persons from whom the House of Representatives may choose a President whenever the right of choice shall have devolved upon them, and for the case of the death of any of the persons from whom the Senate may choose a Vice President whenever the right of choice shall have devolved upon them.

"Sections 1 and 2 shall take effect on the 15th day of October following the ratification of this article.

"This article shall be inoperative unless it shall have been ratified as an amendment to the Constitution by the legislatures of three-fourths of the several States within seven years from the date of its submission."

Also called the Lame Duck Amendment or the Norris Amendment after its prime mover, Senator George Norris of Nebraska, the Twentieth Amendment changed the dates for the swearing in of the president, vice president, and members of Congress. The Constitution originally set March 3 as the date for swearing in members of Congress, and March 4 for the inauguration of the president and vice president. But that was back in the 1700s, when the prime way of getting from one city to another was in a horse-drawn coach bouncing over rutted and often muddy roads. Communication was primarily by letter. Consequently, it was presumed that newly elected officials could need weeks, perhaps months, to get their affairs in order and travel to Washington.

This sometimes left a period of four months when the outgoing—lame duck—administration and Congress could take action and not be answerable to voters. Even if the outgoing president and Congress did not take any action at all, the four-month gap left a leadership void while Washington and the nation waited for their new leaders to take office.

Before long, of course, the telegraph and then the telephone improved communications, and railroads and then the automobile and better highways improved transportation. The incoming officials did not need months to get to Washington. But cutting down the lame duck period did not become a national issue until the Great Depression began with the stock market crash in 1929. The nation was tired of the Hoover administration, and in November 1932 elected Franklin Delano Roosevelt with his promises of a New Deal.

People

After Abraham Lincoln was elected President in 1860, the 11 Confederate states seceded from the United States on February 4, 1861. But neither Lincoln nor the incoming Congress could do anything about it for a month, until they took office in March 1961.

But FDR had to wait four months, until the following April, to launch his eagerly anticipated programs.

In considering the proposed Twentieth Amendment, the Senate Judiciary Committee noted another potential problem with the original March swearing-in dates: if a presidential election was thrown to the House, the election would be decided by the lame ducks rather than the newly elected representatives. "It is quite apparent that such a power ought not to exist," the committee concluded, "and that the people having expressed themselves at the ballot box should through the representatives then selected, be able to select the President for the ensuing term …"

The amendment, which changed the inauguration date for president and vice president to January 20 and the swearing-in date for members of Congress to January 3, was ratified in 1933, after FDR took office. He and his first vice president, John Nance Garner, were re-elected in 1936 and two months later became the first president and vice president to be inaugurated on January 20.

> **People**
>
> John Nance Garner, known as Cactus Jack, was one of the real characters in twentieth-century American politics. Married to a woman whom he defeated for a Texas county judgeship, Garner is remembered for saying the vice presidency was "not worth a bucket of warm spit," but he actually said "a bucket of warm piss," which could not be reported in family newspapers.

The Twentieth Amendment also struck down the Constitution's original requirement for Congress to meet the month after the biennial November elections. Nobody saw much benefit in those lame-duck sessions; Congress did not have time to take any meaningful action, and any legislation enacted would not only be hurried but would be approved by a legislative body whose mandate was expiring. Finally, the amendment said that if a president-elect dies before inauguration, the vice president-elect becomes the president-elect and is inaugurated as president on January 20.

The Twenty-Second Amendment: Presidential Term Limits

"No person shall be elected to the office of the President more than twice, and no person who has held the office of President, or acted as President, for more than two years of a term to which some other person was elected President shall be elected to the office of President more than once. But this Article shall not apply to any person holding the office of President when this Article was proposed by Congress, and shall not prevent any person who may be holding the office of President, or acting as President, during the term within which this Article becomes operative from holding the office of President or acting as President during the remainder of such term.

"This article shall be inoperative unless it shall have been ratified as an amendment to the Constitution by the legislatures of three-fourths of the several States within seven years from the date of its submission to the States by the Congress."

The Constitution originally set no term limits despite the framers' concerns about a monarchy style of leadership. George Washington probably would have been easily re-elected to a third term, and possibly more, but he did not think it was seemly to serve more than two terms. And it wasn't good for the country, he reasoned. If he served longer than eight years, Americans might start thinking of him as a king who served for life. And a long-serving president could upset the delicate balance of power among the three branches of government.

None of the early presidents who succeeded Washington considered a third term, either, and a maximum of two terms became a tradition. President Ulysses Grant, elected in 1869 and re-elected 1873, went on a three-year world tour after his successor, Rutherford B. Hayes, took office.

People

National politics has always been a rich man's game in America. George Washington, considered one of if not the wealthiest man in the country at the time, refused to take his presidential salary of $25,000 a year—the equivalent of more than half a million in today's dollars.

Grant, who had been a much better Civil War general than post-war president, returned from his travels renewed, thinking he had learned much that would make him a better president. Hayes kept his word to serve only one term, so Grant threw his hat in the ring in 1880—insisting that he had honored the tradition against serving three consecutive terms, but there was no tradition against him serving a third term after a break. Whether because he was seeking a third term or because he had not been a sparkling president the first time around, the Republicans refused to nominate Grant. James Garfield, a dark horse, was nominated and subsequently elected.

Vice President Theodore Roosevelt became president in 1901 after William McKinley was assassinated only a few months into his second term. Roosevelt was elected to his own full term in 1904, and had served seven and a half years by the time he left office in 1909. After a series of lusty pursuits such as going on safari in Africa, Roosevelt formed the Progressive Party and ran for president again in 1912. His third-party bid failed, but he drew enough votes away from the Republicans, his former party, that the Democrat Woodrow Wilson was elected.

Franklin Delano Roosevelt had served two terms in 1940, but the two-term tradition went by the wayside because of his popularity for leading the country out of the Depression and because of concerns about a new president coming into office while World War II was heating up in Europe. Roosevelt became the first president elected to a third term. Despite concerns about FDR's "imperial" presidency and that he might set a new tradition allowing president to feel entitled to serve for life, Roosevelt was elected to a fourth term in 1944, when it became clear that United States involvement had tipped the war in the Allies' favor.

When FDR died and then the war ended in 1945, Congress turned its attention to constitutional term limits for president. The Twenty-Second Amendment was approved by Congress in 1947 and ratified by the states in 1951. It said no one could be elected president more than twice, even if the terms were not consecutive. In addition, a vice president who moved up to president because of a vacancy could not be elected more than once if the partial term was more than two years. The practical effect was that no one could serve more than 10 years as president—up to two years of an unexpired term, and then two full terms.

> ◯▷ **People** _____
>
> When the Twenty-Fifth Amendment was approved in 1951, it specifically excluded the sitting president, Harry Truman, who had succeeded FDR only weeks into Roosevelt's fourth term. Truman actually planned to take advantage of the exception and run for another full term, but he scrapped his re-election bid after a disappointing showing in the New Hampshire primary.

Lyndon Johnson could have become the only president other than FDR to serve more than two full terms. He took office in 1963, with less than two years remaining in John F. Kennedy's first term, and was elected to his own full term in 1964. If he had been re-elected in 1968 and served his full term, he would have been president for more than nine years, but he decided against running for re-election amid the turmoil over the Vietnam War.

Proposals to repeal the Twenty-Second Amendment are introduced regularly in Congress, usually by representatives or senators who think the sitting president is doing a wonderful job. One rationale is that every second-term president becomes a lame duck, and the possibility of a third term would preserve some of the president's authority and accountability. On the other hand, some observers say that second lame-duck term is when presidents can reach their crowning achievements, doing things they might not do if they had to worry about political popularity and being re-elected.

Presidents themselves have had mixed thoughts on the Twenty-Second Amendment. In the 1950s, Dwight Eisenhower opposed it, arguing that Americans should be able to elect whomever they want. Bill Clinton, who was only 54 when he left office in 2001, liked the idea of changing the amendment so that a former president could serve consecutive terms, leave office, and then return for a third, nonconsecutive term. Incidentally, two other former presidents, Jimmy Carter and George H. W. Bush, could have been elected again because they each lost their re-election bids and served only one term.

The Twenty-Second Amendment does not mention the vice president, but constitutional scholars presume that since the qualifications are the same for both president and vice president, a former president cannot run for vice president and then become president again if a vacancy occurs. Under that reasoning, comedian Al Franken's tongue-in-cheek idea would not work: Franken suggested that he would run as president with Bill Clinton as his running mate, and as soon as they were sworn in Franken would resign so that Clinton could once again be president.

The Twenty-Third Amendment: D.C. Voting

"The District constituting the seat of Government of the United States shall appoint in such manner as Congress may direct:

"A number of electors of President and Vice President equal to the whole number of Senators and Representatives in Congress to which the District would be entitled if it were a State, but in no event more than the least populous State; they shall be in addition to those appointed by the States, but they shall be considered, for the purposes of the election of President and Vice President, to be electors appointed by a State; and they shall meet in the District and perform such duties as provided by the twelfth article of amendment.

"The Congress shall have power to enforce this article by appropriate legislation."

The Twenty-Third Amendment gives the District of Columbia electors in the Electoral College, which allows D.C. residents to vote for president and vice president.

George Washington, who started his career as a land surveyor, apparently never envisioned the District of Columbia as a major city when he chose the site to become the seat of the new government. And neither did any of the other founding fathers. They saw it as a place where government workers would serve, rather than where hundreds of thousands would live and work.

The original Constitution said that only the residents of states could vote for president. And the District of Columbia was not a state. This amendment recognized that people really do live and work in the District—and that they were American citizens who were not allowed to vote for president, even though they had all the obligations of citizenship, such as paying taxes and serving in the military. The amendment was approved by Congress in 1960 and ratified by the states in 1961, when the District had a population larger than 13 other states. Today the District's population is larger than only one state, barely: Wyoming.

The amendment put a ceiling on the number of electors that the district could have—no more than the state with the smallest population. Since Wyoming, with a population of about 500,000 people, has three electors, that's what D.C. has, too. A proposed constitutional amendment sent to the states in 1978 would have given the district representation in Congress just like a state—a representative and two senators—but that proposed amendment expired, unratified, after seven years in 1985.

The Twenty-Fourth Amendment: No Tax on Voting

"The right of citizens of the United States to vote in any primary or other election for President or Vice President, for electors for President or Vice President, or for Senator or Representative in Congress, shall not be denied or abridged by the United States or any State by reason of failure to pay poll tax or other tax.

"The Congress shall have power to enforce this article by appropriate legislation."

This amendment outlaws the poll tax in federal elections. The poll tax, a fee that citizens had to pay to register to vote or to just vote, dates back to colonial times. The idea was that people who contribute to society, people who were making their way economically and socially, were the ones who should be able to have a say in how the government operates through the vote. Later, it became a way of keeping poor people, especially blacks, from voting.

After Reconstruction, following the Civil War, 11 states in the South enacted poll taxes, largely as a way of keeping black people from voting. By the time the Twenty-Fourth Amendment was approved by Congress in mid-1962, only five states still had poll taxes: Alabama, Arkansas, Mississippi, Texas, and Virginia. The states ratified the amendment outlawing poll taxes in federal elections in early 1964, and the following year Congress outlawed them again as part of the Voting Rights Act of 1965.

That same year the Supreme Court, in a decision in a Virginia case, *Harman v. Forssenius*, threw out the state's attempt to get around the poll tax prohibition. Virginia had a law requiring voters to either pay a poll tax or file a "certificate of residence" six months in advance of an election. The high court was unanimous in overturning the law. The following year, in 1966, in *Harper v. Virginia State Board of Elections*, the Supreme Court relied on the Equal Protection Clause of the Fourteenth Amendment to extend the ban on poll taxes from federal elections only to state elections, too.

The Twenty-Fifth Amendment: Presidential Succession

"In case of the removal of the President from office or of his death or resignation, the Vice President shall become President.

"Whenever there is a vacancy in the office of the Vice President, the President shall nominate a Vice President who shall take office upon confirmation by a majority vote of both Houses of Congress.

"Whenever the President transmits to the President pro tempore of the Senate and the Speaker of the House of Representatives his written declaration that he is unable to discharge the powers and duties of his office, and until he transmits to them a written declaration to the contrary, such powers and duties shall be discharged by the Vice President as Acting President.

"Whenever the Vice President and a majority of either the principal officers of the executive departments or of such other body as Congress may by law provide, transmit to the President pro tempore of the Senate and the Speaker of the House of Representatives their written declaration that the President is unable to discharge the powers and duties of his office, the Vice President shall immediately assume the powers and duties of the office as Acting President.

"Thereafter, when the President transmits to the President pro tempore of the Senate and the Speaker of the House of Representatives his written declaration that no inability exists, he shall resume the powers and duties of his office unless the Vice President and a majority of either the principal officers of the executive department or of such other body as Congress may by law provide, transmit within four days to the President pro tempore of the Senate and the Speaker of the House of Representatives their written declaration that the President is unable to discharge the powers and duties of his office. Thereupon Congress shall decide the issue, assembling within forty-eight hours for that purpose if not in session. If the Congress, within twenty-one days after receipt of the latter written declaration, or, if Congress is not in session, within twenty-one days after Congress is required to assemble, determines by two-thirds vote of both Houses that the President is unable to discharge the powers and duties of his office, the Vice President shall continue to discharge the same as Acting President; otherwise, the President shall resume the powers and duties of his office."

In the original language of the Constitution, Article II says that if the president is unable to carry out his duties, the office "shall devolve upon the Vice President." But it did not clarify whether the vice president actually becomes president or acting president or remains vice president but does the president's job. The Twenty-Third Amendment, approved by Congress 1965 and ratified by the states in 1967, clarifies that the vice president becomes the full-fledged president. It also provides for appointing a replacement if the vice presidency becomes vacant, and sets out procedures in the event that a president is still alive but is unable to carry out the responsibilities of the office.

A precedent was set the first time a president died in office, when President William Henry Harrison was succeeded by his vice president, who became President John Tyler. Questions remained about procedures in the event of presidential vacancy, disability, or inability to serve, but Congress did not address them until after the assassination of

People

President Kennedy's vice president, Lyndon Johnson, was sworn in aboard Air Force One at Love Field in Dallas, the eighth time that a vice president had succeeded a president who died in office. Jacquelyn Kennedy, the widowed First Lady, stood at Johnson's side on the plane as he took the oath of office.

President John F. Kennedy in 1963. But that question was raised: what if Kennedy had survived, incapacitated?

James Garfield, shot by an assassin, had been in a coma for 80 days before he died in 1881, and Woodrow Wilson was an invalid for the last 18 months of his presidency before leaving office in 1921. In either case, the country would have been better served if the vice president had been able to take over, if only temporarily, until it became clear whether the president could recover and resume office. Who would decide if and when a president had recovered sufficiently to resume the office?

While considering presidential succession, Congress also decided to address vacancies in the vice presidency. Besides the eight times a vice president had stepped up to the presidency and left the office vacant, there were seven other occasions when a vice president had died in office and not been replaced. The Twenty-Fifth Amendment gave the president the authority to appoint a vice president, with the confirmation of Congress, if and when the office became vacant.

It did not take long for the Twenty-Fifth Amendment to come into play. Vice President Spiro Agnew resigned amid a scandal in October 1973 and President Nixon, following the procedure laid out in the second section of the amendment, nominated longtime Congressman Gerald Ford, who was promptly confirmed by the House and Senate. When Nixon resigned in disgrace because of the Watergate scandal in August 1974, Ford succeeded him as president. Ford then named former New York Governor Nelson Rockefeller as his vice president.

> **People**
>
> Longtime Michigan Republican Congressman Gerald Ford was the first person to serve as vice president, and then the first person to serve as president, without running for either office. When he did run, in 1976, he was defeated by Democrat Jimmy Carter.

If a president cannot fulfill the duties of the office, the president can send a letter to Congress asking to be relieved. The vice president becomes acting president until the president sends another letter notifying Congress that he is re-assuming the duties. If there is no objection from the vice president, the president is back on the job. However, if there is an objection within four days by the vice president and a majority of the Cabinet—the heads of the administration's executive agencies, all appointed by the president—then it is up to Congress to decide, by a two-thirds vote of both houses, whether the president is fit enough to be returned to office.

The Twenty-Fifth Amendment lays out a comparable process for removing a president who is unable or unwilling to ask Congress to be relieved of the office. If a president is in a coma, for example, or a president goes crazy—which some wags would say has already happened more than once in U.S. history—the vice president and a majority of the Cabinet can invoke the Twenty-Fifth Amendment and notify Congress that the president is "unable to discharge the powers and duties of his office." Congress does not need to do anything right away. Instead, the vice president "shall immediately assume the powers and duties of the office as Acting President." The vice president continues as acting president unless the president objects. Again, Congress then decides by a two-thirds vote whether the vice president should continue to serve as acting president.

When President Reagan was shot in 1981, he probably should have invoked the Twenty-Fifth Amendment and allowed Vice President George H. W. Bush to serve as acting president at least while he was in surgery, and perhaps in the early stages of his recovery. Bush argued against it, saying he did not want to be seen as usurping the president's authority. Constitutional scholars, however, say that was exactly the sort of circumstances for which the Twenty-Fifth Amendment had been designed.

The amendment has been invoked at least twice—there may be other instances that were never made public—in recent history. When Reagan had a colonoscopy in 1985, he transferred power temporarily to Bush as acting president. Similarly, in 2002, Vice President Dick Cheney was briefly acting president when President George W. Bush underwent a colonoscopy.

The Constitution does not list the order of succession after vice president, but the Twenty-Fifth Amendment supplements the Presidential Succession Act of 1947, listing Cabinet offices in the order in which they were created, which sets out the following order of succession:

◆ The vice president

◆ Speaker of the House

- President pro tempore of the Senate
- Secretary of State
- Secretary of the Treasury
- Secretary of Defense
- Attorney General
- Secretary of the Interior
- Secretary of Agriculture
- Secretary of Commerce
- Secretary of Labor
- Secretary of Health and Human Services
- Secretary of Housing and Urban Development
- Secretary of Transportation
- Secretary of Energy
- Secretary of Education
- Secretary of Veterans Affairs
- Secretary of Homeland Security

The Twenty-Sixth Amendment: Voting at Age 18

"The right of citizens of the United States, who are eighteen years of age or older, to vote shall not be denied or abridged by the United States or by any State on account of age.

"The Congress shall have power to enforce this article by appropriate legislation."

Historically, 21 was the age of majority, the age of official adulthood, and the age for voting. But in the 1960s, during the Vietnam War, the age for young men to register for the military draft—and to be drafted, and to go serve, often in Vietnam—was 18. It was not fair, people said, for young men who were giving their lives for the country not to be able to vote for the leaders of that country. President Lyndon Johnson called for lowering the voting age to 18 in 1968, and Congress did so in 1970, as an extension of the Voting Rights Act of 1965. Oregon appealed, and the Supreme Court upheld the appeal, ruling that Congress had the authority to set the age for federal elections only, and not state or local elections.

This presented a dilemma, another issue of basic fairness. It meant that while everyone 18 and older could vote for president, in some states voters still had to be 21 before they could cast ballots for governor or mayor or dogcatcher. Besides the fairness issue, there were logistical problems; with two different sets of voting rolls, state and federal, election officials would have to maintain two sets of records. That would be cumbersome and expensive, and raised the possibility that we might have two sets of elections, state and federal.

The Twenty-Sixth Amendment was approved by Congress in 1971 and ratified later that year, the fastest approval ever for a constitutional amendment. Most but not all states fell in line by lowering not only the voting age to 18, but also the minimum age for signing contracts and other privileges of legal adulthood. Many states lowered their minimum drinking age to 18 as well, but an increase in drunk driving and traffic deaths among teenagers led to a backlash campaign by Mothers Against Drunk Driving and other groups. In 1984, Congress passed the National Minimum Drinking Age Act of 1984, which threatened states with losing a chunk of their federal highway funding unless they raised the drinking age back to 21.

The Twenty-Seventh Amendment: Congressional Pay

"No law, varying the compensation for the services of the Senators and Representatives, shall take effect, until an election of representatives shall have intervened."

This amendment prevents members of Congress from voting themselves pay raises and then starting to collect them immediately. Instead, they have to wait until the next session of Congress, after the next even-year election. The amendment was originally presented to the states for ratification back in the 1700s with the amendments that became the Bill of Rights, but it was ratified by only 6 of the 11 states needed.

That was long before the seven-year time limit for ratification became standard, so in theory the amendment remained pending, even though most constitutional scholars considered it dead in the water, a historical footnote. In 1982, a University of Texas sophomore named Gregory Watson was working on a paper for a government course on the Equal Rights Amendment when he stumbled onto the still-pending amendment. Intrigued, Watson dropped the ERA and wrote his paper about the amendment, arguing that it was still on the table and that if enough states ratified it would become part of the Constitution. He got a C on the paper. The professor said she didn't think he had made the case that the amendment was still alive. Undeterred, Watson undertook a one-man campaign, writing to state legislatures and persuading them to take up the amendment and ratify. Ten years later, in 1992, the amendment was ratified.

The Twenty-Seventh Amendment has largely been ignored by Congress, and it has not kept members of Congress from taking regular cost-of-living increases. But the fact remains: one man, an everyday citizen, amended the United States Constitution. Gregory Watson went on to become a researcher in the Texas Legislature. When the professor who gave him the C learned that the paper had led to actually amending the Constitution, she apologized to Watson. But it was too late to change his grade.

The Least You Need to Know

- Inauguration Day is January 20.

- A president who has been elected twice cannot run for a third term.

- It is unconstitutional to charge poll taxes or other fees to vote.

- If the president is unable to carry out the duties of the office, the vice president can become acting president.

- Gregory Watson was just exercising his citizenship; you should, too.

Chapter 16

The ERA and Other Failed Amendments

In This Chapter

- ◆ Early amendments still pending
- ◆ The Equal Rights Amendment
- ◆ The D.C. Representation Amendment
- ◆ Amendments that never got out of Congress

We know that the Constitution has been successfully amended 27 times since 1789, including 10 amendments—the Bill of Rights—that came out of the first Congress. Besides the 27 amendments that have become part of the Constitution, six other proposed amendments have gone before the states and not been ratified. Two of those amendments are apparently dead beyond revival, but four others are still pending and at least in theory could be approved someday, though that seems impossible because they are moot—a lawyer's way of saying they are outdated, irrelevant, and unnecessary today.

Let's review, briefly, from Article V: two thirds of each chamber of Congress, the House and the Senate, must approve a proposed constitutional amendment for it to be presented to the states for ratification. Three quarters of the states must ratify the proposed amendment for it to become part of the Constitution. Since Alaska and Hawaii joined the Union, that means 38 states must ratify.

So it's rare for the Constitution to be amended. The framers of the Constitution wanted it to be difficult back in 1789, and since then Americans generally have been reluctant to tinker with the supreme law of the land. But attempts to amend the Constitution are far from rare. Besides those 33 proposed amendments that have gone before the states, more than 9,000 other proposed constitutional amendments have been introduced in Congress over the years.

Early Amendments Still Pending

Twelve possible amendments came before the first Congress after the Constitution was approved in 1789. Amendments Three through Twelve were approved by two thirds of both the House and Senate, and then ratified by three quarters of the states—10 of the 13 states at the time—and incorporated into the Constitution as the Bill of Rights.

What about those first two proposed amendments? The second one said that if senators and representatives vote themselves pay raises, they cannot start collecting them until the next session of Congress. That's the proposed amendment that languished for more than 200 years before being revived and becoming the Twenty-Seventh Amendment in 1992.

The Congressional Representation Amendment

The initial proposed amendment to come before that first Congress—it would have become the First Amendment had it been approved, rather than the free speech/press/religion First Amendment so familiar to us today—is still languishing, and is unlikely to ever be revived. No doubt that proposed amendment seemed really important at the time: it was designed to make sure that the House of Representatives reflected the one-man, one-vote principle. It specified that as the country grew, there eventually would never be fewer than 200 members of the House. Here's the text of that proposed amendment:

"After the first enumeration required by the first article of the Constitution, there shall be one Representative for every thirty thousand, until the number shall amount to one hundred, after which the proportion shall be so regulated by Congress, that there shall be not less than one hundred Representatives, nor less than one Representative for every forty thousand persons, until the number of Representatives shall amount to two hundred; after which the proportion shall be so regulated by Congress, that there shall not be less than two hundred Representatives, nor more than one Representative for every fifty thousand persons."

Of course, the House now has 435 members, so there would be little point in trying to revive the proposed amendment aimed at guaranteeing that there would be at least 200 representatives. However, there was no time limit for ratification for those initial amendments—that's why the Congressional pay raise amendment could be brought back and approved two centuries later—so in theory the amendment requiring the House to have at least 200 representatives could be revived someday, too. But don't hold your breath.

The Noble Title Amendment

Another amendment that is technically still before the states for ratification came out of Congress in 1810, and was aimed at keeping U.S. citizens from taking positions or titles in foreign governments, or from taking gifts from foreign leaders. Under this proposed amendment, an American who accepted a British knighthood, for example, could be stripped of his U.S. citizenship:

"If any Citizen of the United States shall accept, claim, receive or retain any Title of Nobility or Honour, or shall, without the Consent of Congress, accept and retain any present, Pension, Office or Emolument of any kind whatever, from any Emperor, King, Prince or foreign Power, such Person shall cease to be a Citizen of the United States, and shall be incapable of holding any Office of Trust or Profit under them, or either of them."

Twelve states had approved this amendment by 1812, not enough for ratification. At least in theory, however, the proposed amendment is still on the table and could be revived in much the same way that the Twenty-Seventh Amendment languished for a couple hundred years before being approved.

There's an arcane, perhaps spurious—and some might say wacky—argument connected to that 1810 amendment. Some claim the amendment actually was ratified, and has been in effect for all those years. Furthermore, the argument goes, since American lawyers sometimes use the "Esquire," honorific, as in "John Lawyer, Esq.," that is a title that could be regarded as illegal under the amendment. Therefore, according to the theory, all lawyers should be stripped of their citizenship. And since so many lawyers served in Congress over the years—illegally, under this theory—all or most of the actions taken by Congress since 1812 have been illegal. Don't count on using this argument to say that the income tax law is unconstitutional, though.

The Slavery Amendment

In 1861, as war clouds were gathering, Congress approved a joint resolution that would have allowed individual states to retain slavery and taken away the federal government's power to outlaw it. The amendment is widely viewed as a last-ditch effort by the Union to keep the South from seceding; the thinking, even among those who hated slavery, was that it was better to keep the Union together and outlaw slavery later, when it was politically more expedient. Besides, it did not appear that the amendment would ever get the necessary approval of three quarters of the states. President Lincoln signed the resolution—it is the only proposed amendment to carry a presidential signature—in hopes that voting on the amendment would head off war.

The proposed Corwin amendment, named after the congressman who introduced it, read:

"No amendment shall be made to the Constitution which will authorize or give to Congress the power to abolish or interfere, within any State, with the domestic institutions thereof, including that of persons held to labor or service by the laws of said State."

Only two states approved the amendment before the Civil War broke out later in 1861. Eventually slavery was abolished by the Thirteenth Amendment, and the proposed Corwin amendment became a historical footnote.

The Child Labor Amendment

Besides the three proposed amendments from the nineteenth century that were never ratified—congressional representation, noble titles, and allowing slavery—there is one other proposed amendment, this one from the twentieth century, that is still on the table, at least in theory. In 1926, Congress sent the states a proposed amendment to pave the way for federal child labor laws and counter the exploitation of children in the workforce:

"Section 1. The Congress shall have power to limit, regulate, and prohibit the labor of persons under eighteen years of age.

"Section 2. The power of the several States is unimpaired by this article except that the operation of State laws shall be suspended to the extent necessary to give effect to legislation enacted by the Congress."

So far 28 states have ratified that proposed amendment, but none since 1937. Ten more states would have to ratify to write the proposed child labor amendment into the Constitution, but that seems unlikely since a great many state and federal rules and regulations are in place, along with court decisions that seem to be adequately protecting child labor.

The first proposed amendment to carry a time limit for ratification was the Eighteenth, otherwise known as Prohibition. Congress said the states had seven years to ratify, or else the proposed amendment would expire and the country would be able to drink to that. The amendment was ratified within the time limit, of course, and nobody drank to that—at least not legally. The seven-year time limit has become standard for ratification, but Congress could change that at any time—and did, for one recent proposed amendment.

The Equal Rights Amendment

Most people think the Equal Rights Amendment was initiated by the feminist movement of the 1960s. In fact, an ERA was first offered in Congress in 1923, when the American women's movement was flush with its biggest victory: ratification of the Nineteenth Amendment, which gave women the vote in 1920.

That original ERA might have had a better chance of passage if it wasn't opposed by so many of the same women who had worked so hard to get themselves the vote. The big fear among the women's movement was that the proposed amendment's "equality" provisions would over-rule existing laws that provided extra protection—protection that men didn't get—for women working in factories and shops.

Five decades later, when the feminist movement captured the imagination and the commitment of so many women—especially baby boomers—Congress approved the ERA in this form:

"Section 1. Equality of rights under the law shall not be denied or abridged by the United States or by any State on account of sex.

"Section 2. The Congress shall have the power to enforce, by appropriate legislation, the provisions of this article.

"Section 3. This amendment shall take effect two years after the date of ratification."

When the proposed ERA went to the states in 1972, it seemed inevitable to many observers that it would be ratified. To many, it seemed like the next logical step in the civil rights movement. Indeed, 22 of the required 38 states ratified the ERA in the first year. But times were changing, and opposition to the ERA grew as the country became more conservative and an economic downturn led to more competition between men and women for jobs. The practical realities of feminism had many people thinking about the changing roles of men and women, and many people decided they didn't like the changes. A Midwestern housewife and political activist named Phyllis Schlafly led a grassroots backlash. Only 13 more states, for a total of 35, had passed the ERA by 1977, and the seven-year time limit meant it would expire in 1979.

> **People** _____
>
> Phyllis Schlafly struck a chord with her newsletter, articles, speeches, and grassroots movement that appealed to many other women—and many men—who made it clear that they did not want the ERA. "I like being a woman, and the protections the law now allows," Schlafly said. She has continued to work for conservative causes, including a constitutional amendment banning same-sex marriage, into the twenty-first century.

In a controversial and much-debated move—was it constitutional?—Congress added three years to the seven-year deadline. But it didn't do the ERA's supporters any good. One of the battleground states was Utah, which had long been at the forefront among states in guaranteeing rights for women; the state had given women the right to vote in 1896. But Mormon church leaders declared that the ERA was a moral issue that would "strike at the family," and many nonreligious leaders in Utah joined the opposition. Amid ardent campaigning by both sides—busloads of women pro and con flooded into the state—Utah considered the ERA twice and defeated it both times.

Schlafly's home state, Illinois, had been considered sure to ratify, but instead rejected it eight times. The Republican Party, which had been on record as favoring equal rights for women for decades, removed that plank from its national platform as Ronald Reagan, an outspoken ERA opponent, defeated incumbent Democratic President Jimmy Carter, whose wife Rosalynn was one of the leading campaigners for the amendment. A number of states that had ratified the ERA earlier tried to rescind ratification.

The ERA officially died on June 30, 1982, after its 10-year limit had expired. If it had somehow garnered 38 states, no doubt there would have been a huge legal battle over whether it was legal for Congress to extend the original deadline, and whether states could rescind ratification. It is doubtful that a new ERA will be presented, at least in the foreseeable political landscape, for a couple of reasons.

The first is that there's no guarantee that it would pass. Second, many of the feminists who would be another ERA's strongest supporters now shrug and say it's not needed. Court rulings under the Equal Protection

Clause of the Fourteenth Amendment, along with the Civil Rights Act of 1964, have accomplished many of the goals of the ERA. Perhaps even more significantly, changes in society, including advances by women in so many aspects of the economic marketplace, have made a constitutional amendment for women seem less urgent.

The D.C. Representation Amendment

The most recent proposed amendment to the Constitution would have treated the District of Columbia as if it were a state in terms of representation in Congress: two senators and a proportionate number of representatives, depending on its population:

"Section 1. For purposes of representation in the Congress, election of the President and Vice President, and article V of this Constitution, the District constituting the seat of government of the United States shall be treated as though it were a State.

"Section 2. The exercise of the rights and powers conferred under this article shall be by the people of the District constituting the seat of government, and as shall be provided by the Congress.

"Section 3. The twenty-third article of amendment to the Constitution of the United States is hereby repealed.

"Section 4. This article shall be inoperative, unless it shall have been ratified as an amendment to the Constitution by the legislatures of three-fourths of the several States within seven years from the date of its submission."

There was never a great deal of support for the proposed amendment anywhere except in D.C., and it died in 1985, when its seven-year time limit ran out.

Amendments That Never Got Out of Congress

It is unusual for Congress to send a proposed amendment to the states, and even more unusual for an amendment to be ratified. But it is not at all unusual for members of Congress to run their ideas for amendments up the flagpole and see if anyone salutes. Several dozen amendments are proposed to Congress in a typical year—more than 800 in the 1990s alone, for example. Some are good old standbys that seem to pop up reliably every session of Congress. Others come and go, depending on the times. When Reagan was elected president in 1980 at age 69—he served until age 77, the oldest president ever—there was some talk about amending the Constitution to set a maximum age limit, but it never got very far.

Here are some proposed amendments that failed to get out of the 2005–2006 Congress:

◆ Guaranteeing women the right to abortion

◆ Restricting abortion

◆ Allowing the president line-item veto power

◆ Allowing the president to serve more than two terms

◆ Restricting the president to one six-year term

◆ Allowing foreign-born citizens (Arnold Schwarzenegger, in other words) to become president

◆ Abolishing the Electoral College in favor of direct voting for president and vice president

◆ Permitting school prayer

◆ Restricting eminent domain

One old reliable, to require the government to balance the federal budget, has had a checkered history, and shows just how political the whole process of amending the Constitution can be. For decades the Democrats were viewed as the free-spending party, and whenever they were in control of Congress the Republicans agitated for a balanced budget. But in recent years, when the Republican Congress and a Republican presidential administration have been running big deficits, the Democrats have been murmuring about an amendment requiring a balanced budget.

The Flag Desecration Amendment

Another suggested amendment that always seems to be around but has yet to get the necessary two-thirds approval of Congress is the so-called flag-burning amendment. In its latest incarnation, in 2006, the text was short and simple:

"The Congress shall have the power to prohibit the physical desecration of the flag of the United States."

The House has approved a flag-burning amendment on a number of occasions, and in June 2006, it fell a mere one vote short in the Senate, getting 66 votes in favor and 34 against. Supporters say the amendment is necessary in the face of Supreme Court decisions that in 1989 overturned a Texas flag-burning law and in 1990 overturned a federal law approved by Congress. In both instances, the high court said the laws violated the First Amendment's guarantees of free speech. The flag-burning issue is a classic illustration of the attitude many Americans have toward the Constitution: polls show people are against desecration of the flag and are in favor of laws against it, but they're not in favor of a constitutional amendment.

> **People**
>
> Daniel Inouye, the Hawaiian senator who lost an arm in World War II, called desecrating the flag obscene. "But I believe Americans gave their lives in the many wars to make certain that all Americans have a right to express themselves—even those who harbor hateful thoughts," he said in opposition to a flag-burning amendment.

The Federal Marriage Amendment

Most states have banned same-sex marriage, but it has been and may well continue to be a controversial possible amendment to the Constitution. The most recent version considered by Congress had this wording:

"Marriage in the United States of America shall consist only of the union of a man and a woman.

"Neither this constitution or the constitution of any state, nor state or federal law, shall be construed to require that marital status or the legal incidents thereof be conferred upon unmarried couples or groups."

> **People**
> Wayne Allard, the Colorado senator who was the chief sponsor of the marriage amendment considered in 2006, urged supporters not to give up on getting it added to the Constitution. "If it's up to me," he said, "we'll have a vote on this issue every year."

Supporters say the amendment is necessary to protect the sanctity of male-female marriage, but opponents note that same-sex marriage is legal only in Massachusetts and that civil unions, with the benefits of marriage but not the name, are legal only in Vermont, Connecticut, and, as of early 2007, New Jersey. Their argument is that the 1996 Federal Defense of Marriage Act already bars federal recognition of same-sex unions and gives the states the authority to ignore same-sex marriages and civil unions from other states—an exception to the "full faith and credit provisions" of Article IV, Section 4 of the Constitution. The amendment came before the Senate in June 2006 and got only 49 of the 67 votes needed. The wording was identical to the proposed amendment that was rejected by both houses of Congress two years earlier.

Like the flag-desecration amendment, polls show that a majority of Americans oppose gay and lesbian marriage, but are not convinced that it needs to be unconstitutional through an amendment.

The Least You Need to Know

◆ Even when Americans feel strongly about an issue, they are reluctant to amend the Constitution.

◆ Thousands of amendments have been proposed to Congress.

◆ The states have ratified 27 amendments.

◆ Six other amendments have been approved by Congress but not ratified by the states.

Chapter 17

The Future of the Constitution

In This Chapter

- ◆ Political hot buttons
- ◆ Social issues that may force a constitutional showdown
- ◆ Changes in society's attitudes and new technology
- ◆ The increasing power of the presidency and the system of checks and balances

The early twenty-first century appears likely to go down as a pivotal time in American constitutional history. The ever-present tensions between branches of government and conflicting constitutional principles were heightened as a result of the government's response to terrorism in the wake of the September 11, 2001, attacks on the World Trade Center and the Pentagon. Beyond terrorism, sharper national debates on a wide range of "values" issues raised constitutional questions concerning crime, education, religion, marriage, race, and the political process.

The future of the Constitution may be affected in a number of ways. A number of constitutional amendments have been proposed, for example. As we've seen, however, amending the Constitution is an arduous process, and Congress has been reluctant to tinker with the law of the land even when changes would seem to make sense and to have popular support among the public. Examples in recent years include proposed amendments to prohibit desecration of the flag and to ban same-sex marriages; both have broad popular support and both came close but fell short of winning enough support in Congress to be presented to the states for ratification.

Instead of amendments, the Constitution—and the rule of law and our system of checks and balances—is more likely to be influenced by the three branches of government, especially the courts. The role of the courts has become more important as national security and moral values—the two main triggers for constitutional conflict in recent years—produce new tensions between society and the law.

If we don't like a new federal law, we say Congress has gone too far. If we don't like a new White House executive order, we say the president has gone too far. If we don't like a Supreme Court ruling, we say the justices have gone too far. And that's what the Constitution is supposed to do: keep any of the three branches from going too far. The Supreme Court's main job is to serve as a "boundary patrol," Justice Stephen Breyer said, to make sure nobody oversteps the bounds of the Constitution, including the court itself. "It's a Constitution that protects a democratic system, basic liberties, a rule of law, a degree of equality, a division of powers, state, federal, so that no one gets too powerful," Breyer added.

There is one benefit that is often overlooked in the national debates over constitutional issues: we become better citizens. When we think about fair trials for enemy combatants versus the war on terror, for instance, or the freedoms of speech and religion versus school prayer, we are participating in the ongoing American experiment in democracy under the rule of law. In learning, considering, and debating the issues, we are practicing exactly the sort of citizenship that the Constitution was designed to accommodate and that the Constitution needs to survive and thrive.

Besides proposed amendments such as flag-burning and same-sex marriage, which were examined earlier in our discussion of failed amendments (see Chapter 16), and other proposed amendments that no doubt will be reintroduced, such as allowing school prayer or requiring the teaching of creationism or intelligent design, let's look at some of the constitutional issues that are likely to be in the headlines.

> **People**
>
> Garry Wills, professor emeritus of history at Northwestern University, in 2007 noted, "The wartime discipline imposed in 1941 has never been lifted .... World War II melded into the cold war, with greater secrecy than ever—more classified information, tougher security clearances. And now the cold war has modulated into the war on terrorism."

Political Issues

The way we elect our leaders, and the way they govern once elected, has always been a constitutional priority in our system. Our needs and expectations have changed with the way that technology and communications have changed, and with the way that political campaigns are conducted.

Elections

New technology and dissatisfaction with the way elections are carried out have brought constitutional concerns—and the courts that interpret those concerns—into play in a number of recent elections, including both the 2000 and 2004 presidential races. Some view the Electoral College as antiquated and outdated, arguing that we should be able to vote directly for president and vice president, and that they should be elected not by state-by-state electors but rather by a simple nationwide popular vote to avoid results such as the 2000 election, when Al Gore won the popular vote but George W. Bush became president by winning more states and more electoral votes (and one crucial 5–4 vote in the Supreme Court).

One interesting development in the weeks of uncertainty following the 2000 election, when it ultimately took a Supreme Court decision rejecting Florida recounts before Bush could be declared the winner, came in the Supreme Court's decision in *Bush v. Palm Beach County Canvassing Board* in December 2000. In that decision, the court reminded us that there is no constitutional right to vote for president; it remains up to the states to determine how their voters choose the members of the Electoral College. Even if the Supreme Court had not cleared the way for Bush to win the election, the court indicated that the Florida Legislature could have simply decided to throw all the state's electoral votes behind Bush to give him the election.

Critics point out that the Electoral College was created in a time when the United States seemed too large and communications too slow and difficult for everyday citizens to become adequately informed about a presidential race. On the other hand, many others say our system of electing a president has worked pretty well for more than two centuries, so if it ain't broke, don't fix it.

What It Means to You

A constitutional amendment to allow a president to serve more than two terms is usually floating around Congress, but rarely gets serious consideration—and it seems unlikely that Americans will lift the two-term limit.

Campaign finance is another area of elections where we are likely to see more court rulings that call upon constitutional principles. We've already had a number of court rulings, of course, including decisions that uphold limits on how much a donor can give to a candidate's campaign, but it is fair to expect more court challenges and more court rulings that set the rules on who can give what and how it can be given, along with when and how—and how much—money can be spent.

A Balanced Budget

Late in the eighteenth century, even before he became president, Thomas Jefferson called for an amendment requiring the United States to operate under a balanced budget and prohibiting the country from deficit spending that ran up a national debt. He warned that deficit spending would allow presidents to wage undeclared wars and would economically cripple the country in the future. "Loading up the nation with debt and leaving it for the following generations to pay is morally irresponsible. No nation has a right to contract debt for periods longer than the majority contracting it can expect to live," Jefferson wrote.

An amendment requiring a balanced budget first came before Congress in 1936, and has been revived periodically, particularly in times when the nation is running large budget deficits. Congressional hearings on balancing the budget were held around the country in 1979, and in 1982 a balanced budget amendment got the necessary two-thirds approval in the Senate but did not come before the House. The one time the amendment came close to being put before the states for ratification was in 1996, when the economy was booming, there was a budget surplus, and the national debt was declining. The House approved a proposed balanced budget amendment, but it fell three votes short of the necessary two-thirds approval in the Senate. New attention was focused on a requirement to balance the budget during the George W. Bush administration, when tax cuts and the war in Iraq combined to create record budget deficits.

On the other hand, opponents of a balanced budget amendment say deficit spending causes no real long-term harm to an ever-growing economy, and point out that instead of proposing a Constitutional amendment, Congress could simply stop appropriating excess funding for government programs and approve a balanced budget each year.

> **What It Means to You**
>
> By 2007, the U.S. national debt was approaching $10 trillion—more than $30,000 for every U.S. citizen. The interest on that debt is paid out of our tax dollars—and the tax dollars our kids will pay in the future.

Social Issues

The mores and morals of society change, along with popular trends and tastes. Whether the Constitution should shift along with those changes, and how much, is a constant question. Strict constructionists say the Constitution should be interpreted exactly as the framers intended in 1791; others believe the Constitution should be flexible, bending with the times. That, they say, is what the framers intended: for the Constitution to accommodate changes in society.

Guns and Gun Control

Perhaps more than any other constitutional issue, people on both sides of gun control say they know what the framers intended. So far, however, gun control has been constitutional kryptonite: the Supreme Court has been markedly reluctant to tackle any aspect of the issue in terms of helping define what people can and cannot do in terms of buying, selling, owning, and firing guns. Similarly, Congress has not been eager to take up this political hot potato; no matter how a lawmaker decides to vote on gun control, a significant portion of the population will be upset, including a significant number of political activists who will campaign against that lawmaker when re-election time comes around.

Both pro-gun and anti-gun forces claim that the meaning of the Second Amendment is clear—it supports their respective, diametrically opposite views—but a few of the more flexible thinkers on both sides of the chasm have called for a new Second Amendment that would, at least in theory, make both sides happier. The key language of the amendment would say, "The right of the people to keep arms reasonable for hunting, sport, collecting, and personal defense shall not be infringed," and at least one version of the proposed amendment would require approval by two thirds of Congress in two consecutive sessions.

Abortion

Like gun control, abortion is an issue that elicits passionate responses. People on either side have difficulty finding any middle ground, and so do the courts. A constitutional amendment banning abortion seems unlikely in the foreseeable future, considering that it has never gotten any appreciable traction in Congress since *Roe v. Wade* in 1973. If it was going to happen, it probably would have happened by now.

That's not to say the law of abortion won't change, however, particularly since the addition to the Supreme Court of Chief Justice John Roberts and Justice Joseph Alito, both of whom are seen by pro-life forces as sympathetic to their cause. On one hand, *Roe v. Wade* has been upheld by the Supreme Court on a number of occasions, and precedent counts for a lot in constitutional law. On the other hand, the courts have approved a number of laws and policies that restrict or limit abortion, and future court rulings could make it harder for women to obtain abortions even if *Roe v. Wade* is not explicitly overruled.

Race

The judiciary, more than the executive or legislative branches, historically has led the way in countering racial discrimination in this country. The courts continue to set the rules—or, more accurately, to tell us which rules can be followed and which cannot—including when the question is whether the rules have gone too far in promoting racial equality. In the 1970s and '80s, for example, the Supreme Court struck down affirmative action rules that discriminated against whites by setting inflexible race-oriented quotas for medical school applications and, in another case, kept black workers on the job while laying off white employees who had more seniority.

In a pair of University of Michigan cases in 2003, the high court upheld affirmative action in higher education, citing the advantages of diversity on campus, but ruled against the school's rating system that gave extra points to black applicants. The court said any affirmative action program requires "individualized consideration" that goes beyond strict quotas.

The Supreme Court heard another case in the 2006–2007 session, combining similar appeals from Seattle and Louisville, where parents challenged school integration programs. School officials said their programs made sure schools were integrated, following the spirit of the landmark 1954 case *Brown v. Board of Education*, while the parents said that children were being assigned to schools according to racial quotas. The Bush administration supported the parents' argument.

Eminent Domain

Since the Supreme Court expanded the reach of eminent domain in 2005 in *Kelo v. New London*, making it easier for governments to take property from private owners, legislators and governors of a number of states have called for amendments to their state constitutions to limit the reach of eminent domain. Some members of Congress think a federal constitutional amendment is needed, too, to shore up the part of the Fifth Amendment that says "private properties shall not be taken for public use without just compensation."

The New London decision expanded the definition of "public use" beyond the traditional park or highway that the public would use directly, and said New London could condemn and take away property to turn over to a private developer for a shopping mall. A proposed constitutional amendment would limit the use of eminent domain for private purposes, such as a new shopping mall, that may offer indirect economic benefits.

Children Online

The government began struggling with how to protect children using the Internet in the 1990s, and is still struggling a decade later. The Communications Decency Act was ruled unconstitutional for being overbroad—and violating the rights of adults—in 1997, and the federal courts later delayed implementation of its successor, the Child Online Protection Act, for similar reasons. COPA, as it is called, sets penalties of up to $50,000 a day for using the World Wide Web for commercial purposes "harmful to minors," but both the Supreme Court and lower federal courts agreed that it presented First Amendment problems while not really accomplishing its goal of protecting children. For example, COPA does not cover inappropriate material that children can see in chat rooms or can receive via e-mail. The Supreme Court said parents might be better able to protect their children themselves by using software to block or filter unwanted messages and images.

Crime and Punishment

As with racial discrimination and affirmative action, the federal courts rolled back some of the earlier court rulings that have been criticized for going too far in handicapping the police and providing too much protection for accused criminals. The exclusionary rule has been refined and restricted, including in a 2006 case where the court decided by a 5–4 vote that evidence is not necessarily excluded even if police violate the "knock and announce" rule for search and seizure. A number of legal scholars have said the court may be moving toward overturning the exclusionary rule entirely, pointing out that only the guilty benefit directly from it and that people who are wronged still have the option of suing for monetary damages.

Other areas of crime and punishment that the courts may address include racial profiling and the death penalty. In previous death penalty cases, the Supreme Court never showed much inclination to declare capital punishment itself unconstitutional, but often refined and tweaked the procedures for when and how it may be administered. One question that the court has yet to answer is when it is permissible to execute a convicted criminal who is mentally ill. The issue is not likely to be intent at the time of the crime or competence to stand trial, but whether the defendant even realizes that he is being put to death, or why.

Presidential Power

The smoke was still drifting over the ruins of the World Trade Center when the government began taking extraordinary measures to fight terrorism. As in past wars throughout American history, some of those measures restricted the civil rights we normally enjoy in peacetime and tested the limits of presidential authority in the system of checks and balances. Some of the anti-terror measures were put into effect openly and publicly. The Patriot Act, for example, was bemoaned—and still is—by civil rights activists, but it was approved and then extended by Congress.

> **People**
>
> As vice president, Dick Cheney often spoke about presidential power. "It was true during the cold war," he said, "as well as I think what is true now, the President of the United States needs to have his constitutional powers unimpaired, if you will, in terms of the conduct of national security policy. So when you're asking about my view of the presidency, yes, I believe in a strong, robust executive authority."

Citizen Surveillance

Some other government anti-terror measures turned out to be more constitutionally troublesome, perhaps partly because they were undertaken in secret and partly because they were widely viewed as constitutionally questionable extensions of presidential authority. Newspapers variously described the Bush administration as creating a "constitutional crisis" or at least igniting a "bruising national debate" over the separation of power.

President George W. Bush signed a secret executive order in October 2001 that authorized warrantless searches and seizures of U.S. citizens' telephone and electronic mail records. A federal court found the wiretapping program was illegal, and the administration subsequently said it would follow the procedures laid out for obtaining warrants in the Foreign Intelligence Surveillance Act of 1978, which allowed the government to obtain warrants in secret, without the possibility of objection or appeal. A congressional investigation continued, however, and so did a lawsuit seeking damages.

Attorney General Alberto Gonzalez told a congressional committee in early 2007 that the administration recognized soon after 9/11 that it could not follow a "strict reading" of the 1978 law. He said the process of obtaining warrants was too slow for the kind of electronic eavesdropping that the government wanted to conduct while investigating terrorist links to American citizens. As a result, Gonzalez said, the administration decided to "push the envelope" of legality. However, he and other government officials continued to argue that the president did not violate the law, and the administration appealed the court ruling that found the wiretapping unconstitutional.

In another legislative-executive showdown, a congressional committee launched an investigation into a program that allowed authorities to inspect bank and credit records. Vice President Dick Cheney said the program was legally authorized by the president to help trace terrorists and terrorist money. "It's a perfectly legitimate activity," Cheney said. "It doesn't violate people's rights."

Prosecuting Terrorists

In another anti-terror move shortly after 9/11, the Bush administration set up a special prison for terrorism suspects at the U.S. military base at Guantanamo Bay, Cuba, and established military tribunals to prosecute enemy combatants. The Supreme Court ruled in *Hamdi v. Rumsfeld* in 2004 that terrorism suspects could not be held indefinitely just because they have been identified as enemy combatants. Justice Antonin Scalia, who was expected by many observers to support the White House, wrote, "Whatever the general merits of the view that war silences law or modulates its voice, that view has no place in the interpretation and application of a Constitution designed precisely to confront war and, in a manner that accords with democratic principles, to accommodate it."

> **People**
>
> Justice Sandra Day O'Connor, writing for the plurality in the Hamdi case that struck down the military tribunals, said, "We have long since made clear that a state of war is not a blank check for the president when it comes to the rights of the nation's citizens."

Congress responded to the court ruling and the administration's requests by approving legislation to allow detention of enemy combatants under special anti-terrorism conditions. For example, the terrorism suspects—the enemy combatants—were deprived of the right of habeas corpus, the right to challenge their detention. The trials under the legislation approved by Congress also would allow hearsay evidence, which is not ordinarily allowed under the rules of evidence, and testimony obtained through coercion—but not through torture. "Torture," however, has been given a broader and not clearly delineated definition by the Bush administration. Given the controversy surrounding the Iraq war in general and the tracking and prosecution of terrorism suspects in particular, legal observers expected more constitutional challenges from the effort to fight terror.

Signing Statements

Beyond terrorism issues, one of the most contentious expansions of executive power under the Bush administration was the president's use of hundreds of signing statements. Past presidents advocated a line-item veto, giving them the power to exercise partial vetoes over legislation, but the Supreme Court in 1998 held that a line-item veto law requested by President Bill Clinton was unconstitutional. The signing statement, which was also used by President Clinton, was the next best thing: a declaration that the president disagreed with some part of the new law he was signing, and perhaps that he did not intend to enforce it.

A Clinton administration memo justifying signing statements put it this way: "If the President may properly decline to enforce a law, at least when it unconstitutionally encroaches on his powers, then it arguably follows that he may properly announce to Congress and to the public that he will not enforce a provision of an enactment that he is signing."

The issue, of course, was whether enforcing laws approved by Congress is the president's job, and the question remained: can a president use a signing statement to legally decline to recognize some part of a new law, and is a signing statement an unconstitutional extension of presidential power?

The Constitution: Our Continuing National Conversation

This has been an admittedly cursory overview of the U.S. Constitution. But if you've gotten this far, you probably know at least a little more about the Constitution than you did. And more importantly, you probably recognize how it has evolved, and continues to evolve. The Constitution represents a remarkable dialogue between a people and a process—between the American people and the United States government. Our experiment in democracy continues to work, sometimes better than others, as long as we continue to buy into the notion that we will participate as citizens to make it work.

The Least You Need to Know

- ◆ A number of amendments may be proposed in the next few years—to ban abortion, allow school prayer, prohibit flag-burning, require the teaching of creationism or intelligent design, among others—but enacting a constitutional amendment is a long and arduous process.

- ◆ Several aspects of the war on terror, including wiretapping and inspecting financial records of U.S. citizens, have raised constitutional questions.

- ◆ The military tribunals for enemy combatants at Guantanamo Bay were declared unconstitutional by the Supreme Court, but then authorized by Congress.

- ◆ The Supreme Court may ultimately have to decide whether signing statements are valid, and how presidents can use them.

Appendix A

Glossary

act   A bill that has passed the legislature and become law.

adjourn   To end a session or meeting.

alien   A resident who is not a citizen.

amendment   A change to existing law.

anti-federalists   A group of early American leaders who opposed the Constitution, including Patrick Henry, George Mason, and George Clinton.

appellate   Pertaining to appeals from lower courts.

apportioned   Distributed proportionately, by percentage.

appropriation   Funds authorized by the legislature for spending.

autonomy   Independence, or self-rule.

bail   A bond or payment to get out of jail, repaid upon appearance for trial.

balanced budget   Government planning so that expenditures will not exceed revenues.

bicameral   Two legislative chambers or branches.

bill   Proposed legislation that has been formally introduced to a legislature.

bill of attainder An act that singles out an individual or specific group of people for punishment without trial.

Bill of Rights The first 10 amendments to the Constitution, aimed at guaranteeing individual rights.

census An official count of the population.

chamber A large room, often refers to the legislative body that meets there; in Congress, the House is the lower chamber and the Senate is the upper chamber.

checks and balances The Constitution's system for the executive, legislative, and judicial branches of government to limit each other's authority.

citizen A member of a nation who enjoys the rights and protection of that nation.

clear and present danger A Supreme Court doctrine giving the government the authority to take action for security purposes that might otherwise violate the First Amendment.

commerce Trade, business, the sale of goods or services, financial dealings.

common law The body of law, largely unwritten, that evolved in England through prevailing customs, widely accepted principles, and decisions by courts rather than through administrative rule or legislative action.

compensation Payment.

compromise An agreement in which both sides give up something.

concur To agree.

concurrent powers Authority shared by the federal government and the states.

confederation A formal governing alliance.

confirmation Verification or approval, as in Senate votes required to confirm a presidential appointee before taking office.

construed Explained, clarified.

counsel An adviser, usually referring to a lawyer.

deficit spending Government expenditures that exceed revenues.

delegate As a noun, a representative; as a verb, to assign.

delegated power Authority specifically enumerated for the federal government in Article I of the Constitution.

democracy A government based on equality for all, with the people choosing their leaders.

discrimination Attitudes or actions denying equal treatment to groups of people.

domestic Pertaining to home or internal national issues.

domestic tranquility Peace at home, referring to a family or a nation.

due process The principle that proper legal rules and procedures must be followed before depriving a person of freedom or property.

duty A tariff or tax.

Electoral College The process (rather than being a physical entity) for the indirect election of the president by electors from each state.

eminent domain The doctrine that allows governments to take over ownership of private property for the benefit of the public.

enumerated Listed or specified.

equal representation The doctrine providing that all the states have equal influence in the federal system.

ex post facto Determined after the fact, retroactively; an ex post facto law, for example, would make an action illegal after it had happened.

excise taxes Taxes on some sort of transaction or event, rather than on property.

exclusionary rule The Fourth Amendment doctrine that makes unlawfully obtained evidence inadmissible at trial.

executive agreement An agreement between the president and another country that does not need Senate approval.

executive branch   The presidency and the administrative arm of the government charged with executing and enforcing the law.

exempt   Not covered by a requirement.

express powers   Powers enumerated in Article I of the Constitution.

federal   Pertaining to the national government.

federal mandate   An order or requirement demanded by the national government.

federal supremacy clause   The stipulation in Article VI of the Constitution that holds federal law to be superior to state laws.

federalism   Regional or state governments arranged under a central or national government.

Federalists   Influential supporters who campaigned for the Constitution to be ratified, including Alexander Hamilton, James Madison, and John Jay.

filibuster   A Senate procedure for blocking a vote with long-winded speeches. Under the rules, a senator who has the floor cannot be interrupted—even to take a vote—so as long as the senator keeps speechifying, so no action can be taken.

full faith and credit   The clause in Article IV of the Constitution that requires the states to respect each other's laws, judgments, licenses, and public documents.

gerrymandering   The manipulation of voting districts by political parties to gain advantages in elections.

grand jury   A group of citizens sworn in to consider evidence and determine whether there is adequate evidence to issue an indictment that forces a defendant to go on trial.

habeas corpus   A writ or document demanding that authorities show there is good reason for holding a person in custody.

hearing   A public session held to gather information.

immigrant   A resident who has come from another country.

impartial   Fair, unbiased.

impeachment A formal legislative accusation against an elected official that could lead to removal from office.

implied power Authority not specifically stated, but understood or assumed.

inalienable rights Natural rights that all humans claim and deserve, and that cannot be taken away by laws or governments.

incumbent An official currently in office.

indictment A formal accusation listing specific charges, usually returned by a grand jury, allowing a prosecutor to take a defendant to trial.

infringe To encroach, violate, or disturb.

inherent powers National authority assumed by the federal government, particularly in foreign affairs, that are not listed in the Constitution.

interest group An organization trying to influence public issues and policies.

judicial branch The branch of the government that interprets laws through courts, judges, and juries.

judicial review The authority of courts to determine whether laws are constitutional, and to void unconstitutional laws.

jurisdiction The right of a court to hear a case or interpret certain laws in certain places.

lame duck Pertaining to an official whose term is expiring but who was not re-elected.

legislative branch The elected officials who propose, debate, and enact laws.

lobbyist A person who works for a special interest.

majority More than half.

militia A military or paramilitary group, typically citizens rather than professional soldiers, that serves temporarily in times of need or emergency.

misdemeanor   A minor or lesser crime usually characterized by punishments of fines only or no more than a year in jail.

naturalized citizen   Someone who was not born a citizen, but has acquired the full rights of citizenship.

necessary and proper clause   The section of Article I of the Constitution that the courts have said gives Congress the authority to pass laws that are not enumerated but are required for the good of the nation.

nominate   To propose or name or give preliminary approval to a candidate.

oath   A statement swearing to keep a promise, as in to testify truthfully.

override   To overrule, as when Congress musters the necessary two-thirds vote to enact legislation despite a presidential veto.

pardon   An executive order to free or dismiss the charges against an accused person.

petition   To ask or request, sometimes but not always with a list of required signatures.

pocket veto   Presidential rejection of legislation not by outright veto, but rather by failing to sign it before the legislature adjourns.

poll tax   A fee paid to vote.

prescribe   To set out a course of action with authority, usually in legislation or a court decision.

preside   To oversee or direct a meeting, session, or hearing.

president pro temporare   The vice president or, if the vice president is absent, a senator who serves as presiding officer.

primary   A preliminary election where parties choose their candidates.

prior restraint   A court order restricting freedom of speech, such as an order blocking the publication of a book or the showing of a movie.

probable cause   The required finding that there is legitimate reason for a certain legal action, such as the search of a home or business.

proportional representation   A system for providing different levels of influence or participation to political entities, such as states, based on their population.

prosecutor   A government official who conducts criminal proceedings against defendants.

public domain   Government-owned property.

quarter   To provide room and board for, as in quartering troops.

quorum   The minimum number of members required to take legal action.

ratification   Formal approval, as when the Senate approves a treaty or the states approve an amendment to the Constitution.

reapportionment   Recalculating according to population shifts, such as the number of representatives each state is determined to have after a national census.

redistricting   Redrawing districts to maintain proportional representation, such as in House districts after census results show population shifts.

redress   To correct or rectify.

referendum   A direct vote by the public on an issue, instead of the usual indirect voting by their elected representatives.

regulatory   Pertaining to government oversight functions, usually of business or industry or professions, carried out by the executive branch.

representative government   A system in which the public elects officials to make and enforce the laws; also called indirect democracy or a republic form of government.

reserved powers   Authority specified in the Tenth Amendment that remained with the states rather than being taken over by the federal government.

resident   A person who lives in a certain state or other area.

revenue   Income from all sources.

rule of law   The principle holding that everyone in society, including the top officials, are equally subject to the law.

security Safety, freedom from danger; also, a financial instrument, a bond, issued by a government or private enterprise.

sedition Attempted overthrow or interruption of a government.

separation of powers The principle delineating three branches of government, and giving them a series of checks and balances to limit each other's authority.

sovereign Superior, as in a monarch or a national government.

Speaker of the House The presiding officer of the House of Representatives, chosen by the majority party.

special interest An organization seeking to influence policy.

states' rights The philosophy that holds that the states have their own sovereignty and at least as much or more authority as the federal government.

strict interpretation A philosophy that takes a conservative view of the Constitution and limits federal authority to powers specifically enumerated in Article I.

subpoena A document issued by a court ordering a person to appear to testify or surrender documents.

suffrage The right to vote.

territory Land controlled by a nation that is not part of that nation.

title of nobility Aristocratic or honorific names banned by the Constitution, such as queen, prince, countess, duke, baroness, etc.

treason Betrayal, usually of a nation.

treaty An agreement between two or among more than two countries.

tyranny An unjust and often cruel form of rule.

unconstitutional A law or rule or administrative action ruled invalid by the courts for violating the principles of the Constitution.

unicameral Pertaining to a single-chamber legislature.

veto An executive's rejection of legislation.

warrant   A document empowering law enforcement authorities, usually to search or seize someone or something for evidence in a possible prosecution.

welfare   As used in the Constitution, the well-being, happiness, and prosperity of the public.

writ   A formal written order, usually issued by a court.

Appendix B

Resources

Further Reading

Academic Solutions, Inc. *The United States Constitution Study Guide*. Academic Solutions, Inc., 2003.

Amar, Akhil Reed. *America's Constitution: A Biography*. Random House, 2006.

Baker, Thomas E. *Constitutional Analysis: In a Nutshell*. West Group, 2003.

Berkin, Carol. *A Brilliant Solution: Inventing the American Constitution*. Harvest Books, 2003.

Currie, David P. *The Constitution of the United States: A Primer for the People*. University of Chicago Press, 2000.

Fink, Sam. *The Constitution of the United States of America*. Welcome Books, 2006.

Jordan, Terry L. *The U.S. Constitution: And Fascinating Facts About It*. Oak Hill Publishing, 1999.

JusticeLearning.org. *The United States Constitution: What It Says, What It Means: A Hip Pocket Guide*. University of Oxford Press, 2005.

Monk, Linda R. *The Bill of Rights: A User's Guide.* Close Up, 2004.

———. *The Words We Live By: Your Annotated Guide to the Constitution.* Hyperion, 2004.

Vile, John R. *A Companion to the United States Constitution and Its Amendments, 4th ed.* Praeger Publishers, 2006.

Websites

American Library Association: The First Amendment
www.ala.org/ala/oif/firstamendment/firstamendment.htm

American Memory: Historical Documents from the Library of Congress
http://memory.loc.gov/ammem/help/constRedir.html

Bill of Rights Institute
www.BillofRightsInstitute.org

The Constitution: Government Printing Office
http://caselaw.lp.findlaw.com/data/constitution/articles.html

Emory School of Law
www.law.emory.edu/cms/site/index.php?id=3080

FindLaw: The Constitution
http://supreme.lp.findlaw.com/constitution

Legal Information Institution
www.law.cornell.edu/constitution/constitution.overview.html

This Nation: American Government & Politics Online
www.thisnation.com/constitution.html

The National Archives
www.archives.gov/national-archives-experience/charters/constitution.html

National Constitution Center
www.constitutioncenter.org

Optimus Law Library Online
www.lawlibraryonline.com

A Roadmap to the U.S. Constitution
http://library.thinkquest.org/11572

The U.S. Constitution: About.com
http://americanhistory.about.com/od/usconstitution/United_States_
Constitution.htm

The U.S. Constitution Online
www.usconstitution.net/const.html

U.S. House of Representatives, Educational Resources
www.house.gov/house/Educate.shtml

U.S. Senate References: The Constitution
www.senate.gov/civics/constitution_item/constitution.htm

US.Info.Gov: United States Government Information Programs
http://usinfo.state.gov/products/pubs/constitution/constitution.htm

Wikipedia: The U.S. Constitution
http://en.wikipedia.org/wiki/United_States_Constitution

Yale University: The Avalon Project
www.yale.edu/lawweb/avalon/usconst.htm

Index

T

U

V

W-X-Y-Z